The Coming Captivity and Restoration of Israel

by

Messianic Rabbi Allan Moorhead

AjON MULTIMEDIA

"The Word is Eternal" Isaiah 40:8

ISBN:0-9915657-7-0

Printed in the United States of America

Published by Aion Multimedia
20118 N 67th Ave
Suite 300-446
Glendale AZ 85308
www.aionmultimedia.com

This book is a result of eleven messages taught on this subject at Arrowhead Messianic Congregation in Peoria, Arizona, in the fall of 2015.

For Book Signings, Speaking Engagements, and more info:
Rabbi Allan Moorhead (623)780-0172, Email: info@myamc.org

Table of Contents

Introduction

Nobody has a complete handle on how prophecy works, so if you have a different opinion of what I'm saying, well, bless the Lord! I'm glad you're studying and I'm glad that you've come to an understanding how you think it's going to work, and that's fine. I'm not saying I'm right. You may be right, but all I can do is use the Scriptures and understanding that I know and present them as I view them.

It's like putting a puzzle together. One problem some prophecy writers make is that they start assembling a puzzle, but they're lacking some pieces. So what do they do? They look for one that looks close and force the piece into a wrong position. Well, you know their finished picture is not going to look right. So when you have a puzzle piece (prophetic scripture) that doesn't fit, what do *you* do? You wait on the Lord until you see where it fits. That's very important. Otherwise, your picture is distorted. If you don't build a well-structured foundation, whatever you build on that foundation is not going to work. This is also very important. I'm one who will flat-out tell you we don't have all the pieces yet. So if you've read materials and books that say "This is exactly how it's going to be," you should immediately say, "No. We don't know." You should know right off the bat they will probably be wrong because we don't have all the pieces. We do the best we can, however, to understand all the pieces, especially when it pertains to Israel.

I came across a phrase that says, "From there you will seek the LORD thy God, thou shall find him if thou seek him with all thy heart and with all thy soul," in Deuteronomy 4:29. This is what got me started on this book because of the words "from there." What is "there"? I needed to explain what the "there" is. "From there" will Israel come back to the land. I started researching and from there things grew (and grew, and grew...). I began to understand that God was giving me a series of messages dealing with the coming captivity and restoration of Israel. There's a reason, best known to Him, why He suddenly wants this taught.

Maybe something's getting ready to happen in the land or in the spirit. But I felt suddenly impressed that I had to do it, and I had to do it *now*. That led to this book about Israel: what's going to happen to them prophetically, where they're going to be driven into their captivity once again, and about the restoration when Israel, as a nation, comes out.

While reading and studying this book, it is important to know what definition of LORD as opposed to Lord. The word LORD is the name of God using the four Hebrew letter consonants that spell out his name: *yod-hey vav-hey*. The translators chose to use LORD because they don't know how to pronounce the four letters together since there are no vowel points. If you add vowel points there would be many ways to pronounce the name. So as you study, be aware that LORD is the substitutionary word for the almighty's name. The word Lord with the last three letters in lower case is Adonai or master and not His name, although sometimes this word is used to speak of the LORD in phrases, such as Lord God. Some people actually prefer to use Adonai when speaking of the name of the LORD. Why is it important to understand the distinction here? Because there are many Lords in the world. Even the false god Baal was called Lord. So to be precise, you need to understand that LORD is talking about the God of Abraham, Isaac, and Jacob and none other. Even Yeshua is called LORD.

Chapter 1:

Why Study Prophecy?

As you study the Word of God—particularly from the prophets who speak about the coming captivity and the coming restoration of Israel —there are certain things you have to understand such as shadow types, symbolism, and cryptic concepts. You have to also know the parallelism or the way God so masterfully put His Word together. He gave a word that was the word in season at that time, and yet will also have a greater fulfillment of it in the future. Much of the prophecies of Isaiah and Zechariah and others had some fulfillment with the Babylonians, but yet you see other tidbits throughout the scripture of things that were not fulfilled. That's a clue that there is another similar event in the future that's going to happen. That's what you have to watch really closely. When you start seeing things that were not fulfilled, that's when you start taking heed that God is using parallelism in His Word. Instead of repeating himself twice, He says it once through that particular prophet (and He pretty much said it through all the prophets), but one particular prophet may state what is going to happen when the Chaldeans and Babylonians come from the north. Then you begin to see there are other things involved in it. When you see that, then you realize this is history repeating itself again, only in a greater fulfillment of His judgment upon, not only Israel, but also upon the world.

Now when I mention judgment upon Israel, we cringe because we love Israel, we support Israel, and we pray for Israel. But, nonetheless, God is not mocked. When you break His commandments, there will be consequences. I don't care if you're Israel—and poor Israel has certainly seen its judgments by God—the United States or any other nation, there will be consequences for breaking God's commandments. Like Daniel 8:23 says, when the transgressors are full, then he will send the "evil one" from that area up north that we talked about upon the Earth to start executing judgment upon the whole Earth. He will send him—or it, whatever you want to call it—upon the whole world, but it begins in the Middle East when the transgressors are full.

Many times, I've asked the LORD, "What do you actually mean by when the transgressors are full?" Basically, it's the same concept that affected the Amorites. The Hebrews were in Egypt for 400 years until the sins of the Amorites came to a fullness as mentioned in Genesis 15:13 and 16. So in other words, when sin reaches its fullness, it's time to destroy it; it's time for God's complete judgment. That's exactly what the Hebrews did to the Amorites; they wiped them out. They took over their land because God no longer had mercy on them. This is a sobering thought that when the transgressors get full, God's mercy no longer falls out to them. Now, we as believers have the mercy of God by our confession of faith in Him and His Messiah Yeshua. We're sanctified by Him, we're justified by Him. However, if we're alive when this begins to happen, we're going to see such terrible things occur all over the world.

I found it very interesting that groups of people today (mainline denominational, and some seminary college professors from different universities) think all of the last day's prophecies—especially the book of Revelation—has already happened. That usually comes from people who haven't studied Revelation or the prophets in detail. One of the reasons they say that is they don't want to think it may be in their day. They don't want to think they may have to answer for it, and see this fearful thing that's coming upon the Earth. They don't even want to imagine those things. So they say it's already done and things will get better and better.

What world are they living in? I've heard some of them say it was all completed during the time of Nero. I answer by saying, "Well, that's very interesting, because the book of Revelation wasn't even written during the time of Nero. There is a big debate on when the book of Revelation was written. Some say it was the time of Domitian around 90 A.D. Regardless, there are other questions that need answered like: When does Israel get led back into captivity and come back in restoration? When did the oceans and the rivers all turn to blood? When did the stars all fall from heaven? When did the locusts with the tails of scorpions and the faces of man come out of the bottomless pit and torment and sting men for five months? When did burning hail fall, with all these other judgments Revelation talks about?"

You know what their answer usually is? *That's just hyperbole.* What do you mean it's hyperbole or even symbolism? How do you read into God's word from the prophets or Revelation that all of it is hyperbole or symbolism? Some things are symbolism but not all. The Bible says the bottomless pit will open up, and these creatures will come out and have the face of a man, a tail of a scorpion, and fire that comes out of their mouth. When they go around and sting and torment men for five months, how do you say that's just hyperbole or symbolism?

Now, I know some prophecy writers say this it refers to helicopters. Well, there's a problem with that. Helicopters cannot distinguish between those who have the mark of God and those who have the mark of the beast. Helicopters indiscriminately blow stuff up or spread their poison upon everyone when they attack, let alone just torment for five months.

It says those with the mark of God will not be hurt by these scorpions. Also, if it is attack helicopters, how do you just torment men and not kill them when you're doing deadly stuff like that? This is why you sometimes just have to use spiritual common sense. Look at these scriptures and see what they're talking about. When was there ever a great earthquake in which every city on Earth was leveled (see Revelation 16:17-20)? That has not happened. *Well, that's just symbolism.* Okay then,

5

explain to me how the symbolism works. How do you say that there's going to be a great earthquake and every city is going to be leveled and tell me how it's symbolism. Explain it to me. Sometimes we don't want to believe the things we read, so we symbolize it to death, particularly by saying it doesn't apply today. It's dangerous to think those things. That's why scripture says Israel will come back out of captivity and rebuild all the waste places. Basically, the whole world becomes a waste.

I used to think that in 1948 when the Jews came back in the land and began to rebuild some of the old cities, that it was a total fulfillment of scripture. But that's not true. They mostly rebuilt new cities next to the old cities. So what does it mean that when they come back out of captivity, they'll rebuild the waste cities? Some of these cities were still being inhabited even after the Israel final dispersion in 135 AD. The great earthquake in Revelation 16:18 will level every city in the world and in Israel. When Israel comes back out of captivity of the last days, they will quickly rebuild those cities. So we're talking about a very short time frame when all this starts happening.

When the Jews began to gather in the land at the end of the nineteenth century, the land surrendered to them and it prospered. Before this, the land was a curse when the non-Jews controlled it. The land belongs to Israel, and there have always been Jews in the land, but it didn't begin to blossom until the times appointed and the Jews came back into the land. The waste places being rebuilt and the land blossoming today is just a taste of what is going to happen during the final restoration of Israel when there will be real peace. Yes, there is some fulfillment going on now and Israel is blessing the world with its products. But this is not the end of the story.

Some biblical teachers will tell you that all prophecies concerning Israel have happened already so we shouldn't even bother studying it. These people are going to be very surprised. I've heard people say, "I don't understand prophecy so I'm not going to read it." I tell them, "Why don't you just take a third of the Bible and throw it away?" If God did not want you to read it and try to understand it, why did He put it in there?

He didn't say we have to *completely* comprehend it. We comprehend the scriptures better the more we study. Also, as we get closer and closer to the final days, God reveals more to us. He wants us to know; He wants us to study these things.

So don't push it aside and say it's too confusing and there are too many opinions. There's nothing wrong with opinions, as long as we continue to study and try to rightly divide the word of truth. We must ever learn God's Word as it is revealed to us and not become rigid and refuse to admit that maybe a previous interpretation of prophecy was wrong. It is all right to have an opinion as long as you can back it up with scripture. Be very careful of random teachings of men who make something out of scriptures that is not there, or teach the doctrines of men.

I coined a word called "Scripturelate." It is when you take unclear prophetic scripture and speculate with the best of your knowledge because there is not a clear answer to it as you understand—yet. In that case you have to Scripturelate. There's nothing wrong with scripturelating when things are not completely clear, but when things are clear, why do we deviate from those things? We need to know prophecy and we need to understand. Remember that "the fear of the LORD is the beginning of wisdom" (Psalm 111:10). James 1:5 tells us, "If any of you lack wisdom, let him ask of God... and it shall be given him." Ask God for understanding when you are seeking His Word. Being filled with the Holy Spirit is also important to understand God's word, especially prophecies.

What did people believe before 1948? There was a concept called Replacement Theology, and the people who believed in that concept say all those prophetic positive scriptures had to do with the church today and not Israel, and all negative scriptures still apply to the Jews. Well, that's interesting. When did the church ever get kicked out of their land, and when are they going to come back to their land? That doesn't make any sense. One of the problems with old prophecy writers is that they didn't have all the puzzle pieces together. Now they see what happened in 1948 and that changed everything. When they saw things differently, they began to understand God's plan for Israel.

We cannot accurately figure out everything that's going to happen in prophecy until it happens. So if anyone ever says to you, *Yeah, I got it all figured out, this is the way it is,* go somewhere else, because they don't. Of the myriads of end-time prophecy writers, none have been perfectly accurate because they can't be. That's the way God's prophetic word works. There's a reason behind why it's not always perfectly clear. You're dealing with evil forces (Satan's bad angels) and God cryptically put things in there so that they can't even figure it out. Otherwise, they can do greater harm. That's why some of these things are cryptic. Satan's angels would love to completely understand everything God wrote so they could try to ambush all these things. These cryptic things are revealed sometimes just before or right after it happens, and everybody says, "That's what that scripture meant!" You see it after the fact.

It's the same thing when Israel became a nation in 1948. A lot of people did not know that was going to happen. A few prophecy writers did, but many of them did not. Satan wasn't sure because he cannot read God's mind. He's not omnipresent, he's an individual; he's not God. That's why we don't say things like, "The devil made me do it." Well, that's interesting. The devil didn't make you do anything. However, a demon could have interfered or influenced you because you let him. More than likely, the devil is not messing with you as he has bigger fish to fry. He's not going to personally come and interfere with my life. He's going after the big ones, the big fish. Now, he may send his demons over to mess with us. That happens all the time, but he, himself, is not going to do it.

Sometimes we treat Satan as though he's God and has God attributes like he's omnipresent and can read thoughts. No! Satan and the demons can't read your thoughts— they watch what you say, they watch what you do. Once they see that and you open the doors or windows of your soul, here they come. We must not open spiritual doors by our eyes, ears, mouths, or any actions that allow demonic world to harass us. This is why it is so important we walk in righteousness and seek God's Word at all times. Deuteronomy 6:5-9, known as the V'ahavta, says that you shall "love the LORD thy God with all thine heart, and with all thy soul, and with all thy might." It also says to teach the word to your children and bind the word of God upon your hands and on the doorposts of your heart. In other words, the Word of God guards the spiritual doors in your life— your eyes, your ears, your mouth, your hands. The Word of God will guard those doors when you apply it appropriately. If you do things you're not supposed to do and you think nobody's seeing, first of all, God sees. A demon may also see and it helps inflict the pain when you do wrong. So don't ever think you're alone in doing things you shouldn't be doing because they can see it.

Chapter 2:

History of Israel

It's important to understand a little history of Israel. First, what happened to Israel? You probably know they formed as a nation when they came out of Egypt. There were up and down times—righteous kings and bad kings back and forth—and then came God's judgment on them. The Assyrians of the Assyrian Empire were finally unleashed on them from the north and they hauled away the ten northern tribes of Israel captive to the land of Assyria. The initial boundaries of the Assyrian Empire were from the eastern Turkey, Armenia, and Georgia area, northern parts of Iran and Iraq and Syria. From there, the ten tribes were scattered among the nations.

Judah and Benjamin continued to exist with good kings and bad kings. Then a bad king rose up called Manasseh who offered children in sacrifice to the god Molech. They actually built a slide (a ramp) with fire at the base. The slide would be constructed in the arms of Molech and the parents would bring their young children up, offer them to the priests of Molech, and while the children were alive, they'd drop them children on the slide and down into the fire. This was the worship of Molech which made God very angry. Manasseh began to build temples and idols in high places, gardens, and everywhere else for the worship of Molech. God said that He was going to finally, and completely, judge Judah based on what Manasseh did.

Believe it or not, Manasseh repented later on in his life, and turned

11

to God. However, the LORD forgave him but He would not hold back his judgment against Israel because of what Manasseh had done previously. So due to the wickedness of Manasseh, the Babylonians came. When they first came around 606 B.C., they led away captive the individuals that Nebuchadnezzar the Babylonian king thought he could use in his empire, along with a lot of the prophets including Daniel and Ezekiel. So the books you have, particularly the book of Ezekiel, were written while the prophet was in captivity in Babylon. It was the same with Daniel.

The land of Judah still existed, but then they rebelled against Nebuchadnezzar under King Jehoiakim. Later under King Jehoiachin, the children of Judah rebelled again, and the Babylonian king came again, put down the rebellion, and took King Jehoiachin captive. Now under a new king, Zedekiah, Judah rebelled again. This time the city and temple were burnt by Nebuchadnezzar in 587 B.C. Later the governor (Gedeliah) that Nebuchadnezzar had appointed to rule over the land was killed by some of his own people and the frightened remnant fled to Egypt. Then Nebuchadnezzar came with his full fury and chased the remnant into Egypt and conquered Egypt also.

Jeremiah was writing his book during that period of time and God told him to tell the people to remain in Judah and not flee to Egypt as He would protect them. But if they fled to Egypt, God would destroy them. So Jeremiah told the people, but they ignored him and they brought him with them into Egypt. We never heard any more about what happened to Jeremiah, but Nebuchadnezzar chased them all the way into Egypt and destroyed that remnant. So being disobedient to God even in hard times, even though they were under captivity, God promised them that He would protect them if they would just remain in the land. But no, they couldn't do that.

So after 70 years, as promised by Jeremiah (Jeremiah 25:11) and spoken of in Daniel (Daniel 9:2), that particular captivity came to an end. However, it is not *the* captivity that we're going to talk about. This one is

12

yet to come.

Did you know only about 40,000 Jews came back out of the land of Babylon after 70 years? The rest of them stayed in Babylon. What a sad state of affairs! They had a chance to be released by the Persian king who found favor with the Jewish people after he conquered the Babylonians, and only 40,000 came back! Tens of thousands of others remained in Babylon who were hauled off starting in 606 B.C., twice more, and also in 587 B.C. So after 70 years in Babylon, a remnant returned to the land to rebuild the city and temple. However, it was not the final return the Bible talks about. That group did come back and built what we know as the Second Temple, Zerubbabel's Temple.

Sometime later came the Maccabean period with Antiochus Epiphanes who was a shadow of the false Messiah to come. He did great harm to Israel as many Israelis died and had their temple violated. Then came the rule of the Maccabeans after they conquered Antiochus. Then Herod showed up on the scene after the Roman general Pompeii came in and pretty much took over the land. Herod rebuilt Zerubbabel's Temple into what is known as Herod's Temple—the temple Yeshua would come to. Then Yeshua came and warned His disciples at that time, saying, "When you see the armies surround the city of Jerusalem, flee into the wilderness." That's exactly what happened in 70 A.D.

What happened to Herod's Temple? Josephus, the Jewish historian at that time, writes quite a lot about it, but the Romans weren't the only ones who destroyed the city. The inhabitants of Jerusalem also played a major role. When the Romans approached, the violent Zealots began to fight the priests and the Pharisees because both groups wanted to surrender to Rome. However, the Zealots said, "No way! We're not going to allow Rome in here. We're going to fight them." So the Zealots fought against the Pharisees and the priests and thousands were killed fighting among themselves. Finally, the priests were able to throw the Zealots out of the city and close the gates after thousands perished and died.

What happened next? Well, the Zealots weren't done. So they went south to a place called Edom, found the Edomites, and convinced them to fight with them for spoils. Josephus wrote that the Edomites would run to a battle quicker than they would hurry to a feast! They loved to fight and they loved to shed blood! So about 20,000 Edomites joined with the Zealots who still had people inside the city walls. At night these insiders opened the gates, and the 20,000 Edomites fled into Jerusalem and began to slaughter, throwing people off the walls of Jerusalem—women, children, men, everyone. As a matter of fact, it got so bad even the Edomites said, "We're sick of this blood; we're leaving." That's saying something about Edomites because they're a bloodthirsty group of people! Even they got tired of the blood. So at night, the Edomites fled from Jerusalem.

Meanwhile, Titus, the Roman general, had the city pretty much surrounded. Not much is recorded concerning what was said, but I can imagine these generals saying, "They're fighting each other in the city!" Of course, any leader of a military group would say, "Fine, let them keep fighting and kill each other off. It makes our job easier." So Titus stood off and watched the bloodshed taking place, and when it finally came to an end, he came in. But the small amount of priests that were still there at the temple mount fought against the Romans at the temple, and then the Romans burnt the temple down. The story says that someone set fire to the curtains, all the wood inside began to burn, and all the gold began to melt and flow into the stones.

When Yeshua said not one stone will be left unturned (Matthew 24:2), the reason was that not only did the Romans want to utterly destroy everything because they were mad at the revolt of the Jews, they wanted the gold that went down in the rocks. So they were flipping all the rocks and pulling all the melted gold out of the cracks of the rock. There was no stone that was not turned over in the temple itself. They also did a heck of a job to the walls around there, too, but it was the temple Yeshua was talking about when He said that no stone would be left unturned.

So the Messianics (Jews who believe that Yeshua is the Messiah which were at that time in the tens of thousands) fled into the wilderness. Remember, Yeshua said when they saw the armies surrounding Jerusalem, they were to flee. So they fled to a place across the Jordan River called Pella and there they remained until the Romans had completed putting down the revolt while killing hundreds of thousands of Jews. Afterwards, the remaining Jews and Pharisees were very angry at the Messianics because they didn't help fight. The Messianics said, "The Lord told us to flee and leave when the armies surrounded Jerusalem so we did."

After things calmed down, the Messianics and the non-Messianics began to worship in the synagogues together. Then along came another fellow called Bar Kokhba, "Son of the Star." One particular rabbi, Akiva, declared him to be the Messiah. They revolted against Rome again in 132 A.D. So the Jewish leaders called on thousands of Messianics and asked them to come help fight the Romans! But the Messianics basically said, "Not if you call Bar Kokhba the Messiah. We will not fight under his banner. He is not the Messiah." Of course, Rabbi Akiva and the rest of them held firm and continued to declare Kokhba the Messiah so the Messianics refused to fight under his banner. They then fled again across the Jordan River to safety.

In 135 A.D., Hadrian, the emperor of Rome, put down the rebellion, killed Bar Kokhba and massacred hundreds of thousands of Jewish people. All the rest of the Jewish people were scattered all over the Roman Empire at that time as the Romans didn't want any more possibility of them gathering together and they were forbidden to enter Jerusalem.

Jerusalem was renamed Aelia Capitolina, and the land of Israel was renamed Philistinia, which is where we get the word "Palestine" today. There never was a Palestine before, and it's named after the Philistines, Israel's archenemies. Hadrian added insult to injury by doing that and no longer letting it be called Israel. Since 135 A.D., the Jews have been scattered all over the known world, although there have always been small pockets of Jews living in Israel and even in Jerusalem. This has led to a lot of conflict, especially when the Arabs came in the seventh century. There was conflict with the Byzantines, there was conflict all the time. Scripture says that if Israel doesn't obey the commandments of God, they will have terror. Of course we need to know it applies to us also and not just Israel.

Deuteronomy 28:62-66
And you shall be left few in number, whereas you were as the stars of heaven for multitude; because you would not obey the voice of the LORD your God. And it shall come to pass, that as the LORD rejoiced over you to do you good, and to multiply you; so the LORD will rejoice over you to destroy you, and to bring you to nothing; and you shall be plucked from off the land whither you go to possess it. And the LORD shall scatter you among all people, from the one end of the Earth even unto the other; and there you shall serve other gods, which neither you nor your fathers have known, even wood and stone. And among these nations shall you find no ease, neither shall the sole of your foot have rest; but the LORD shall give you there a trembling heart, and failing of eyes, and sorrow of mind; And your life shall hang in doubt before you; and you shall fear day and night, and shall have none assurance of your life."

This is why the Inquisition in Spain occurred, the pogroms in Russia, the Holocaust of Nazi Germany, and many other incidences from the Mid-East to all over Europe constantly going after the Jewish people. The first scattering occurred with the Babylonians followed by the Romans and then afterwards Israel was constantly in fear and their life was in doubt, but God said that He would not forget them. He said that He will remember them, and He will bring them back into their position one more time permanently.

So Israel was scattered and then along came the latter part of the nineteenth century, and a Hungarian Jew named Theodor Herzl who began promoting "The Zionist Movement," the idea of Jews going back to the land of Israel. Bit by bit, the Jewish people began to go back in their land. They began to drain the swamps that were full of malaria and to work the land. However, they needed workers, but the only workers they had were the Arabs in the area and in the surrounding countries who starting coming to Israel to work as migrant workers.

Then, because of World War I, a Jewish man, Chaim Weizmann, helped England win the war by creating synthetic acetone. They could not make bombs without acetone, and Germany secured all the natural sources of acetone they could get in that area. Weizmann, a Jewish biochemist scientist, figured out how to make synthetic acetone and so helped England win the war against Germany. After the end of the war, and after England defeated the Ottoman Empire and chased the Ottoman Turks out of the land of Israel, England came to Weizmann to thank him and wanted to know how to repay him. Weizmann asked for a homeland for the Jews and requested Palestine. England agreed and the Balfour Declaration was established.

The Foreign Secretary of England at that time, Arthur James Balfour, created a right for the Jewish people to have the land of Israel right after WWI. All the Arab nations were really uptight about that. They didn't want a Jewish nation in the middle of land that belonged to their god Allah. In Islam, Muslims believe once a land has been conquered in the name of Allah, it is always Allah's land, and it is their duty to chase anybody who is not Muslim out of it. The Arab nations threatened an oil boycott against England over this Balfour Declaration. About that time, Hitler was beginning to rise up and England knew it needed oil to be able to fight him. So, under pressure from the Arab countries, England created what they called "The White Paper" which cancelled the Balfour Declaration.

Do you remember the phrase, "The sun never sets on the English Empire"? They controlled property all around the world. As soon as they issued that White Paper, that all began to crumble. One nation after nation after nation began to fall out of England's control until they came down to the little island they have now. It all fell apart. God humbled England. Why? Because England poked their finger in the eye of God by coming against Israel and the Jewish people. When the Jewish people revolted against God, it was God's business to take care of them how He sees fit. It is not anybody else's business to harm them. Scripture after scripture says, "I will punish you, but I will also punish those nations who come against you" (Jeremiah 9:25, Amos 3:2, Isaiah 34:2 and Zechariah 12:9). So it's a warning to everybody; don't harm Israel even though we may not agree with everything Israel does.

You may not be aware of this, but Israel's abortion rate in 2012 was 117 per 1000 pregnancies. While this is low compared to Europe and the United States which is almost double that amount, Israel's abortion rate has been steadily dropping every year, most likely due to the influx of Muslims into the nation. However, Israel has one of the higher homosexual rates in the world. Tel Aviv is known as the gay capital of the world. Is Israel a righteous nation? No! It is not, but it does have something most people don't have—a promise, a prophetic word that God will one day restore the nation. Nonetheless, the nation of Israel has blessed the world and there are some righteous that live in the land, but they are far from righteous according to God's standards. They need Yeshua for the forgiveness of sins.

After World War II, England tried to stop all the immigration to Israel, especially the Jews. Finally, in 1948, England—tired of the problem between Arabs and Jews concerning the land—turned the problem over to the United Nations. In 1948 the UN voted and a majority of the nations of the world voted for the establishment of Israel and a partition plan in which part of the land was supposed to be Palestine for the Arabs and part for Israel. As soon as Israel made the declaration as an independent state, the nation was attacked by five Arab armies. When the smoke finally cleared, Israel had a little bitty strip of land along the Mediterranean and down the Negev (south), and a small area in the north, and just a little pointed area that touched Jerusalem. That's all they had; smaller than the state of New Jersey. The rest of the land originally given to them by the Balfour Declaration was swallowed up by Jordan, including the land for the Palestinians.

A large portion of the country of Jordan is the land of Arab Palestine today that the UN partition plan said should belong to the Arabs. The Jordanians don't want to give it up, but why do all the Arab nations want Israel to give up their little stretch of land? Because of the same religious concept; it was once conquered by Muslims, so it remains Muslims' land and they are supposed to fight any infidel who tries to take that land. This is why we see the conflict going on over there today.

In 1948 Israel was declared a nation. Was that the beginning of the release and captivity of Israel the Bible talks about? No. We know Israel had to be formed as a nation again because of all the prophecies that talked about the existence of Israel. There are also many prophecies that talk about Jerusalem existing under Israel's control in the last days. So yes, prophecy was fulfilled when Israel became a nation, but it is not the promised end of captivity and the restoration of Israel that we are still awaiting to see take place.

Unfortunately, a lot of prophecy writers after 1948 wrote all kinds of books saying that Israel becoming a nation again was the fulfillment of all these scriptures, but it's not. As we go over the Israel prophecies, their captivity, and many other aspects of what's going to happen in Israel, we'll see what happened in 1948 was not the fulfillment of those scriptures. There's actually only a handful of scriptures in the Bible that even can be referred to the 1948 incident. All of the rest of them are still yet future. Things like when the LORD said, "When they come to their land, they will never be taken from their land again" (Jeremiah 24:6). Since 1948, that's all they've been doing is fighting over the land!

Other scriptures say they will come into the land knowing God and keeping His commandments. Did you know that in 1948, most of Israel that came into that land were atheists and communists? There were a handful of religious Jews, but most of them were secular. Why do you think they built all those kibbutzim? They were communist communes; that's what a Kibbutz was, a communist commune.

Israel came into the land in unbelief, but there are scriptures saying they will come in the land knowing God—in full belief in the LORD God, the God of Abraham, Isaac, and Jacob, and serving the Holy One of Israel, which would be Yeshua. Many scriptures talk about these things. So if that's the case, what can we expect in the future? Well, Israel is going back into captivity. You can't have scriptures that say they're coming out of captivity if they're not in captivity to start with. Their captivity would be due to the beast of Revelation. When this beast comes, it says in Daniel, he will sweep through the promised land. Zechariah says he will come in and take the land of Judah, and then he will attack Jerusalem. This is the beast; this is what we are going to see in the future. He will haul Israel off into captivity, mainly to two areas—Assyria and Egypt—as well as other nations. Then, he will attack Jerusalem and take most of the city. But before he can take the whole city, the Messiah will come back and defeat him. It's all in the book of Zechariah which I'll be talking about later in this book.

It is very important that you understand what is getting ready to happen in that land. Folks, there are going to be a lot of believers who thought 1948 was the end of the captivity. Then, all of a sudden, Israel is going to be hauled away again and confuse believers and prophecy buffs. People will claim, "Oh, you can't trust anything you read! I was told this, I was told that. You can't believe God's Word!" They're going to lose faith because of incorrect teachings they heard over the last 30 to 40 years. A lot of great prophecy writers talked about many things that may or may not come to pass as they see it, but they're wrong about this category. Israel will go back into captivity again. There are even scriptures which said that the gentiles will bring their children back into the land on their shoulders. That didn't happen in 1948; it's something that's going to occur in the not-too-distant future.

God is going to restore Israel, but during that Tribulation period when the beast comes into the land. This is one of the reasons we must strongly pray for Israel and the Jewish people. We have to lift them up and ask the LORD to deliver as many as possible because many will faint and will fall to their death during that period of time because of the beast and the nations that will come and attack with it. They will be deceived and receive the mark of the beast and face the judgment of God!

Now you'll probably hear me say this many times, but whatever happens to Israel happens to the rest of the world. So don't think that it's just Israel; it's the rest of the world, too. Israel and the world run a parallel course. So if judgment's coming in the land of Israel, it is also coming upon the nations of the world. We cannot think otherwise. We can't think, "Oh, poor little Israel. I'm glad I'm over here!" That isn't the way it's going to work. When judgment falls in Israel, it will fall on the rest of the world. We're going to see this in the very near future, and it's going to happen at lightning speed.

Chapter 3:

Reason for Captivity

Deuteronomy 28:58-68

"If you don't observe to do all the words of this law, I will send plagues on you, diseases of Egypt, sickness until you are destroyed. You'll be few in number. You'll be plucked from the land, you'll be scattered among other nations. You will serve other gods. You will find no ease, no rest, and a trembling heart; failing of eyes, sorrow at mind. Your life will be in doubt, you'll let fear day and night, no assurance of life, and you'll be sold to the enemies as bondsman. No man shall even buy you, they'll be so rejected by you."

The LORD warned Israel to obey His commandments. Failure to do so would result in plagues, diseases, and being scattered from the land. Unfortunately, this has been their lot since leaving Egypt 3,500 years ago. Israel was regathered due to the time God set. He brought them back for His glory, not for their righteousness. Israel is still not where God wants them but His plans for them are fast approaching.

Deuteronomy 30:1-3

"And it shall come to pass, when all these things are come upon thee, the blessing and the curse, which I have set before thee, and thou shalt call them to mind among all the nations, whither the LORD thy God hath driven thee. And shalt obey his voice according to all that I command thee

23

this day, thou and thy children, with all thine heart, and with all thy soul; That then the LORD thy God will turn your captivity and have compassion on you, and will return and gather you from all nations, whither the LORD thy God hath scattered thee. If any of thine be driven out unto the outmost parts of heaven, from thence will the LORD thy God gather thee, and from thence will he fetch thee: And the LORD thy God will bring thee into the land which thy fathers possessed, and thou shalt possess it; and he will do thee good, and multiply thee above thy fathers. And the LORD thy God will circumcise thine heart, and the heart of thy seed, to love the LORD thy God with all thine heart, and with all thy soul, that thou mayest live. And the LORD thy God will put all these curses upon your enemies and them that hate you, which persecute you, and you shall turn and obey the voice of the LORD and do all his commandments."

There will come a day in which Israel will recall God's words. Many in Israel could fall into this category but it's a small group. Once they call on the Messiah, they will begin to follow and obey, then the LORD will gather them and they will prosper and have their hearts changed. This hasn't happened in full yet. This is still in the future with another captivity. It can't yet be said that all of Israel loves the LORD their God with all of their heart.

In the last chapter, I talked about the history of Israel and brought you up to current times. Now we'll move on. Israel will go back into captivity in the upcoming years. But the question arises, *Why will they go back into captivity?* It's because in Ezekiel 39:23, it says, "The house of Israel went into captivity for their iniquities and their trespasses against God." Now you have to understand that Ezekiel 39 covers the end of the Gog and Magog War. It's right before the beginning of the millennial reign of the Messiah on Earth. A thousand years of peace will fill the Earth.

24

Ezekiel tells us that Israel will go into captivity because of their wickedness. Isaiah 13:11 also says, "I will punish the world for their evil and the wicked for their iniquity." So not only does Israel get punished, the whole world is going to be turning to iniquity and gets punished also. Where Israel goes, the whole world goes. Isaiah 26:21 says, "The LORD comes out of his place to punish the inhabitants of the earth for their iniquity." Isaiah also says that their feet (talking about the feet of mankind on the Earth) run to evil (59:7), and we're beginning to see this in the world today. It's slowly coming down upon us.

Matthew 24:12 says, "And because iniquity shall abound, the love of many shall wax cold." So we know that iniquity is going to wax worse and worse in the entire world. That flies a little bit in the face of those people who say the church is going to overcome, the world's going to be great, and we're going to hand over a saved world to the Messiah. That concept is being taught by orthodox churches today. I'm here to say, from my analysis of scripture, that will not be the case. Things will get worse, not better.

We also learned in Revelation 8:11 that Jerusalem, the city of our Lord itself, is called "Sodom and Egypt" during this time. So even Jerusalem is not considered holy by God during this period of tribulation. Daniel 8:23 says that the bad guy that is to come upon the Earth is a king of fierce countenance and will come when the transgressors are full. What does that mean? When we have reached a point where the world, the nations, and people have finally reached the fullness of their sin, the coming of judgment of God will be launched.

As the world decays and there is less righteousness, the Lord is getting His horse ready. The angels and the saints that will come with Him will soon be behind Him. This is all beginning to come to fruition as we see sin spiraling upward in the world as the transgressors are becoming full.

This does not mean that there may not be moments of revival. It may not mean that there will be times that God will stay His judgment and righteousness will rule for a short season again and many will be saved in the world. It is certainly possible. During the tribulation many will get saved. So there will be revivals during the last days but under dangerous and martyrdom situations. But this for sure, God's Word will be accomplished and will not fade away or change until all is complete. The LORD can delay judgment, but eventually the transgressors will become full in the Earth and judgment will begin.

Now concerning Israel today, many people are surprised about the sins of Israel that exist today. I say this not to be harmful to Israel, God forbid. I have spent my entire life being a blessing to Israel and helping them. I love Israel and the Jewish people, and I pray and desire for them to understand and receive the gospel message. All believers that call upon the LORD should have a heart for Israel. However, just because they're called physical Israel does not mean they walk in righteousness. There are righteous in Israel and the world has been blessed by Israel. The nation has a great heart in helping others. Yet we must remember that God's criteria for righteousness is the important thing and not our own set of rules of righteousness. We need to understand that.

Basically, in Israel today, less than 10 percent are even what you would call Ultra-Orthodox religious Jews. According to the 2010 Israel Central Bureau of Statistics, about 12 percent are what are referred to as just religious Jews, and 13 percent are traditional Jews who follow some form of Halakha laws of mostly kosher and attend one or two of the feast days such as Passover or Yom Kippur during the year. This amounts to only about 35 percent of Israelites who have some form of religiosity. The rest are nonreligious or secular. 20% of this group are outright atheists. However, when asked about the existence of God, about 80% say there is probably a god.

In 1948 when Israel became a nation, the amount of people who actually believed in and served God was probably around 10 percent as compared to the 2010 survey of about 35 percent So Israel is beginning to have some kind of a waking-up taking place. When Israel came in existence in 1948, most of the Jews were secularists—atheists, communists—and not truly believers in God.

These stats are just talking about the Jewish people; we're not talking about the Muslims, Christian populations, Druze, or other non-Jews which make up about 24 percent of the population. Remember, just because someone says they believe in God doesn't mean they have a personal relationship with the Creator. All around the world there are people who say they believe in God but are far removed from Him. One must also understand that God does not like to see the so-called religious Jews persecute those who serve the Messiah. This makes Him very angry.

As mentioned in chapter 1, the Israel abortion rate is high per capita. It's around 40,000 every year. If you consider, they only have 8 million people in that land, that's a pretty high percentage of abortion of .5 percent—higher than the United States which is at .3 percent. Israel's abortion rate is less than most European countries.

As also mentioned earlier, Tel Aviv is touted by many as the gay capital of the world. Just recently the news reported that gays wanted to march at one of the universities in Tel Aviv and the leaders of that university forbid them to do it. Now it's being taken to court. They were saying, "We're a university that raises up people that are of religious thought. Why would we want to allow that?" But many orthodox Jews today are accepting the gay lifestyle that's taking place in Israel. Same-sex activity became legal in 1988, and they were one of the first countries to recognize cohabitation of the same sex. They allow gays to serve openly in their military. The United States is just slightly behind Israel in the gay community, but we're fast closing and catching up with them. As Israel gets drawn down into wickedness, so the rest of the world follows. Many Christians are also falling away too.

This is why Jerusalem will be called Sodom in the Tribulation period. Revelation 11:8 says the city where the Lord (Yeshua) was crucified will be called Sodom which is Jerusalem. Israel's iniquity is getting worse. That's why we pray for Israel, the Jewish people, and for Jerusalem, as well as for those who call upon the Lord but are not obedient to Him. We want their unrighteousness to stop, and for them to start seeking the Lord God with all their heart and all their mind. Now there will always be a remnant there that believe, and even when judgment comes upon that land, a remnant will be spared which will be predominantly gathered at the city of Jerusalem.

Even though the beast of Revelation will march into the land of Israel with the nations and conquer the land and lead many into captivity, he cannot completely take Jerusalem. Zechariah 14 says the nations will take half the city of Jerusalem, and the rest will either be killed or led into captivity. However, in that city of Jerusalem a remnant will survive until delivered by the Lord, the Messiah (Revelation 12). It's funny how the LORD always has a remnant.

There's a phrase I like to use called "The Elijah Syndrome." When Elijah killed the priests of Baal, and Jezebel decided she was going to kill him (see 1 Kings 19), he fled to Horeb—which is at Mount Sinai, hid in a cave, and began to cry there to the LORD: "I even I only am left; and they seek my life, to take it away." Sometimes, we get into our own spiritual self-pity parties. *I'm the only one that's really serving God. I'm the only one that's doing it like it's supposed to be.* What did the LORD do? He spoke to Elijah in a still, small voice and said, "I have seven thousand who have not bowed their knee to Baal." So the LORD basically said, "Get out of here and get back to work!" Sometimes we all find ourselves involved in the Elijah Syndrome. *I'm the only one!* No, no, no. The LORD has a bigger remnant than that, and we have to remember that there may be a larger remnant than we think that still follow Him.

Chapter 4:

The Fig Tree

Before we begin, let's talk about the fig tree concept that is used many times to prove Israel's establishment in 1948. This concept tells of the fig tree tender leaves coming forth as mentioned in Mark 13:28-30.

> *"Now learn a parable of the fig tree; When her branch is yet tender, and puts forth leaves, you know that summer is near: So you in like manner, when you shall see these things come to pass, know that it is near, even at the doors. Verily I say unto you, that this generation shall not pass, till all these things be done."*

First, what or who is the fig tree? And second, what is a generation? Over the years, books have been written that Israel is the fig tree and a generation is forty years. Well, obviously a generation was not forty years if the establishment of Israel was the fig tree in 1948. We are well past that. Is Israel truly the fig tree? In Psalm 80:8:`14, God makes it clear that the vine represents Israel.

> *"You have brought a vine out of Egypt...O God look down from heaven and visit this vine."*

Obviously, God brought Israel out of Egypt. So the vine is Israel. So if the vine is Israel, what does the fig tree represent? In the book of Judges, chapter 9, we see the sons of Gideon—a judge in Israel who had died—vying to be the new judge in Israel. One of the sons, Abimelech—

born from a concubine of Gideon—killed all of Gideon's sons so he could be judge over Israel. However, the youngest son, Jotham, survived. When the people gathered to make Abimelech judge, Jotham spoke to them from a distance on a hill. What he said gives us a hierarchy of the importance of certain trees. Jotham began with the olive tree and said, "And the people said to the olive tree saying 'Rule over us' and the olive tree said 'Should I leave my fatness, wherewith by me they honor God and man'" (Judges 9:9). The olive tree is most important and its oil represents the Holy Spirit.

Next he mentions the fig tree in importance, then the vine. Last on the list was the bramble bush in reference to his older brother Abimelech. The youngest son of Gideon mentioned the thorny bush, or the bramble. The trees said unto the bramble, "Rule over us!" and the bramble replied, "Okay." So the olive tree, the fig tree, and the vine turned down being the ruler of Israel, but the thorny bramble accepted the offer. This was in reference to Gideon's older son who killed all of his brothers except the youngest who escaped. Of course, the bramble represents bad kings. There were several bad kings in Israel and Judah that eventually fell and God's judgment came upon them.

Let's look at the first three trees. We have here a hierarchy of olive, fig, and vine. If the olive tree represents the Holy Spirit and the vine represents Israel, what does the fig tree represent? We have to look elsewhere in the scriptures to make the comparison.

The first mention of figs is in Genesis 3:7 when Adam and Eve saw they were naked and sewed fig leaves together for clothing. The best concept here is they used fig leaves because they were large enough to cover their private parts. Is there another reason? They needed something to cover their nakedness. This is similar to Torah, or the law of God. Before Yeshua came, man needed laws to learn how to get along with one another, understand God, and hear the promises that are to come. Torah is a covering. Torah is the schoolmaster who leads the children safely to school until the teacher, who is Yeshua, appears (Galatians 3:24-25).

In Matthew 21:19-21, Yeshua and his disciples were going to the temple, Yeshua saw a fig tree and went to gather fruit from it to eat. When it had no fruit, he cursed it. The fig tree immediately withered away and the disciples were amazed about it.

Yeshua went on to say, "If you have faith and doubt not, you shall not only do this which is done to the fig tree, but also if you shall say unto this mountain, Be you removed, and be you cast into the sea; it shall be done." What is "this mountain"? What is He talking about? Where was He? He was getting ready to enter the temple, so He talking about that mountain. So basically, the fig tree became symbolism of that mountain upon which the temple stood.

If the fig tree was representing the temple at that time, why was Yeshua cursing it? It wasn't even time for the fig tree to bear its figs yet. Yeshua was very unhappy with what was going on in the temple mount, that it was not producing fruit. So when He got to the fig tree and there was no fruit, He used it for a message against what was happening at the temple. It was symbolic of the priests, the Pharisees and Sadducees, and all the groups that were worshiping at the temple mount who were not producing the sweetness of a fig like it should be—- like the fathers were when they first came out of Egypt (Hosea 9:10). This new nation of Israel became, after some trials in the wilderness, an obedient people serving God in the wilderness for many years, just before they entered the promised land. The LORD referred to them as first ripe figs and sweet. Then they turned to Baal at the Jordan river and were punished (Numbers 25 and 31). Then they showed forth rotten fruit. Or, as in this case, rotten figs. Figs are sweet and they're full of seed, but the seeds can be eaten; they're really easy to chew on. In this case, the fig represents being obedient to the commandments of God. It could also represent the temple and a holy priesthood as well as leaders of Israel. So we have a temple reference here.

In Jeremiah 29, the prophet placed a basket of good and bad figs before the temple. The good figs represented those who were obedient to God, and the bad figs represented those that did evil and were subject to judgment. This is like blessing and curses of the law. If you obey the law, it is a blessing and if you disobey the law, it's a curse. Again, another reference to the temple.

The temple was the representation of the law. This is where the sacrifices and celebrations of the Torah (law) took place. Could it be that the fig tree represents the temple being rebuilt? Perhaps a generation won't pass once the temple is rebuilt. The fig tree is the second most important tree as far as symbolism is concerned. The vine is Israel as mentioned and may not be the concept of the fig tree as so many teach.
The Torah or the word of God is the most important thing in anyone's life outside of the presence of the Holy Spirit (olive tree).

In the scriptures, a generation can be the life given by God on Earth which can be 70 to 80 years (Psalm 90:10) or perhaps 100 years based on the idea that the Hebrews stayed in Egypt for 400 years, or four generations for the sins of the Amorites to reach its fullness before leaving Egypt (Genesis 15:13 and 16). In the first chapter of Matthew, when considering the 14 generations three times from Abraham to Messiah, the average generation would be about 48 years. So using generational concepts to determine the return of the Lord can be a wide range, anywhere from 48 to 100 years from the time the fig tree leaves are tender as stated in Mark 13:28-30. Thus, the fig tree could be when Torah is back in force and/or when the temple is rebuilt. Some writers think it may have begun in 1967 when Israel took the Temple Mount back in the 6-day war. We will see.

Joel 1:7
"He hath laid my vine waste, and barked my fig tree: he hath made it clean bare, and cast it away; the branches thereof are made white."

Here we have a scripture mentioning an enemy that comes and destroys the nation of Israel and the temple, using the same concepts of the vine and fig tree. No doubt Nebuchadnezzar of Babylon did this. He led most of Israel into captivity but not all and destroyed the Temple completely. He certainly laid the temple bare. Yet it is also a declaration of the Day of the LORD in verse 15. Also in Joel 2:2 we are told that an enemy is coming unlike ever has been seen nor shall be. This would put Joel in a different scenario than what Nebuchadnezzar had done.

Let's look further into to the fig tree. We read in Joel 1:7 that the vine was laid waste. So the whole nation of Israel will be laid waste by this strong army that is coming, and he barked the fig tree. It's important to understand exactly what the fig tree is all about. You have to look at a lot of scriptures and concepts to understand what's taking place here. In Exodus 15:25, the LORD brought Israel to the waters of Marah ("bitterness"). He took a tree there and threw it in to make it sweet. Exodus 15:26 says, "If thou wilt diligently hearken to the voice of the LORD thy God, and wilt do that which is right in his sight, and wilt give ear to his commandments, and keep all his statutes, I will put none of these diseases upon thee, which I have brought upon the Egyptians: for I am the LORD that healeth thee."

We see right here the example of a tree. It doesn't say it's a fig yet, but the writer tells us it's a tree that God used to make the water sweet. At that point, when this tree made the waters sweet, God says "If you obey me and follow my commandments, then none of these diseases will come upon you." Psalm 119:103 also tells us that God's words are sweeter than honey. If one disobeys God's word, it is bitterness, but if he obeys God's words, it is sweet. So the tree of Marah was like God showing His grace and telling the Hebrews to follow His word, which is very much like the concept of the fig tree.

Micah 4:4
"But they shall sit every man under his vine and under his

33

*fig tree; and none shall make them afraid: for the mouth of
the LORD of hosts hath spoken it."*

This has been repeated many times in the scripture: Every man
under his own vine and every man under his own fig tree. In this case, the
vine and fig tree are talking about prosperity. Every man will have his own
vine, every man will have his own fig tree. Truth be known, not every man
has or will have a vine and not every man has or will have a fig tree. This
scripture is about symbolism. What is he talking about? What does it
represent? The vine, of course, represents Israel. As we know, in John 15:1
Yeshua said, "I am the true vine," and we are the branches.

If you're a gentile who believes in Yeshua, you are engrafted into
Israel. If you're Jewish and you are part of Israel, then the root of that vine
is Yeshua. We are only the branches. We know the whole household of
Israel is represented by the vine. So it seems this scripture is indicating a
presence in the land of Israel (vine) and following Torah (fig tree) for
blessings.

Proverbs 27:18
*"Whoso keepeth the fig tree shall eat the fruit thereof: so he
that waiteth on his master shall be honoured."*

That's a nice statement which could be said about any tree. If the
tree is yours, you get to eat the fruit of it. But why is he particularly
mentioning the fig tree? In Hosea 9:10 the LORD said, "I found Israel like
a grape in the wilderness." This, again, is the vine concept. "I saw your
fathers as the first ripe in the fig tree at her first time." But they went to
worship Baal. So God saw the leaders of Israel—the fathers anyway—as
figs because they obeyed the voice of the LORD. But then they turned and
started worshiping Baal. So when you see that "But they went," they were
like figs and now they were not. Something happened there. They're still
the vine, they're still Israel, but they are no longer like the fig when they
started turning against the commandments of God, worshiping other gods,

and becoming disobedient.

So when God talks about the vine being laid waste in Joel 1:7, He's talking about the whole nation of Israel. Even the fig tree, the temple, got barked.

In the future when the fig tree leaves are tender, this could be about the rebuilt temple and the new priesthood and/or leaders who follow the commandments of God. Without Yeshua, even those who try to follow torah will be removed from the land by an enemy yet to come. It is in their captivity that this remnant will call upon Yeshua and they will be delivered.

Luke 13:6 says (concerning the fig tree that was planted in this farmer's vineyard), this farmer came and looked at it and said, "There's no fruit on it! Tear it down!" But the workers said, "Well, Lord, give me a little chance, a little bit longer, to dig up the soil and give it one more year and maybe then it will produce figs." This is talking about the Lord God in heaven looking down upon this fig tree and looking for fruit (just like the tree that Yeshua cursed at that time). The keeper of the trees said, "Give me one more year to try to get it to produce fruit." That could be an example of the Lord in our lives looking down and saying, "You're not producing any fruit!" Let Yeshua be the dresser through the Holy Spirit and work through your life to get you to start producing fruit. If there's no fruit, the scripture says that He will cut down the unfruitful trees and burn them (Matthew 3:10, 7:19). We have to be fruitful.

In Psalms 119:103 we learn that the Word of God is sweet to our taste, yea, sweeter than honey to our mouths. Figs are referred to as honey. So another definition of good figs could be speaking of those who follow the Word of God and bad figs could represent those who do not.

In 2 Kings 20:7, the LORD is speaking to Hezekiah. Hezekiah was told to get his house in order because he was about to die. Hezekiah, very humbly, went with it, right? No! Hezekiah whined and cried! "No! I don't want to die!" So he went to Isaiah, and Isaiah interceded for him with the LORD, and the LORD gave Hezekiah 15 more years. But in that 15 additional years, that's when Manasseh was born—the worst king Judah ever had. Hezekiah would have been better off if he would had just gone when it was his time. When the LORD promised him 15 more years, He said, "Take a lump of figs and lay it on the boil." He recovered, then the LORD said, "and on the third day, you shall go to the house of the LORD." There's a clue here. That fig healed Hezekiah, and on the third day he went to the house of the LORD.

Prophetically speaking, a day is a thousand years with the LORD. So Yeshua, being also a fig tree for us—He is the one who heals us—and then on the third day, we will go to the house of the LORD also. Hezekiah did not die because he put fig on his boils. We know that Yeshua heals, and we have eternal life. We shall not also die, and we shall go to the house of the LORD due to the fig tree. If the fig is the Word of God or even the temple of the LORD, that is Yeshua, then the Word of God is what heals. The third day concepts are prevalent throughout the scriptures. The Hebrews prepared themselves for two days and on the third day the LORD met them at Sinai. Yeshua was in the tomb for three days. One of the more pronounced examples is shown below in Hosea.

Hosea 5:15–6:2

"I will go and return to my place, till they acknowledge their offence, and seek my face: in their affliction they will seek me early. Come, and let us return unto the LORD: for he has torn, and he will heal us; he has smitten, and he will bind us up. After two days will he revive us: in the third day he will raise us up, and we shall live in his sight."

Hosea is speaking here of the Messiah Yeshua. He is the only one who came, returned to His place (heaven at the throne of His Father), and then promised to come back—in this case after two days. Since prophetically speaking a day with the LORD is a thousand years (Psalm 90:4 and 2 Peter 3:8), this means on the morning of the third day, or just after 2,000 years, He will come back. And when He comes, those who trust and believe will certainly receive their full healing.

The fig tree is a lot more than just a nice little fruit tree that's mentioned in the Bible. The vine represents Israel, the fig represents all the goodness of God, the commandments of God, the priesthood of God, the temple of the LORD, and the healing of God. This is all involved with the fig tree.

Jeremiah 24:1-2

"The LORD shewed me, and, behold, two baskets of figs were set before the temple of the LORD, after that Nebuchadnezzar king of Babylon had carried away captive Jeconiah the son of Jehoiakim king of Judah, and the princes of Judah, with the carpenters and smiths, from Jerusalem, and had brought them to Babylon. One basket had very good figs, even like the figs that are first ripe: and the other basket had very naughty figs, which could not be eaten, they were so bad."

One basket will be good figs, and one basket will be bad figs, or as the scripture says, very bad figs, rotten figs, stinky figs. He's supposed to lay those two bags on the porch of the temple. Again, this is related to the temple. The good figs, the LORD says, represent the good of Judah and He will acknowledge (remember) them when they are carried away by Nebuchadnezzar to a land of the Chaldeans. "And I will bring back and give them a heart to know me. I will be their God, and they will be my people and they will return with their whole heart" (Jeremiah 24:7). That's what the good figs represented.

Now, we don't know if that really ever happened. We do know that a remnant came out of Babylon, but did they really come back with a whole heart toward God? We don't know. However, it says the bad figs represent those who are going to remain in Jerusalem, particularly Zedekiah, king of Judah, and his princes; those left in Jerusalem; those in the land; and those hiding in Egypt (Jeremiah 24:8-10).

The LORD will remove them unto all the kingdoms of the Earth for their hurt and make them a curse in all the places where He will drive them. He will send the sword, famine, and pestilence, until they are consumed even off the land. Wow! That's what the bad figs represent. If the good figs are supposed to represent the sweetness of the LORD through His laws and His commandments through the temple ordinances, then a stinky, bad fig will be those who rejected the LORD, who worshiped other gods, who are disobedient and breaking the laws of God. But a good fig would be the opposite; he'll be obedient to the things of God.

In Joel 3:17 it says "the mountains shall drop down new wine and the hills shall flow with milk." What did the prophet mean by milk? It could be milk by a cow or milk by a goat, but do you know what the general description of milk is? Fig juice. So here we have the fig tree and the vine represented again as wine and milk—another concept of walking in righteousness and holiness.

In John 1:45-51, a soon-to-be disciple of Yeshua, Nathanael, saw Yeshua and came to him. When Yeshua saw Nathanael, He said, "Behold, an Israelite indeed, in whom is no guile." Yeshua then said, "When you were under the fig tree, I saw you." What did Nathaniel say? "You are the son of God; you are the King of Israel." What would cause Nathanael to say this to Yeshua? Certainly Nathaniel wouldn't call Yeshua the Son of God just because Yeshua saw him at a distance under a fig tree. Something miraculous happened here. More than likely Yeshua was stating that He knew Nathanael's spiritual condition. He said this was a man with no deceit and no guile. Nathaniel was a righteous man.

When Yeshua said He saw him under the fig tree, that goes back to the analogy of "every man having his own vine, and having his own fig tree." Those who are walking in righteousness will result in spiritual prosperity, and He saw Nathaniel sitting under the fig tree. Where will God see you sitting? Will you be sitting under the fig tree? Will you sit under a thorny bush, a tumbleweed, or even dandelions? We need to be found under a fig tree, indicating that we are righteous and obedient to God.

The Bible says every man will have his own vine and fig tree during the millennial period. Every believer is part of Israel; that's the vine being grafted in if you are a gentile. If you're walking in holiness and the commandments of God, you're under the fig tree. As mentioned before, remember that Jeremiah put out two baskets of figs, both good and bad. The bad had all kind of judgments pronounced on them, but the good—even though they're going to be led into captivity—God said "I will return them back to their land for their good." That means you don't always escape your problems, but God's got his hand on you and He's watching you all of the time. This is why we need to rend our hearts, not our garments, and dwell under the fig tree.

The fig leaf represents the commandments and the law of God. It was important to keep people straight, to lead them as a schoolmaster until the teacher, which is the Messiah, comes and redeems them (Galatians 3:23-25). The first tree mentioned other than the tree of life in the Bible is the fig. Adam and Eve had to sow and wear fig leaves after their sin in the garden as a covering over their nakedness.

That's where we get the concept, "Under the law." It's good to be under the law; otherwise, one is lawless. We've really made it sound like it's something like a curse to be under the law, but it's not. Disobedience to the law is a curse! But Israel was under the law until the Deliverer came and showed them grace and mercy and wrote the laws in their heart through the Holy Spirit. Until that time, God had to keep them straight and that's why He put them under the law. Without Yeshua, man is still under the law and will be judged through it. Why would one neglect a great opportunity and reject the Messiah and have their life judged by the law? Adam and Eve were put under the law by the fig leaves. Following the law and being obedient to the law still applies today but grace and mercy of our Messiah Yeshua should be number one in our lives as everyone sins, and He is faithful to forgive us of our sins. Being judged by the law can be without mercy. Strive for the better way.

We all need to be under our own fig tree. If you have Yeshua, if you love (which is the fulfillment of the law) and you're under your own fig tree and your own vine, it doesn't mean you go out and do whatever you want to do. He's faithful and just to forgive us of our sins *if* we confess them. That's where we have an advocate in Yeshua. When we do something wrong, we can say, "LORD, forgive me!" and it's done. That's the magnificent plan of God, but if we keep doing what we want to do, our hearts will start to turn hard, we won't ask for forgiveness anymore, and we'll be subject to judgment. We've got to dwell under our fig tree.

Actually, we need to be part of the olive tree (Holy Spirit), the vine (Israel), and the fig tree (Torah or law of God, even the temple). As believers, we are now the temple of the LORD, and the law should be written in our hearts by the Spirit of God. We've got to be part of the vine —part of Israel—part of the fig tree (holiness), and obedient to the laws that are applicable today. The pomegranate tree was another tree that has meaning. What does the pomegranate tree represent? Priesthood. The high priest has pomegranates sown on the bottom part of his garments. A pomegranate has a crown on it and all the seeds inside are surrounded by red juice, indicating the unity of believers saved by the blood of Yeshua.

Joel 1:12 also mentioned the apple tree which indicates fruitfulness. We've got to produce fruit. Any fruitful tree that doesn't produce fruit will be cut down. All the trees of the fields represent people and their spiritual condition. What kind of tree are you?

Chapter 4 | The Fig Tree

Chapter 5:

The Evil Nations

Jeremiah 30:7
"Alas! for that day is great, so that none is like it: it is even the time of Jacob's trouble, but he shall be saved out of it."

Have you ever heard the term "Jacob's trouble"? That's what the Tribulation's all about. That word "trouble" is a noun and it can mean *enemy or rival?* So when you say, "Jacob's trouble" it doesn't just mean someone is having a hard time; it means the enemy overflows into the land, leads them into captivity, and persecutes them. You can see it today — "Jacob's trouble" is presently knocking at the door of Israel. This term is specifically speaking of an enemy that is coming.

Daniel 12:1
"And at that time shall Michael stand up, the great prince which standeth for the children of thy people: and there shall be a time of trouble, such as never was since there was a nation even to that same time: and at that time thy people shall be delivered, every one that shall be found written in the book."

Trouble is coming upon the Earth—and especially Israel, unlike anything ever seen before. Because of that trouble, Israel will call upon the LORD and be delivered.

Enoch 90:2

"And after that I saw in my vision all the birds of heaven coming, the eagles, the vultures, the kites, the ravens, but the eagles led all the birds, and they began to devour those sheep (Israel), and to pick out their eyes and to devour their flesh."

Note, Enoch will be quoted several times in this book. The quotes come from The book of Enoch or 1 Enoch as translated by biblical scholar R.H. Charles in 1893. The book of Enoch was found in the Ethiopian and Eritrean Bibles over 200 years ago and brought to the western world, although there were some who claimed to already have copies of it. The book of Jude quotes from Enoch and the early Christian Fathers, such as Clement of Alexandria, Irenaeus, and Tertullian, quoted from it. Several fragments of the book of Enoch were found in the Dead Sea Scrolls. It was at one time an important book.

This particular scripture of the book of Enoch describes Israel as sheep. There are carnivorous animals such as lions, tigers, wild boars, foxes, as well as wolves and hyenas which are the enemies of Israel in the flesh that surround them today. But the carnivorous birds—eagles, vultures and others—are bad angels which will come and begin to destroy many in Israel. They are getting ready to arrive on the scene. As a matter of fact, Enoch 56:5 says, "And the angels [talking about the bad angels that have been locked up] will be released. Shall return and hurl themselves to the East among the Parthians and the Medes? And they shall stir up the kings with a spirit of unrest and they shall break forth as lions and wolves." What starts all of this? These bad angels. Of course, we're waiting for the transgressors to be full, but bad angels are also coming and they're going to begin at the land of the Medes and the Parthians.

Let's take a look at the countries that play a major role in the last days.

Israel is the major target of the nations in the last days. North from Israel is Turkey which is also a major player. A major city in Turkey is Istanbul which controls the waterway between the Black Sea and the Mediterranean Sea. East of the Black Sea is the largest freshwater lake in the world, the Caspian Sea. The areas of interest we're going to be talking about are the Mediterranean area to the Black Sea over to the Caspian Sea and everything in between. Russia is north of the Black Sea and the Caspian Sea. The country of Georgia is between the Black Sea and the Caspian Sea, with Azerbaijan and Armenia and eastern parts of Turkey, northern Iran, northern Iraq, and northern Syria. These lands make up the land of Magog and the old Assyrian empire, and this is where Gog of Ezekiel Chapters 38 and 39 will come from—the land of the Parthians and Medes. On the northern border of Georgia is the Caucasus Mountain Range that separates Georgia from Russia. There are only a few passes here that allow people to travel from Georgia to Russia. Alexander the Great actually built a gate across the main pass and called it the gate of Magog to keep out the people that are on the north side of the gate. That area used to be called the land of the Scythians. Today it belongs to Russia.

According to Enoch, the bad angels are coming to the land of the Medes and the Parthians. That's where it will begin. They will come flying into the land of Israel and stir up everybody around there. These are bad angels that God had locked up from a previous engagement back during the time of Enoch, and now they will be let out for judgment against the world. Of course, this is the area of ISIS also today. One has to wonder whether or not the viciousness of ISIS is because of these bad angels that may already be here.

It's important to understand how this all begins. They are bad angels. Then you read a little bit further in Enoch 57:1 (after that event of those bad angels) where it says that the dispersion of Israel will come to an end. The LORD will begin to gather them from the East and the West in wagons, and it says the noise of those wagons will be great and the whole world will know that He is the LORD God. Now, I don't think they're covered wagons. It's probably talking about ships and so on. Whatever, it's going to be a loud noise so the whole world recognizes that God is regathering Israel at this time.

This is why it mentions in the scriptures that no longer will people say great is the LORD who brought the Hebrews out of Egypt, but great is the LORD who brought them from all the countries of the world (Jeremiah 16:14-15). There will be miracles; there'll be outstanding events that will take place, and everybody will be saying great is the God of Israel when this takes place. What happened in 1948 was a pretty big deal, but the world doesn't proclaim God over that event; however, they will on this event. That's why 1948 was not the final regathering of Israel.

Psalm 2:1

"Why do the heathen rage, and the people imagine a vain thing? The kings of the earth set themselves, and the rulers take counsel together, against the LORD, and against his anointed, saying, Let us break their bands asunder, and cast away their cords from us. He that sitteth in the heavens shall laugh: the LORD shall have them in derision. Then shall he speak unto them in his wrath, and vex them in his sore displeasure. Yet have I set my king upon my holy hill of Zion."

Here, the heathen are raging. One of the reasons why they are raging is that they don't like the cords and bonds and they want to break them. What are they talking about? What do they consider cords and bonds? They are the commandments of the LORD. The heathen want to be able to do what they want to do without feeling guilty or living by a law that says they can't. They want to break those bonds away from the LORD and His anointed, which is none other than Yeshua.

We see this today; people rising up everywhere, coming against anything that might be of the law of God. Even the heathens want release and to break those bonds that are shackling them from their own selfishness and lust. They want free access to abortion at anyplace, anytime. They want free access to engage in all kinds of sexual immorality. They want to break these bonds and cords that believers see as a strengthener, a fortress, and a guidance to live a proper, righteous life before the LORD. The heathen don't see it that way; they think it's something restrictive, but we see it as valuable to our lives. So the heathen are going to gather in a mass in the last days against Israel because they see Israel as the custodian of the Torah or law of God, especially if the temple has been rebuilt by then. The temple of God represents the law of God just as believers today represent the law of God since believers are the true temple of the LORD.

Chapter 6:

Gog

Ezekiel 38:1-2
"And the word of the LORD came unto me, saying, Son of man, set thy face against Gog, the land of Magog, the chief prince of Meshech and Tubal, and prophesy against him."

We now have an individual called Gog coming on the scene from the land of Magog as the worse of bad guys. I believe this Gog is one of those angels and he's coming real soon. I believe he's also the beast of Revelation and he will stir up all the nations to come against Israel and Jerusalem. Look at the ancient map on page 66.

Notice on the ancient map that the Caucasus Mountain range is between the Black Sea and the Caspian Sea. The modern countries of Georgia and Azerbaijan line the southern range. North of the Caucasus Mountain Range is where the Scythians ruled. It is also part of the land of Magog. Alexander the Great built a wall and a gate here he called the Gate of Magog to keep the Scythians out. The land of Magog existed on both sides of this range. South of this range is not only the land of Magog but also the land of Meshach. The land just east of this is the land of the Parthians and Medes which is modern Iran.

The modern country of Turkey would be west of this area and south of the Black Sea. East of Turkey would be Armenia and Iran (Persia). South of Turkey would be Iraq and Syria. Looking again at the ancient map, we see that Gomer is on the north and south side of the Black

Sea. Notice that Tubal, Meshech, and Togarmah are all listed in the eastern Turkey and Armenia area. Every nation mentioned in Ezekiel 38 confederation for Gog is mentioned right here in eastern Turkey, northern Iran, northern Iraq, Armenia, and Georgia with the exception of Ethiopia (eastern Africa) and Libya (northern Africa).

Now I don't disagree with the concept that maybe some of these nations migrated to other places, including Russia, which is north and east of the Black Sea. Today Russia borders the Caucasus Mountain Range on the north. Is Russia one of these nations of Ezekiel chapters 38 and 39? I don't know. Many believe that Russia is Gog the chief prince of Meshech and Tubal as mentioned in Ezekiel 38:2-3 and 39:1. One must consider that the Gog war appears to be the last battle before the coming of the Messiah. Israel is redeemed after this and brought out of captivity and they all know the LORD God (Ezekiel 39:27-29). Also, keep in mind that the following chapters of Ezekiel 40-48 are all about the millennial reign of Messiah. No more wars are mentioned. So it makes sense that Gog must be the Beast of Revelation. Now the Hebrew term for "chief" of chief prince that Ezekiel speaks of is the word "Rosh". Now Rosh sounds close to Rus for Russia. However, we must remember that the "s" in Rus is a different Hebrew letter than the "sh" in Rosh. It is still possible that Rus is Rosh but not likely. We must be careful when trying to link words that are similar in spelling. Such as trying to link Moscow to Meshech just because there are similar letters.

Again, serious hermeneutic problems arise when you try to compare things like that. I'm not saying Russia won't be involved. All I'm saying is be careful how you take these words and try to make them something that they're not. As far as I can tell, the bad guy (Gog) will begin in the area of Eastern Turkey, Armenia, Georgia, and/or Iran.

Now the angels that come there and stir up the kings, they can certainly stir up Russia, and they can certainly stir up all the kings of the

Earth, but this is where it starts, not Russia. Keep in mind, however, that Russia is currently in the area fighting ISIS, the radical jihadist group. It is the opinion of this writer that ISIS is what Islam is all about. One just has to look back to the early days of Islam and understand that it's the initial spread was due to forced conversion, death, and violence. ISIS is true Islam. It is not a peaceful religion. When the Islamic Messiah or Maadi shows up, he in fact may be the Gog of Ezekiel which I believe is also the beast of Revelation. All Muslims will follow him and those who don't will be labeled worse than an infidel and will be killed as the Islamic writings state.

Ezekiel 38:3
"And say, Thus saith the Lord God; Behold, I am against thee, O Gog, the chief prince of Meshech and Tubal."

Again, that term "chief prince" is Rosh Nasi. The word "chief" is Rosh, not "rus", which Russia gets its name. It is not a good comparison to try and make Rosh "rus". Rosh doesn't appear to have anything to do with Russia.

Ezekiel 38:4
"And I will turn thee back, and put hooks into thy jaws, and I will bring thee forth, and all thine army, horses and horsemen, all of them clothed with all sorts of armour, even a great company with bucklers and shields, all of them handling swords."

It is interesting the phrase "turn thee back." This word *shuwb* has many meanings and one of them is "return" or "bring back." Could this be an indication that God is returning the bad angels we saw in Enoch? Otherwise, who is it that will be turned back or return which indicates a past presence?

It then goes on to say some of the nations that will be joining with

Him at that time—Persia (that's Iran), Ethiopia...

On a modern map (page 65), Egypt is south of Israel, Ethiopia is further south of Egypt, Sudan is between Egypt and Ethiopia, and Somalia is east of Ethiopia along the Red Sea. At one time all of these eastern African nations were all part of a larger Ethiopian empire. Egypt was just a province of Ethiopia. The nation of Egypt came out of the Ethiopian empire. Everything in Egypt originally came from Ethiopia. So when it says Ethiopia, it means that whole area of Egypt, Sudan, Ethiopia, Somalia — all the east side of Africa.

On the other side of Egypt is Libya. Did you know that the Libyan Empire pretty much controlled all of northern Africa at one time? So if the Ethiopian empire is on the east side of Africa and the Libyan Empire is on the north, all the way to the west part of Africa, this is why many ancient writers once called Libya, Africa. However, it's really a word referring to Northern Africa.

Ezekiel 38 goes on to say many nations will join with Gog at that time which will be Persia (Iran), Ethiopia (Eastern Africa), Libya (Northern Africa), Togarmah (Turkey), and Gomer (areas around Black Sea). This will include many other nations too

I believe that when Gog arrives on the scene, he will proclaim himself to be The Twelfth Imam, or the Mahdi of Islam. Being an angel, he will work miracles and do all kinds of false wonders and amazing things. He'll have 1.4 billion Muslims at his fingertips who will believe that he is the Muslim messiah and his followers will do anything and everything he says. The whole world will then go into turmoil because one of the things he's going to do is to make Islam the religion of the world and kill the infidels who don't follow suit. The whole world will go into chaos and with much violence and bloodshed.

Matthew 10:21 tells us that brother will be against brother, sister

52

against sister, children against parents, parents against children. People will slay each other all over the world and deliver each other up to be put to death. This will happen because those who become Islamic will feel it's their duty to kill everybody around them, including family members. The whole world will go into a tremendous upheaval at this time.

If you read the book of Revelation, you realize that this beast of Revelation, Gog, also hates Islam, but he will use this religion for his purpose until he controls the world. In Revelation he says that he burns the harlot Babylon which is a city (Revelation 17:16) and it's a good indication that the Babylon of Revelation is not in Iraq. The original Babylon has not been rebuilt. More than likely this Babylon is Mecca, the center of Islam. Why does he burn her? The woman who sits on the beast in Revelation, the religion Islam is telling the beast what to do.

Once he's in control, he doesn't want to be told what to do anymore. Now he's proclaiming himself God in the temple at Jerusalem and no longer needs Islam. He used it for his own purposes to get control of the world. Now he will burn the city of Mecca. That's what it talks about in Revelation and he will actually take control of the whole world at this time.

By the way, the mark of the beast are three Greek letters: *chi, xi,* and *sigma,* translated as 666. However, according to those who know Arabic, they can be translated in Arabic to symbols that say, "In the name of Allah, Jihad." The same three Arabic letters look very similar to the three Greek letters 666. Is that what John saw? I don't know, it could be. Apparently, many jihadists have these symbols on the headbands and flags they use. The X symbol or *chi* in Greek is similar to an Arabic symbol representing the crossing of swords which is symbolic of jihad.

Ezekiel 38:5-6
"Persia, Ethiopia, and Libya with them; all of them with shield and helmet: Gomer, and all his bands; the house of

Togarmah of the north quarters, and all his bands: and many people with thee."

Gomer goes from the northwestern part of the Black Sea near Greece to the north of the Black Sea, including the country of Ukraine today. Togarmah is south of the Black Sea in the eastern part of today's Turkey. Turkey is a major player in the last days, just as it was during the Ottoman Empire.

You have to understand, too, that Ezekiel knew all of these places, but he knew nothing of Russia or Moscow. He didn't even know anything about China, but he knew these places and he didn't question the LORD on any of them. Many times these prophets received information, and if they don't understand, they'll say, "LORD, will you explain?" Ezekiel knew exactly the countries God was talking about; he didn't question any of it. So it looks like all of it begins right up in those areas.

Ezekiel 38:8

"After many days thou shalt be visited: in the latter years thou shalt come into the land that is brought back from the sword, and is gathered out of many people, against the mountains of Israel, which have been always waste: but it is brought forth out of the nations, and they shall dwell safely all of them."

After a time, Gog will be visited. This can mean attended to, reckoned with, or sought out. Another clue that it may be a fallen angel who will come into the land of Israel.

In 1948, Israel was gathered out of all the nations and the people are dwelling somewhat safely today. The LORD is putting the hook in the jaw of Gog and saying, "Come into the land to a people that are now dwelling safely that were gathered from the nations." It's talking about what began in 1948 until now, and He's getting ready to come into the land.

Ezekiel 38:9

"Thou shalt ascend and come like a storm, thou shalt be like a cloud to cover the land, thou, and all thy bands, and many people with thee."

What does he mean by "ascend"? Is it just a poetic statement, or is it truly saying you shall ascend out from where I had you imprisoned before I released you? The book of Enoch talks about how the bad angels were hidden in the bowels and the valleys of the Earth. Can that be the ascending where He lets them out and they come onto the scene from the lands of the Medes and Parthians and from there start trouble?

Ezekiel 38:10

"Thus saith the Lord God; It shall also come to pass, that at the same time shall things come into thy mind, and thou shalt think an evil thought:"

What is Gog thinking? What is his evil thought? Let's find out.

Ezekiel 38:11-12

"And thou shalt say, I will go up to the land of unwalled villages; I will go to them that are at rest, that dwell safely, all of them dwelling without walls, and having neither bars nor gates, To take a spoil, and to take a prey; to turn thine hand upon the desolate places that are now inhabited, and upon the people that are gathered out of the nations, which have gotten cattle and goods, that dwell in the midst of the land."

You know this has to be at a time where the cities are not in fortresses or have big walls, so you know it's in modern times. To "take a spoil" means *to rob of possessions; gold, silver, whatever somebody wants.* But to take a prey, if you look up the definition, it means *people and beasts*. So Gog is coming in the land to not only rob it, but to take people into captivity. That's why I said Israel will go back into captivity and Gog will do it. He will take most of the land of Israel and half the city of Jerusalem. He cannot take all of Jerusalem because the LORD will not allow him to do it. There's a remnant in the city that He will protect.

Ezekiel 38:13

"Sheba, and Dedan, and the merchants of Tarshish, with all the young lions thereof, shall say unto thee, Art thou come to take a spoil? hast thou gathered thy company to take a prey? to carry away silver and gold, to take away cattle and goods, to take a great spoil?"

Dedan is in the area of Sheba; some people say the other side where Ethiopia is, is also Sheba. Dedan is in the Arabia area as well as Sheba. So basically, the Arabians seem to be complaining here about the invasion of Gog. Perhaps they feel that Gog is coming to take their oil. Then we have the merchants of Tarshish. Who or where is Tarshish? Nobody knows. There's a lot said in the Bible about Tarshish, and I wish there was really good, scriptural evidence that we could identify it, but we cannot. Some people believe it was the Phoenician area; some believe it was Spain; and others believe it could be England because even Solomon sent the ships of Tarshish out to collect goods from all over the world. Tarshish was visited by Phoenician ships as the Phoenicians were great sailors. There's even evidence that Phoenicians were here in the United States. Of course, we all know that Columbus wasn't the first one here. Historians say the Norse were here first up in Canada, but there's good evidence that the Phoenicians were here long before Columbus. When you put all this stuff together, there is also good evidence that the Chinese were here long before Columbus.

So who are the ships of Tarshish? Who are they? I won't get into big detail about Tarshish, but when the tribulation finally ends, Isaiah 60:9 says, "The ships of Tarshish will be the first to bring Israel's sons from far." So whoever this Tarshish is seems to have great honor in bringing the children back to the land first. Although many nations will assist in bringing the children of Israel back to the land, the ships of Tarshish will be the first ones. If Tarshish is Spain and England, like some historians say, what two countries founded the United States? Spain and England? Can the United States be the ships of Tarshish? Has the United States earned the honor to bring the children of Israel back to the land? Maybe. Even though we find ourselves going downhill pretty fast, will we have that honor in the last days? We don't know who Tarshish is, it's just a thought.

It says here, *with all the young lions thereof and say unto you, are you come to take a spoil? Have you gathered your company to take a prey; to carry silver and gold and take away cattle and goods and take a great spoil?* So Sheba, Dedan, and Tarshish aren't doing anything about it, but they're all saying, "What are you coming down here for? What are you trying to do? Are you trying to rob the people?" It sounds like they're wanting to play ambassadors, but at a distance and all they want to do is talk. They're not going to do anything about it because they're all afraid of this guy.

It also says in Revelation 13:4, "Who is able to make war against him (the beast)?" No one. So if the beast was just a mere man, the nations of the world could rise up against him. With the weaponry we have today, they could destroy him. However, if he's not a mere man, why is it that we cannot fight him? No one can make war against the beast because he's not a mere man, although he may take on the form of a man. He's going to sweep into this land.

Ezekiel 38:14-16
"Therefore, son of man, prophesy and say unto Gog, Thus saith the Lord God; In that day when my people of Israel dwelleth safely, shalt thou not know it? And thou shalt come from thy place out of the north parts, thou, and many

people with thee, all of them riding upon horses, a great company, and a mighty army: And thou shalt come up against my people of Israel, as a cloud to cover the land; it shall be in the latter days, and I will bring thee against my land, that the heathen may know me, when I shall be sanctified in thee, O Gog, before their eyes."

So this guy Gog is coming against Israel from the northern parts and will be pretty much successful. Now *north* has other meanings that may be interesting to know. *North*, or *tsaphown* in Hebrew, also means "dark and hidden." Could it be the prison where God had the fallen angels or is it just north as in direction? What does it mean to *be sanctified before you, O Gog?* That means that God is going to allow Gog to come down, take Israel, take half of Jerusalem, and then He is going to destroy him so the whole world will know that the God of Israel is the God is Abraham, Isaac, and Jacob, the Mighty One of Israel. At that point, He's going to show the whole world that he is God.

Ezekiel 38:17-19
"Thus saith the Lord God; Art thou he of whom I have spoken in old time by my servants the prophets of Israel, which prophesied in those days many years that I would bring thee against them? And it shall come to pass at the same time when Gog shall come against the land of Israel, saith the Lord God, that my fury shall come up in my face. For in my jealousy and in the fire of my wrath have I spoken, Surely in that day there shall be a great shaking in the land of Israel."

It is important to understand this great shaking taking place at this time in the land. Typically, what do you associate a great shaking with? Earthquakes. Did you know there are great earthquakes in the book of Revelation that are judgments of God? The last one in Revelation 16:18 is called a Great Earthquake which will level all the cities of the world. You don't think bad things are coming? A lot of bad things are coming! It is the seventh vial poured out by the wrath of God upon the world; the last judgment, a great shaking before He actually comes to destroy the army of Gog the beast. It'll be a great shaking. That's why it says in verse 20, "So that the fish of the sea, and the fouls of the heaven, and the beasts of the field, and all creeping things that creep upon the Earth, and all the men that are upon the face of the Earth, shall shake at my presence, and the mountains shall be thrown down, and the steep places shall fall, and every wall shall fall to the ground."

This is really scary. If you think about the great earthquakes you've seen happen around the world and the utter destruction they cause, they're nothing compared to this. This will blows the Richter scale off the top. When we look at great earthquakes around 9 on the Richter scale and the horrible destruction they create, this one will be far greater and probably not measurable. It will be unlike anything anyone has ever seen or heard.

Ezekiel 38:21
"And I will call for a sword against him throughout all my mountains, saith the Lord God: every man's sword shall be against his brother."

When God's judgment begins on Gog and the beast with all the Islamic hordes, He will do like He's done before—cause them to fight each other. Every sword will be against his man's brother also. God has done this throughout the Bible when He sends angels among them and causes everybody to fight each other. This happened in the time of King Jehoshaphat when the armies of Moab, Ammon and Edom fought each other to death (see 2 Chronicles 20). They didn't trust anybody; they thought everybody was their enemy, and they all began to fight against each other. Now this may not be only against Gog and his army in the land of Israel, but it'll probably be this way all over the world.

Verse 22 says, "And I will plead against him with pestilence and with blood; and I will rain upon him, and upon his bands, and upon the many people that are with him, an overflowing rain, and great hailstones, fire, and brimstone." Understand that the word "plead" is better translated as "judge".

Here's clear evidence that this Gog is also the beast of Revelation. What else is poured out during this time? We read in Revelation 6:2, "Swords are poured out upon all who have the mark of the beast." That's the pestilence. "The sun will scorch mankind" (Revelations 16:8; darkness will come (Revelation 16:10); a great earthquake (Revelation 16:18), and great hail burning will fall upon mankind. It repeats a lot of those given in Ezekiel 38. So the same kind of judgments in Ezekiel that's falling on Gog are the same judgments falling on the beast of Revelation.

This is a good place to understand that Gog and the beast are one and the same taking place.

Ezekiel 38:23
"Thus will I magnify myself, and sanctify myself; and I will be known in the eyes of many nations, and they shall know that I am the LORD."

Ezekiel 39:2
"And I will turn thee back, and leave but the sixth part of thee, and will cause thee to come up from the north parts, and will bring thee upon the mountains of Israel."

In other words, all the nations that will gather together to do battle in Israel, God will leave one-sixth of those nations behind because He doesn't intend to completely wipe out the inhabitants of the world. He will spare one-sixth of the inhabitants of those invading nations at that time. Now there's a good chance that many of these will be women and children. That's why Isaiah 4:1 says that in the last days, seven women will grab hold of one man and say "Take away our shame." (In other words, "marry me".) This is because there will be so few men by the time this is over with.

The LORD said he's going to cause Gog and his hordes to come up from the north parts and will bring them upon the mountains of Israel. You ask, "What are the mountains of Israel?" These mountains of Israel are not only the northern mountains of Israel, but they're also the mountains in southern Israel at the Dead Sea. So where is this battle going to take place that He's going to bring them into the mountains of Israel where God wipes them out?

Chapter 7:

The Assyrian

Isaiah 11:11
*"And it shall come to pass in that day, that the Lord shall set his hand again **the second time** to recover the remnant of his people, which shall be left, from Assyria, and from Egypt, and from Pathros, and from Cush, and from Elam, and from Shinar, and from Hamath, and from the islands of the sea."*

Here we have an example of the nations where Israel will be scattered. The LORD speaks about a second time. The first time was during the Hebrew's Passover exodus out of Egypt. So when is the second time. It's not 1948. Did the sign of the Son of Man appear yet? No, so we're talking about future concepts, something that has yet to happen. When this second time, occurs the Lord will begin to gather His elect from the four corners of the Earth and bring them back into the land at this time (see Matthew 24:31).

As we move on, we're going to see two predominant countries that God talks about bringing his people out of—Assyria and Egypt. Why Assyria and why Egypt? The book of Daniel mentions a conflict between the kings of the East and the kings of the North. This is the conflict between Egypt and Assyria. This is mostly talking about the Greek Syrian king Antiochus Epiphanes in approximately 162 BC before the Maccabean revolt.

However, Daniel is also letting us know that a similar incident will occur in the future. Somehow, Egypt and Assyria are going to be greatly involved in the final day's conflicts. The bad guy in the last days is referred to as the Assyrian. You may be shocked to learn what the Bible says about him and others in the last days. Enoch 56:5 tells us that the bad angels are coming back to the land of Parthia and Medes. Parthia is that land from northern Iran to the eastern Turkey area which the Romans were never able to conquer. Media is the land just east and south of Parthia and includes a part of Iran today. Enoch says the bad angels are coming back into that land and from there they will begin to build their forces. God imprisoned these angels before the flood of Noah. Or perhaps these bad angels are part of Satan's angels that are waiting for the opportunity.

One of those angels, I believe, is the beast of Revelation. In fact, it might even be the angel of Enoch called Azazel. This angel taught men to kill and make weapons of war and he might be coming back, perhaps in the form of a man, but he'll be a very wicked violent angel. He will come from the land of the Parthians where the old land of Assyria is. The Bible says "beware of The Assyrian." Many of these references had to do with the last days and not during the eighth century BC attack against Israel and Jerusalem by the old Assyrian empire when they took the northern tribes of Israel captive. This is an Assyrian of the last days.

When we talk about the Assyrian, I want to show you why he's called that just by looking at a Middle East map (page 65). This individual will come from the old Assyrian empire which would today be eastern Turkey, northern Iran, northern Iraq, Armenia, Georgia, and northern Syria. I believe that this Assyrian is one and the same Gog of Magog mentioned in Ezekiel 38 and 39, not the same Assyrian that attacked northern Israel and led them into captivity in the eighth century BC. Later another Assyrian king attacked Judah but he was defeated, and his army was destroyed near Jerusalem before he had a chance to attack the city. Later he was killed in his own homeland and eventually the empire fell to the Babylonians. Although he did a lot of damage in the land, he was

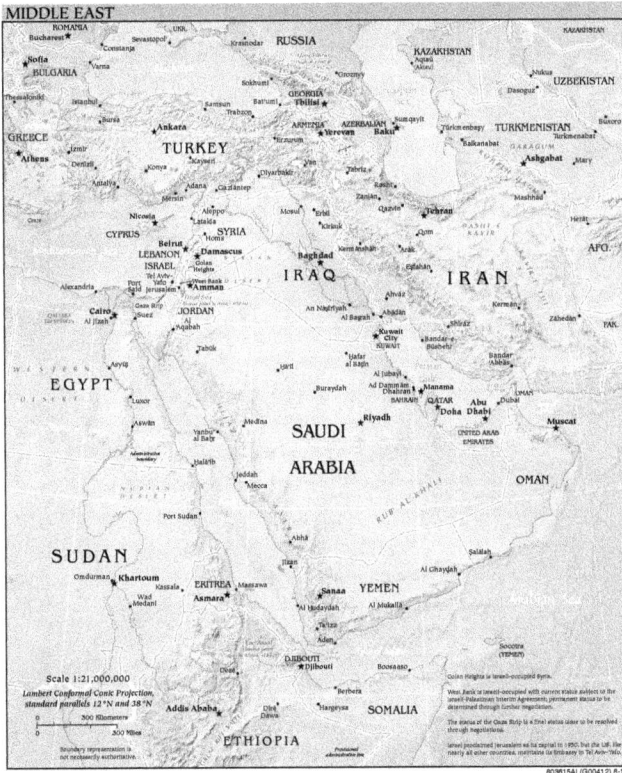

"Middle East - 2013." *University of Texas Libraries*. U.S. Central Intelligence Agency, n.d. Web. 22 June 2016.

destroyed.

If you look at an ancient Middle East map (page 66), Israel is south of Assyria. Don't confuse Assyria with today's Syria. Although the land of Syria was part of the Assyrian and Babylonian conquests, it is not Assyria. Most of the nations mentioned in Ezekiel 38–39 is the land that The Assyrian is going to come out of, anywhere from northern eastern Iran, northern Iraq, eastern Turkey, and the Georgia-Armenia area, which is the land of the Medes that the Bible talks about. As mentioned before, the bad angels are going to be released again and the first place they're going to head for is to the land of the Parthians and Medes, which is part of the old Assyrian Empire. All the evidence indicates this area is going to get stirred

From The Historical Atlas by William R. Shepherd, 1923

up in the last days. So anytime the prophets talk about the Assyrian in the Bible in the last days, it's the guy that rises up out of here (probably Gog from the Gog–Magog War) and he's going to sweep down to Israel from there. His army will be defeated in southern Israel by the valley of the passengers (or the King's Highway) and the dead will be buried in the Dead Sea area on the east side of the Dead Sea as stated in Ezekiel 39:11.

And it shall come to pass in that day that I will give unto Gog a place there of graves in Israel, the valley of the passengers on east of the sea: and it shall stop the noses of the passengers: and there shall they bury Gog and all his multitude: and they shall call it The valley of Hamongog.

Look at the attached old map (left) from 1854 that shows many of the names of nations involved in the Gog campaign of Ezekiel 38 and 39. There are many opinions of where each of these nations were located. For the sake of discussion, I will use this 1854 map which is called The World As Known To The Hebrews. Notice that this map shows that the land of Magog is between the Black Sea and the Caspian Sea. Above this is the land of the Scythians. Notice that Gomer is above the Black Sea and also below the Black Sea in the middle of Turkey. Meshach and Tubal are part of Togarmah which is in eastern Turkey. Madai, the land of the Medes, is northern Iran and northern Iraq. This area is the land Ezekiel is talking about. The prophet knew these places; he knew where they were from. He didn't ask any questions about them, he just wrote down the details as God told him because he understood the area that was being talked about. Now having said that, it doesn't mean that they didn't expand north into part of Russia now. And it doesn't mean they didn't expand west and be part of eastern Europe or anything like that. It's possible that could have happened, but speaking of the very root of those countries, it's all right in here— the same as the Assyrian Empire.

Isaiah 10:12

"Wherefore it shall come to pass, that when the LORD hath performed his whole work upon mount Zion and on Jerusalem, I will punish the fruit of the stout heart of the king of Assyria, and the glory of his high looks."

The LORD is going to do something to this arrogant prideful king of Assyria after He delivers Jerusalem in the last days.

Isaiah 30:31

"For through the voice of the LORD shall the Assyrian be beaten down, which smote with a rod."

The very voice of the LORD will destroy this Assyrian.

Isaiah 31:8

"Then shall the Assyrian fall with the sword, not of a mighty man; and the sword, not of a mean man, shall devour him: but he shall flee from the sword, and his young men shall be discomfited."

The Assyrian will fall not by sword but by the LORD, yet his men shall die by the sword.

Isaiah 10:17

"And the light of Israel shall be for a fire, and his Holy One for a flame: and it shall burn and devour his thorns and his briers in one day."

I find it interesting here that it says "The light of Israel." This light is used so many times in Hebrew to talk about the glory of God, the light of the LORD. It's very possible that this term refers to the saints coming back with the Messiah as it says that we're going to be coming back to help judge with Him. But we also know, looking at scripture, that God will empower the Israelites living at that time to be able to fight also. So, we may see a combination here. We may be known as believers as the light of Israel, but God will cause physical Israel to fight back also.

Zechariah 14:5

"...and the LORD my God shall come, and all the saints with thee."

1 Thessalonians 3:13

"... at the coming of our Lord Yeshua Ha Maschiach with all his saints."

Jude 1:14

"...Behold, the Lord cometh with ten thousands of his saints."

68

Also, in 1 Corinthians 6:2 it says the saints shall judge the world. Revelation 19:14, when speaking of the Messiah, says his armies which were with Him in heaven will come with Him clothed in white linen.

At the same time the physical redeemed of Israel—and particularly the house of David—will fight her enemies as David fought (see Zechariah 12:8).

"In that day shall the LORD defend the inhabitants of Jerusalem: and he that is feeble among them at that day shall be as David; and the house of David shall be as God, as the angel of the LORD before them."

Israel will fight like David, yet the house of David shall be as God, as the angel of the LORD. This appears to be a reference to the saints which are the temple of the LORD and the body of Messiah.

Isaiah 10:18-19

"And shall consume the glory of his forest, and of his fruitful field, both soul and body: and they shall be as when a standard-bearer fainteth. And the rest of the trees of his forest shall be few, that a child may write them."

Isaiah is speaking of the last days of Assyrian. His forest is all the people that he gathers together. It appears to be, too, that he will muster other nations including the Arabia and African area (northern Africa and eastern African). They will all be joining with him to surround Israel. So by the time the LORD gets done judging them, it says that his forest (or his people) will be so few that even a child can number it. So the hundreds of thousands, if not millions, that are going to come and attack Israel, God will wipe them out even so much that a child can count the remaining people from those nations. That's a tremendous amount of judgment. Has that ever happened before? No, that's never happened before. This is another one of the clues that this is still in the future.

Isaiah 10:20-22

"And it shall come to pass in that day, that the remnant of Israel, and such as are escaped of the house of Jacob, shall no more again stay upon him that smote them; but shall stay upon the LORD, the Holy One of Israel, in truth. The remnant shall return, even the remnant of Jacob, unto the mighty God. For though thy people Israel be as the sand of the sea, yet a remnant of them shall return: the consumption decreed shall overflow with righteousness."

A lot of Israelis will perish during the Tribulation period as well as many more gentiles. The whole world is under judgment. What the Assyrian had in mind to completely destroy Israel will now turn into an overflow of righteousness because God came in and destroyed the enemies, and righteousness will begin to prevail. Is Israel living in righteousness now? No! There are some righteous in Israel today, but as a nation they come up short. As said before, however, the nations of the world also come up short. So you know that period is coming where the whole nation of Israel will become a righteous nation.

Isaiah 10:24-27

"Therefore thus saith the Lord God of hosts, O my people that dwellest in Zion, be not afraid of the Assyrian: he shall smite thee with a rod, and shall lift up his staff against thee, after the manner of Egypt. For yet a very little while, and the indignation shall cease, and mine anger in their destruction. And the LORD of hosts shall stir up a scourge for him according to the slaughter of Midian at the rock of Oreb: and as his rod was upon the sea, so shall he lift it up after the manner of Egypt. And it shall come to pass in that day, that his burden shall be taken away from off thy shoulder, and his yoke from off thy neck, and the yoke shall be destroyed because of the anointing."

The above verse describes something that is going to happen similar to the slaughter of Midian at the rock of Oreb by Gideon mentioned in Judges 7. There are various opinions about this, but the location will be right around the area east of the Jordan river, northeast of the Dead Sea. Some Bible scholars say that word "Oreb" really should be "Horeb" which is Mount Sinai. If that's the case, we're talking about the Mount Sinai in the Arabian Desert in Midia east of Edom. That's possibly where the slaughter's going to be, possibly. We're not sure; we're only guessing on that one there.

Isaiah 14:25
"That I will break the Assyrian in my land, and upon my mountains tread him under foot: then shall his yoke depart from off them, and his burden depart from off their shoulders."

Isaiah 19:16-19
"In that day shall Egypt be like unto women: and it shall be afraid and fear because of the shaking of the hand of the LORD of hosts, which he shaketh over it. And the land of Judah shall be a terror unto Egypt, every one that maketh mention thereof shall be afraid in himself, because of the counsel of the LORD of hosts, which he hath determined against it. In that day shall five cities in the land of Egypt speak the language of Canaan, and swear to the LORD of hosts; one shall be called, The city of destruction. In that day shall there be an altar to the LORD in the midst of the land of Egypt, and a pillar at the border thereof to the LORD."

Something will take place in the land of Judah that Egypt is going to be very afraid of. One of the cities is going up in smoke. I don't know if that's Cairo, but one of the cities is going into destruction. Remember, Egypt will be joining forces with this Assyrian. God cares as much about

71

the Egyptians as He cares about the Assyrians after he destroys this army. So there will be an altar in the middle of the land of Egypt to the LORD. Is there an altar in the land of Egypt today to the LORD? If there is, we don't know about it. A pillar should also be at the border of Egypt and Israel to the LORD. Is there a pillar there today? We don't know of a pillar there today.

Isaiah 19:20-22

"And it shall be for a sign and for a witness unto the LORD of hosts in the land of Egypt: for they shall cry unto the LORD because of the oppressors, and he shall send them a saviour, and a great one, and he shall deliver them. And the LORD shall be known to Egypt, and the Egyptians shall know the LORD in that day, and shall do sacrifice and oblation; yea, they shall vow a vow unto the LORD, and perform it. And the LORD shall smite Egypt: he shall smite and heal it: and they shall return even to the LORD, and he shall be intreated of them, and shall heal them."

The LORD is going to judge Egypt, then He's going to heal them, and then they shall know the LORD. Has that ever happened? No, it has not ever happened.

Isaiah 19:23

"In that day shall there be a highway out of Egypt to Assyria, and the Assyrian shall come into Egypt, and the Egyptian into Assyria, and the Egyptians shall serve with the Assyrians. In that day shall Israel be the third with Egypt and with Assyria, even a blessing in the midst of the land: Whom the LORD of hosts shall bless, saying, Blessed be Egypt my people, and Assyria the work of my hands, and Israel mine inheritance."

The Egyptians and the Assyrians are going to be serving Israel.

They will come to know the LORD after the judgment that takes place, and they will actually be servants unto Israel. That has never happened. We do know that the LORD has never built a highway from Assyria to Egypt as the scriptures say. These are in the future.

Isaiah 30:30-33

"And the LORD shall cause his glorious voice to be heard, and shall shew the lighting down of his arm, with the indignation of his anger, and with the flame of a devouring fire, with scattering, and tempest, and hailstones. For through the voice of the LORD shall the Assyrian be beaten down, which smote with a rod. And in every place where the grounded staff shall pass, which the LORD shall lay upon him, it shall be with tabrets and harps: and in battles of shaking will he fight with it. For Tophet is ordained of old; yea, for the king it is prepared; he hath made it deep and large: the pile thereof is fire and much wood; the breath of the LORD, like a stream of brimstone, doth kindle it."

Tophet is a special place of judgment for this king. Revelation 19:20 tells us that the beast of Revelation is thrown into the lake of fire; he's the first inhabitant of this lake, along with the false prophet. There's a good chance this is what Tophet is all about—the lake of fire. God has great anger at this Assyrian because of what he does to Israel during that time.

Isaiah 31:7-9

"For in that day every man shall cast away his idols of silver, and his idols of gold, which your own hands have made unto you for a sin. Then shall the Assyrian fall with the sword, not of a mighty man; and the sword, not of a mean man, shall devour him: but he shall flee from the sword, and his young men shall be discomfited. And he

shall pass over to his strong hold for fear, and his princes shall be afraid of the ensign, saith the LORD, whose fire is in Zion, and his furnace in Jerusalem."

Israel will begin to repent and serve the LORD in their captivity and will cast out their idols. This Assyrian king will flee to his land, but all his people, his army, will fall and die. Then the LORD will take that king. He will not be killed by the hands of man; he will be killed by the hands of the Messiah Himself—exactly the same situation of the beast of Revelation. The Messiah will take the beast and throw him into the lake of fire. It appears also that the LORD will take this Assyrian and throw him into Tophet—this place of judgment of fire and brimstone. This king will be destroyed by the LORD Himself, just like the beast of Revelation was destroyed by the LORD Himself. The Assyrian princes will be afraid of the ensign. This will be the sign of the Son of Man, Yeshua.

Micah 5:2
"But thou, Bethlehem Ephratah, though thou be little among the thousands of Judah, yet out of thee shall he come forth unto me that is to be ruler in Israel; whose goings forth have been from of old, from everlasting. Therefore will he give them up, until the time that she which travaileth hath brought forth: then the remnant of his brethren shall return unto the children of Israel."

Who is Micah talking about here? Yeshua, who came out of Bethlehem. In other words, Micah is saying that the LORD will give up Israel for a period of time until she which travails breaks forth. Many scriptures talk about Israel being under travail waiting to give birth. For example, in Revelation 12, we see the woman finally giving birth from being in travail. The woman is Israel and it is the time that a remnant of the woman comes to know the Lord and is born again. Israel is waiting for this birth to take place.

Many think this chapter is talking about the birth of Yeshua, but this doesn't make sense. The book of Revelation starts with the resurrected Lord. Why are we talking about the birth of Yeshua in the middle of Revelation? Also after Yeshua was born, Israel, the woman flees into the wilderness with wings of an eagle to be protected by God for three and a half years. That did not happen after Yeshua's birth. This child has to be someone else who will rule the nations with a rod of iron. Is there another thought on this? Revelation 2:27, speaking of the church of Thyatira, says that he who overcomes will rule the nations with a rod of iron. The saints who overcome will have a throne and crown and will rule with the Messiah.

It is also interesting to note that the word here in Greek for man (*arrhen*) in Revelation 12 has a root (*airo*) that means to raise up, lift up, take off, remove, and to draw up. Could this be talking about the rapture of the saints? This cryptic example could indeed be when the rapture will take place. Jews and Gentiles who follow the Lord could be raised at this time. This also fits what the apostle Paul says in 2 Thessalonians 2:3 that the gathering unto the Lord will not take place until the man of sin is revealed, this son of perdition. Certainly, when the beast of Revelation attacks Israel, this man of sin is revealed. According to Paul, the rapture should come shortly afterwards and thus Revelation 12. Also the Revelation 12 incident is after the seventh trump of judgment so it could be the last trump that 1 Corinthians 15:52 speaks of.

So according to Micah 5:2, the LORD will give up on Israel until Israel gives birth to this rapture group who will rule the nations. The rest of the remnant will then return.

Micah 5:5
"And this man shall be the peace, when the Assyrian shall come into our land: and when he shall tread in our palaces, then shall we raise against him seven shepherds, and eight principal men."

It tells you right here it's the Assyrian that's coming, but the Man born of Bethlehem shall be our peace when He rises up against them. Yeshua Himself will rise up against the Assyrian and then we'll have this odd combination of seven shepherds and eight princely men. When you look this up in a lot of commentaries, they say this seven and eight is an idiom concept of perfection and eternalness. The number seven means completion or perfection and the number eight is new beginnings or eternity. The Messiah will make those who believe in Him perfect with eternal life.

So who are these seven shepherds and eight princely men? They are rulers, chiefs, princes, and kings—saints of God—who are coming with Yeshua to help destroy the Assyrian's army. Jude 1:14 says the Lord will come back with ten thousands of His saints. We've been made perfect in the Messiah and we have eternal life.

Micah 5:6

"And they shall waste the land of Assyria with the sword, and the land of Nimrod in the entrances thereof: thus shall he deliver us from the Assyrian, when he cometh into our land, and when he treadeth within our borders."

We need to understand that even the land of Nimrod would be the Babylonian–Chaldean area south of Assyria, so the land of Assyria will also reach down to the land of Babylon. We see the whole aspect— the Chaldeans, the Assyrians, the Babylonians—all of it is one large area in this middle east area as mentioned on the map and talked about earlier.

So it's the Assyrian that is coming to attack Israel and to lead most of them into captivity, only to be brought out of captivity a short while later by the Messiah who is our peace.

Today this area is a trouble spot for the whole world. The

Ottoman Empire ruled this area for hundreds of years. ISIS is from this area. Gog (probably the beast of Revelation) will come from this area. Watch and be aware.

> ### Isaiah 27:12-13
> *"And it shall come to pass in that day, that the LORD shall beat off from the channel of the river unto the stream of Egypt, and ye shall be gathered one by one, O ye children of Israel. And it shall come to pass in that day, that the great trumpet shall be blown, and they shall come which were ready to perish in the land of Assyria, and the outcasts in the land of Egypt, and shall worship the LORD in the holy mount at Jerusalem."*

There will be a trumpet sound and a sign that will appear (see Isaiah 5:26; 11:10, 12; 18:3; 31:9). This sign or ensign will appear and that begins to bring the outcasts back to Israel. There will be a sign in heaven, and I believe it is that sign that Yeshua talked about in Matthew 24:30, the sign of the Son of Man. This sign will appear, the outcasts will look into that sign and realize that Yeshua is the Messiah. They will call upon His name and the LORD will touch them and bring them from the north and the south back into the land of Israel, rejoicing. They shall worship the LORD in the holy mountain at Jerusalem and a great trumpet will go along with it at the time.

This is why on the feast of trumpets—or better known as Yom Teruah, the Day of Shouting—I teach that the sound of the trumpet on that feast is probably not the firstfruits rapture concept. It's the trumpet that blows to bring the children back into the land of Israel and, in fact, may be another rapture. There is more than one rapture, but that's another teaching.

The children of Israel will come back after being led into captivity into Assyria and Egypt. That hasn't happened, folks. It didn't happen in

1948, and it didn't happen after the Babylonian captivity. None of those things happened. We're still looking for that day to take place for those who were ready to perish in the land of Assyria and in Egypt. (More on this subject on the chapter of the Ensign or the sign of the Son of Man.)

The following scriptures of Jeremiah describe unusual concepts—what is called double-fulfillment in God's Word. There would've been one initial fulfillment, but not all, which tells you there will be another fulfillment. This happens a lot. This is one of the prophetic principles of studying prophecy. Many times, God will speak a prophecy of something that was going to happen within a very short period of time, but then you realize not all of it was fulfilled. So it tells you that either the rest is going to be fulfilled later, or the whole thing is going to be repeated again in a proper, complete fulfillment. The following is a type of the double fulfillment:

Jeremiah 50:17
"Israel is a scattered sheep; the lions have driven him away: first the king of Assyria hath devoured him; and last this Nebuchadnezzar king of Babylon hath broken his bones."

This is true, this did happened.

Jeremiah 50:18
"Therefore thus saith the LORD of hosts, the God of Israel; Behold, I will punish the king of Babylon and his land, as I have punished the king of Assyria."

Has that had historic fulfillment? Yes, it has.

Jeremiah 50:19
"And I will bring Israel again to his habitation, and he shall feed on Carmel and Bashan, and his soul shall be

satisfied upon mount Ephraim and Gilead."

That is only partial. Only about 40,000 Jews left Babylon and Persia while many more stayed. They didn't all come out of Babylon and Persia. Maybe it was fulfilled, maybe it was not fulfilled. However, by looking at the next verse, we know it was not fulfilled.

Jeremiah 50:20
"In those days, and in that time, saith the LORD, the iniquity of Israel shall be sought for, and there shall be none; and the sins of Judah, and they shall not be found: for I will pardon them whom I reserve."

Were the sins of Israel forgiven after the Babylonian captivity? No. Were the sins of Israel forgiven in 1948? No. This is why we know there's a double-fulfillment taking place here because not all of that prophecy was fulfilled. True, the Assyrians and Babylonians did attack Israel, and God did judge both of those kings; but as far as the iniquity being taken away, it was not. Israel continued to sin against God. There's only one way to take away the iniquity and that's through Yeshua, and Yeshua wasn't there during the first captivity of Assyria and Babylon.

Daniel 8:23
"And in the latter time of their kingdom, when the transgressors are come to the full, a king of fierce countenance, and understanding dark sentences, shall stand up."

We're talking about all of those empires coming together. In the vision Daniel had, the Assyrian, Babylonian, and Egyptian kingdoms are all coming back together again to form one united kingdom, which is yet to happen. In the latter time of their kingdom, verse 23 says, "when the transgressors are come to the full…" In other words, when the sins of the world and of these kingdoms that are joined together have come to a full, then the king of fierce countenance will come. The world today is fast becoming full of sin, so soon the things the prophets wrote about will come to be.

As far as when the transgressors are full, the same thing happened to the Amorites. The LORD said he kept the Hebrews in Egypt until the iniquities of the Amorites were full. When he released the Hebrews from Egypt and while going to the Promised Land, they were going to wipe out the Amorites. So God waited for the Amorites' sin to become full so that they were worthy of total destruction.

That's what God is waiting for in the world today—and it's a terrible thing to be waiting on, but this is what's going to happen. God is waiting on the world's transgressors to become full. When they have finally reached that point and there are very little righteous left in the world, God will begin His judgment to judge the world. He's going to use Gog and Magog to execute it when the transgressors are full. Then a king of fierce countenance who understands dark sentences shall stand up. This is a king who understands parables and proverbs. He has a twisted mind, but he understands these things. I don't know what this guy's going to look like, but he has a fierce countenance. He's not going to look like a businessman in a nice three-piece suit like you see in movies about the Antichrist. He's not going to be nice to look at; he's going to be scary and he's going to be mean looking. His whole plan is destruction. This is the king of fierce countenance.

Daniel 8:24

"And his power shall be mighty, but not by his own power: and he shall destroy wonderfully, and shall prosper, and practice (perform), and shall destroy the mighty and the holy people."

Revelation 13:4 says Satan will give his power to the beast. This is the same concept. This guy of a fierce countenance will not be operating by his own power; he'll be operating by the power of Satan. I like the King

James translation: "And he shall destroy wonderfully." Well, I've never heard "wonderfully" used in such an aspect as this, but he shall destroy wonderfully at this time. What it really means is that there's no stopping him. It will be incredible the extent of the damage this guy does. We have to remember, God is allowing this guy to execute judgment upon the world. Now whether he is one of those fallen angels that has taken on the form of a man or whether he is a man himself, we don't know, but he receives power from Satan. We know the bad angels are coming out of that area and are going to be with him and supporting him at that time.

Revelation tells us that the beast will be given power over the saints. So during that period of time, the people still on the Earth who believe in Yeshua—the saints—are going to come under his attack. The beast is going to make war against them. God will pull the covering back from the saints for a short period of time, and the beast will begin to go after the saints and literally make millions of martyrs out of them during this period.

Since this teaching is not about the rapture, I will not go into details about it at this time. But keep in mind that most likely there will be a firstfruits rapture earlier and then a martyr rapture followed by a rapture of multitudes who came out of the tribulation (Revelations 7:9-17). When the first rapture takes place—probably when the woman (Israel) gives birth— millions of people will see it and repent and become believers (Enoch 50:1-3). This is most likely the group that the beast goes after. Remember Paul says the rapture will not occur until the son of perdition has been revealed. This is that time with the beast. Rapture discussions can be quite lengthy and require its own study. For instance, the 24 elders of Revelation 4 are taken out of the nations and are given white raiment which indicates resurrection and awards. This is before any seal or trumpet is blown. Who are these elders? Are they a group of believers raptured earlier? There is a lot to ponder over. I believe 24 is a symbolic number representing Jew and Gentile believers, two groups of 12 which is the number of the government of God.

Daniel 8:25
"And through his policy also he shall cause craft to prosper in his hand; and he shall magnify himself in his heart, and by peace shall destroy many: he shall also stand up against the Prince of princes; but he shall be broken without hand."

I always thought it was an interesting concept that this fierce-looking king understands dark sentences so well in his manner of speech that he can make you think he's making peace at the same time he's killing you. I tell you, I have to think about some of the things I've heard recently in this country about Islam. *"It's a religion of peace."* But yet, they kill, and kill in brutal ways. What is going on here? Is Islam part of the concept Daniel is talking about? "By peace, he will kill many." It's an odd statement, but you can actually see it before your eyes taking place in the world even now. "He shall also stand up against the Prince of princes; but he shall be broken without hand." Islam believes that Yeshua never died or was resurrected, nor was He the Son of God and yet He will come back to convert Christians to Islam. But they also believe that this Yeshua the saints are looking for is really the Antichrist. This is why the beast will gather the nations to attack Yeshua. They are convinced that Yeshua is the bad guy, and this is being preached among the Muslims today. What convoluted logic.

We see in Revelation 17:14 that when the heavens open up and the Lamb of God begins to descend, the beast gathers the nations to make war against the Lamb! How insane can you be? They have been brainwashed and told that's the Antichrist. The nations have to fight Him because they are now convinced that the beast of Revelation is the messiah and they now must fight against the One whom is coming in the heavens. How distorted can we get in these concepts? This is yet to happen; this is going to come. It says he'll be destroyed without hand. In other words, this guy will be destroyed without the hand of another man. He'll be destroyed by the real Messiah Himself.

Daniel 8:26

"*And the vision of the evening and the morning which was told is true: wherefore shut thou up the vision; for it shall be for many days.*"

So the LORD's telling Daniel it's a long time yet before it's going to happen, but it is going to happen.

Daniel 8:27

"*And I Daniel fainted, and was sick certain days; afterward I rose up, and did the king's business; and I was astonished at the vision, but none understood it.*"

This vision affected Daniel to the point that he became sick and passed out. He just could not believe what he was seeing and what was getting ready to happen. Daniel 12 tells us that there will be a tribulation coming (unknown to mankind) like we've never seen before. So we take all the things that's already happened in this world—the terrible things of World War I and II and the communist takeover where millions were slaughtered in both Russia and China. Then think about the holocaust, the pogroms, the Inquisition; the things that happened in Cambodia and the killing fields. We're talking about hundreds of millions of people slaughtered already in our history! Yet, Daniel 12 says we haven't seen anything yet. This is coming upon the world and it happens when the transgressors have reached a full. Incredible things are getting ready to happen on the world's scene.

Chapter 8:

The Army of Joel

When talking about the bad guys in the last days, we can't ignore the army of Joel. There are similarities in Joel that can be compared to the Babylonians when they destroyed Israel, but not all. What we don't know is exactly who they are. Are they part of Gog? Or the Assyrian concepts? Are they the bad angels coming? Is it an army of saints? Can they be a special spiritual army of the judgment of God—for instance, the armies of the four horsemen of the Apocalypse? Or perhaps a special contingent of God's angels waiting for this day? No one really knows but they must be talked about.

Joel 1:6
"For a nation is come up upon my land, strong, and without number, whose teeth are the teeth of a lion, and he hath the cheek teeth of a great lion."

So we see here a great nation is coming upon the nation of Israel that has teeth like a lion. This could be the Babylonians.

Joel 1:2
"Hear this, ye old men, and give ear, all ye inhabitants of the land. Hath this been in your days, or even in the days of your fathers?"

In other words, the LORD is saying there has never ever been anything like this that's coming; nothing. That's why we see in Daniel 12:1

that a tribulation will come upon the Earth unknown and never seen by man; a tribulation we've never even imagined. All the horrible things that have already happened in the Earth, now there are even greater things that are getting ready to happen.

Joel 1:12

"The vine is dried up, and the fig tree languisheth; the pomegranate tree, the palm tree also, and the apple tree, even all the trees of the field, are withered: because joy is withered away from the sons of men."

All the crops are destroyed. Spiritually, this is talking about the land of Israel the vine and the temple which is the fig tree, the priesthood which is the pomegranate, the palm tree which is the righteous, and the apple tree talking about the fruitfulness of land.

Joel 1:15

"Alas for the day! for the day of the LORD is at hand, and as a destruction from the Almighty shall it come."

This is the day of the LORD. Although it can refer to the Babylonian attack, it is much more than that.

Joel 1:20

"The beasts of the field cry also unto thee: for the rivers of waters are dried up, and the fire hath devoured the pastures of the wilderness."

There is a strong army coming which is going to destroy everything in its path. All the trees, all the grass, everything is going to be burned up. You say Nebuchadnezzar did a lot of that, but he left a lot of the farm fields and trees to produce fruit and substance to help feed Babylon. So he didn't wipe out the fields and the trees. He certainly destroyed the cities, but something else is taking place here. Certainly the rivers were not dried up. These are last days events.

Joel 2:2

"A day of darkness and of gloominess, a day of clouds and of thick darkness, as the morning spread upon the mountains: a great people and a strong; there hath not been ever the like, neither shall be any more after it, even to the years of many generations."

Whatever this army is, there's been no other army that can match it, ever. It doesn't matter what nation's army you're talking about; this hasn't happened yet. This army is greater and bigger than any army before it. Better than Nebuchadnezzar's army, better than the Assyrians, better than the Russians, better than Chinese, better than the United States army. When I say "better," it means more destructive than anything in the past.

Joel 2:3

"A fire devoureth before them; and behind them a flame burneth: the land is as the garden of Eden before them, and behind them a desolate wilderness; yea, and nothing shall escape them."

You can have a garden in front of you, and after they go by, it's like a wilderness. Whatever it is, they destroy everything in their path. This is the calling card of the army of Joel.

Joel 2:4-8

"The appearance of them is as the appearance of horses; and as horsemen, so shall they run. Like the noise of chariots on the tops of mountains shall they leap, like the noise of a flame of fire that devoureth the stubble, as a strong people set in battle array. Before their face the people shall be much pained: all faces shall gather blackness. They shall run like mighty men; they shall climb

the wall like men of war; and they shall march every one on his ways, and they shall not break their ranks: Neither shall one thrust another; they shall walk every one in his path: and when they fall upon the sword, they shall not be wounded."

Any army that has men in it will die, but this army doesn't die!. They marched and they moved forward. They destroy everything in their path and they don't die. Has that happened yet? No. We've not had an army like that yet. This is something that's yet to come. It seems to be a spiritual army or an army of robots. Laugh if you will, but nations are trying to make robot warriors today. Once it is perfected, they can make millions of them. Perhaps the movie "Terminator" isn't so farfetched after all.

Joel 2:9
"They shall run to and fro in the city; they shall run upon the wall, they shall climb up upon the houses; they shall enter in at the windows like a thief. The earth shall quake before them; the heavens shall tremble: the sun and the moon shall be dark, and the stars shall withdraw their shining: And the LORD shall utter his voice before his army: for his camp is very great: for he is strong that executeth his word: for the day of the LORD is great and very terrible; and who can abide it?"

Let's talk about the army of the horsemen of Revelation 9:16: it says, "And the number of the army of the horsemen were two hundred thousand thousand: and I heard the number of them." This is 200 million! The scripture say, "army of the horsemen." What horsemen? The four horsemen of the Apocalypse that were mentioned in Revelation 6. They are the generals, and their army is 200 million that comes with them. Can it be them? Maybe, it's very possible. We all like to think that maybe we're part of that army. Remember that even Nebuchadnezzar was called the army of the LORD. If the army is doing what the LORD desires, then he calls it His army. That doesn't mean it has to be a righteous army. So who knows, but there is a 200-million-person army that is coming.

Some prophecy writers say it is the army of the communist China. They say that's the only nation that can put together an army that size. Well, there's a problem with that. Number one, logistically, can you imagine what it'd be like to take 200 million people and march them across the land? All the food and camps and latrine services you would need? That's crazy. One nuclear weapon could wipe them out and it's over with. Chinese can die and this army doesn't die. There's no indication that it's Chinese at all; however, we can't dismiss the concern that China is actively building a robot army. If they can build a 200 million army of robots, that could fit the scripture. Only time will tell.

More than likely it's a spiritual army of some sort. It is certainly a possibility that the saints are coming back with Yeshua for battle as indicated in Joel 2:11. Some may balk at this since the appearance of these creatures is terrifying and look like horses like the 200 million in Revelation. Remember that the Devil and his angels are being thrown out of heaven to the earth in Revelation 12:9. It is possible that the army of Joel are these angels who also join the army of the beast. Whoever they are, they don't die; they march on the walls, they march on the cities. How many have heard the song "Blow the Trumpet in Zion?" It's a fun praise song, but a lot of people don't realize what they're singing.

"Blow the trumpet in Zion, Zion.
Sound the alarm on My holy mountain.
Blow the trumpet in Zion, Zion.
They rush on the city; they run on the wall,
Great is the army that carries out His Word."

They're talking about these guys—utter destruction! In worship, everybody's up clapping and singing the song, everybody's happy with the song, but the song is about utter destruction and death! Most people don't realize that what they're singing is coming out of Joel 2.

Joel 2:12-13

"Therefore also now, saith the LORD, turn ye even to me with all your heart, and with fasting, and with weeping, and with mourning: And rend your heart, and not your garments, and turn unto the LORD your God: for he is gracious and merciful, slow to anger, and of great kindness, and repenteth him of the evil."

The LORD is saying, "I want to see your hearts change, I want to see your lives change! I want to see you repent." There was a custom when people would mourn or be upset about something, they'd take their garments and rip them like when the high priest questioned Yeshua during the Lord's trial. Many times that was an outward expression of an inward sorrow. However, it was most likely an outward expression just to show off in front of people. God is saying, "Don't rip your garments. Rip your heart, change your heart." That's what He wants—a changed heart, not outward signs or mourning but He requires inward or heart changes. Those alive on Earth at this time will be the ones in great sorrow when they see this army of Joel coming.

Joel 2:18

"Then will the LORD be jealous for his land, and pity his people."

We're talking about Israel here, about how he'll be zealous for his land and pity his people. So this army of Joel is coming, sweeping across the land (maybe the whole world, but certainly in Israel also). At that time, God will pity His people and be zealous for His land after the army of Joel has finished its work. Afterwards, God will call for and cause the captivity of Israel to return.

Joel 2:20

"But I will remove far off from you the northern army, and

will drive him into a land barren and desolate, with his face toward the east sea, and his hinder part toward the utmost sea, and his stink shall come up, and his ill savour shall come up, because he hath done great things."

Scholars say that the East Sea is the Dead Sea while the utmost (behind) sea could either be the Mediterranean or the Red Sea. Again this northern army of the beast is going to be down in the southern Israel area. That's where the final battle will take place, in southern Israel, not northern Israel. People say, *Well, Armageddon, that's northern Israel. That's where it's going to happen.* Not so. What does "Armageddon" mean? It means *the mountains of Megiddo.* There is supposedly a Solomon Chariot Fortress in the valley of Jezreel called Megiddo, so they call the whole valley the Valley of Armageddon. The problem is, why don't they translate Megiddo also? If you translate the whole word, "Armageddon" means "The mountains of the place of gathering," where God decides to gather the nations. There are other scriptures that say the cities of Edom called Bozrah and Teman is where all these battles will take place and then the LORD comes out of Edom with His garments dipped in blood. This is not northern Israel, but Edom which is to the southeast of Israel, and from the cities of Teman and Bozrah. This is where the final battle will be. The northern army—which is the Gog-Magog army—may come from the north. They will be driven into southern Israel and from there God will destroy that army.

Remember what it said when we were studying Gog-Magog? It would take seven months just to bury the dead of Gog. Where does it tell you they'll bury the dead? At a place called Hamongog (Ezekiel 39:11-15), which is near the Dead Sea and near to the valley of the passengers. They're not going to haul the bodies from northern Israel down to the Dead Sea. They're going to bury them where they fell.

Some say that Edom represents the Arabian Peninsula and so judgment is coming also on them. This is where the center of Islam is and where the cities of Mecca and Medina are located.

Joel 2:21-23

"Fear not, O land; be glad and rejoice: for the LORD will do great things. Be not afraid, ye beasts of the field: for the pastures of the wilderness do spring, for the tree beareth her fruit, the fig tree and the vine do yield their strength. Be glad then, ye children of Zion, and rejoice in the LORD your God: for he hath given you the former rain moderately, and he will cause to come down for you the rain, the former rain, and the latter rain in the first month."

This passage goes on to say that the LORD will now pour out His Holy Spirit upon all flesh. What happened at Pentecost was just a small outpouring compared to what is coming. By the time the tribulation is over with, He will pour out the Holy Spirit to all those that survived, and upon all flesh including Israel.

Joel 3:1

"For, behold, in those days, and in that time, when I shall bring again the captivity of Judah and Jerusalem,"

Israel had gone back into captivity except for a small remnant from Jerusalem that fled into the wilderness. But now the LORD will bring back all who survived.

Joel 3:2

"I will also gather all nations, and will bring them down into the valley of Jehoshaphat, and will plead with them there for my people and for my heritage Israel, whom they have scattered among the nations, and parted my land."

Now, God is going to bring all the nations down into the Valley of Jehoshaphat that will attack Israel, take their land, and will lead them off into captivity. There He will plead (judge) with them and destroy them. Where is the Valley of Jehoshaphat? Around the fourth century A.D., some writer decided that the Valley of Jehoshaphat was the Kidron Valley right outside of Jerusalem. That's where they get the idea that all these armies are going to be brought into the valley of Jerusalem and slaughtered there. Most likely that's not where the Valley of Jehoshaphat is. Who was Jehoshaphat? He was a king, a righteous king. What was he famous for? I'll give you the storyline.

In 2 Chronicles 20, Jehoshaphat received a report that the armies of Ammon, Edom, and Moab were gathered at Engedi at the Dead Sea and were coming to conquer Jerusalem. He knew he couldn't beat them, so he called for a fast for all of Jerusalem and then called upon the LORD. Of course, he was a righteous king so the LORD listened to him. If you want the LORD to listen to your prayers, a criterion is to be obedient! The LORD said, "The battle is not yours but God's." The LORD then told him, "You need not to fight in this battle: set yourselves, stand still, and see the salvation of the LORD with you." So Hezekiah, the Levites, and the people went to Tekoa, and from there they began to sing praises unto the LORD and to watch what the LORD would do.

Where is Tekoa? It is at the southwestern edge of the Dead Sea overlooking a cliff above the Dead Sea. So Jehoshaphat and his men looked off the cliff toward the southern end of the Dead Sea, and there were the armies of Edom, Moab, and Ammon ready to march forward and take Jerusalem. Jehoshaphat and the Levites began to sing, jump up and down, and shout, and the LORD sent His judgment to these armies and killed every one of the Ammonites, Edomites, and Moabites. King Jehoshaphat didn't have to do anything but watch and sing praises unto God. Do you want to win in battle? Sing praises unto God! Give Him the glory and He will fight the battle. How important it is to understand that concept! The battle is the LORD's.

In my opinion, the Valley of Jehoshaphat is the very place where

Jehoshaphat looked at the armies of Ammon, Moab, and Edom by the Dead Sea. Again, this judgment is in the southern end of the Dead Sea area. Now it is possible this is where the judgment of the goats and sheep will also take place (see Matthew 25:31-46), or it could just be a repeat of the destruction of the nations that come against Jerusalem.

There's no evidence that Armageddon is going to be in northern Israel. Every time one goes to Israel, the tour guides all mention that there have been a lot of battles fought in the Valley of Jezreel. It looks like a good place for a battle, and such-and-such general said this is a great place for war. But the scripture says that there have been lots and lots of battles in the southern Dead Sea area also. So you can't say just because there have been battles fought in the Jezreel valley that likely it makes it the place of Armageddon. What do the scriptures say? I am convinced through scripture that the final battle is going to be in the southern Dead Sea area. Then, God will cause the return of the captivity of Israel to take place.

Joel 3:3

"And they have cast lots for my people; and have given a boy for an harlot, and sold a girl for wine, that they might drink."

When they take Israel into captivity, this is what they're going to do. They will sell a boy for a harlot and a girl just for a glass of wine. Pretty cheap. No doubt, Nebuchadnezzar's people probably did some of the same things, but this is going to be even worse at this time.

Joel 3:4

"Yea, and what have ye to do with me, O Tyre, and Zidon, and all the coasts of Palestine? will ye render me a recompence? and if ye recompense me, swiftly and speedily will I return your recompence upon your own head;"

That word "Palestine" is the English translation of the word

Philistinia. Israel was named that in 135 A.D. by Hadrian the Roman emperor after the last Israel revolt against Rome. He called the land Philistinia, so the King James Bible used the English version of the word "Palestine.". The word Philistinia is in reference to Israel's arch enemies, the Philistines. The Roman emperor called it that in his anger to erase any reference to Israel.

Tyre and Sidon (that's Lebanon), and the coast of the Philistinia, known today as Gaza, will be joined in this battle against Israel. They are two trouble areas today. In Lebanon today, the Hezbollah guerrillas control that area, and are continuously threatening Israel. The coast of Philistinia is where the Hamas are that keep launching rockets at Israel. So God's warning them right here, "Your time is coming. Are you going to pay to Me all the damage you did to My people Israel? I don't think so! If you recompense me, swiftly and speedily will I return the recompense upon your head." This is because what they will do and have done to Israel, they did to the LORD.

Joel 3:5-6
"Because ye have taken my silver and my gold, and have carried into your temples my goodly pleasant things: The children also of Judah and the children of Jerusalem have ye sold unto the Grecians, that ye might remove them far from their border."

The King James version says "Grecians," but it's actually Yavan— the grandson of Noah who settled the Turkey-Armenia area all the way to the Greece area. All of that is Yavan. It begins in the Armenian area, the eastern part of Turkey, and the northern part of Iran. That is where Yavan settled.

Joel 3:7
"Behold, I will raise them out of the place whither ye have sold them, and will return your recompence upon your own

head: And I will sell your sons and your daughters into the hand of the children of Judah, and they shall sell them to the Sabeans, to a people far off: for the LORD hath spoken it."

What you sow is what you reap! God doesn't forget that, because they sold the Yavanites a boy for a harlot and a girl for a glass of wine. So He's going to recompense it. In other words, He's going to take their children and sell them to the Sabeans or Sheba (that's around Yemen), or way down in the tip of the Saudi Arabian Peninsula, or even the eastern side of Africa. That sounds kind of harsh but at this point, God has finally had enough and He's going to recompense what everybody deserves. If the enemies of Israel sold the children of Israel, then He's going to take their children and give them to the hands of Judah, and Judah will sell them to a land far away. That's the kind of judgment that's coming. It's kind of hard to grasp that sometimes, but this what the LORD is going to do! Has that happened? No! It's coming! This has not happened before.

Joel 3:9-12

"Proclaim ye this among the Gentiles; Prepare war, wake up the mighty men, let all the men of war draw near; let them come up. Beat your plowshares into swords and your pruninghooks into spears: let the weak say, I am strong. Assemble yourselves, and come, all ye heathen, and gather yourselves together round about: thither cause thy mighty ones to come down, O LORD. Let the heathen be wakened, and come up to the valley of Jehoshaphat: for there will I sit to judge all the heathen round about."

So the LORD is calling all the gentile nations to come down. Actually, He is going to bring all the heathen armies down into the Valley of Jehoshaphat for judgment. Like I said before, in the fourth century A.D. one writer said that this judgment will be in the Kidron Valley just outside the eastern wall of Jerusalem and will involve perhaps millions. The

Kidron Valley is very small and short. How can one get that many people in that? So more than likely, it's not the Kidron Valley. As explained before, it will be in the Valley of Jehoshaphat in the southern end of the Dead Sea as it is a wide area and can hold millions of people. It certainly possible that this is a reference to the Matthew 25 sheep and goat judgment of how the people treated Israel. "Because you didn't do it to my brethren, you didn't do it to me" is a reference to Israel.

Joel 3:13-16

"Put ye in the sickle, for the harvest is ripe: come, get you down; for the press is full, the fats overflow; for their wickedness is great. Multitudes, multitudes in the valley of decision: for the day of the LORD is near in the valley of decision. The sun and the moon shall be darkened, and the stars shall withdraw their shining. The LORD also shall roar out of Zion, and utter his voice from Jerusalem; and the heavens and the earth shall shake: but the LORD will be the hope of his people, and the strength of the children of Israel."

The Messiah will come and He will deliver them. Many will perish, but He will deliver the remnant, those that are left alive. The Valley of Decision is most likely a reference to the Valley of Jehoshaphat.

Joel 3:17

"So shall ye know that I am the LORD your God dwelling in Zion, my holy mountain: then shall Jerusalem be holy, and there shall no strangers pass through her any more. And it shall come to pass in that day, that the mountains shall drop down new wine, and the hills shall flow with milk, and all the rivers of Judah shall flow with waters, and a fountain shall come forth out of the house of the LORD, and shall water the valley of Shittim."

God dwells in Zion which will be the heavenly Zion and also Jerusalem will be holy. No one will pass by her that doesn't believe. New wine and milk will flow which is speaking of the vine and fig tree. The land will produce and righteousness will rule the day. A river will flow from the house of the LORD and flow to the Dead Sea.

Chapter 9:

Into Captivity

When speaking prophetically of Israel's future, certain scenarios and situations must be considered. One can't lump all of Israel into one scenario as many things will happen about the same time. It is easy to get confused trying to understand all of what God's Word is saying to us.

• Scenario one: When Gog the Assyrian attacks there will be a large section of Israel that will be led into captivity, particularly into Assyria and Egypt.

• Scenario two: There will be a remnant that will be cornered in Jerusalem by the beast. This remnant is known as the woman of Revelation 12 and Zechariah 14.

• Scenario three: There will be a remnant in Jerusalem that will be raptured unto God. This is seen as the child born of the woman of Revelation 12 after she gives birth or a rapture of believing Jews.

• Scenario four: The woman then will flee into the wilderness to be taken care of by God for three and a half years (Revelation 12:6).

• Scenario five: Many will die during the Tribulation and many will receive the mark of the beast to be judged.

That's what makes it so difficult for prophecy writers to understand what's going on because they try to lump it all up in one scenario. However, a lot of things are going on at the same time.

Let's look at scenario one closer:
Ezekiel 38:8 says that Gog will come into the land that is brought back by the sword. This is Israel. Gog will ascend and cover the land like a cloud. He will come up to unwalled villages and attack them that are at rest. He will come to take a spoil. God will rise against him with great fury. Chapter 39, verse 23, says that Israel will go into captivity for their iniquity. Verse 25 says that the LORD God will bring again the captivity of Jacob and have mercy on the house of Israel. He says then He will not hide his face from them anymore. Some say this might be about the Gog invasion after the thousand-year reign of Messiah, but it doesn't seem to fit that thought.

In Zechariah 12:2-3, Jerusalem and Judah will be in siege by the nations. Verse 7 says the LORD will save Judah first before Jerusalem. verse 9 also tells us that the LORD will seek to destroy all the nations that come against Jerusalem. Then in verse 10 the LORD pours out His spirit of grace and of supplication on them and they will look upon the One whom they have pierced.

Scenario two begins in Zechariah 14:2; Jerusalem is surrounded and half the city will go into captivity. Verse 3 says the LORD will go forth and fight the nations.

Scenario three begins when a small remnant at Jerusalem will be raptured as seen in Revelation 12 by the child that is born of the woman. This child is not talking about the birth of Yeshua but a raptured remnant from Jerusalem.

Scenario four is the woman (Israel) of Revelation 12 who flees Jerusalem when the LORD comes and splits the Mount of Olives in two and the woman will flee to the wilderness of Azal (Zechariah 14:4-5). She will flee into Jordan toward the Arnon River as seen in Isaiah 16:1. There she will be taken care of, then they flee to Petra, and then to the Mount. This mount must be Sinai where God takes care of them for three and a half years while the beast causes havoc on the world. The beast tried to get the woman but God protects her.

The Jerusalem woman remnant that flees into the wilderness (see Revelation 12) will be chased by the army of the beast of Revelation. However, God will protect that remnant group by destroying part of the beast's army with a flood. He will watch over them for three and a half years. This will be the group at Mount Sinai as mentioned before.

Scenario five is the group that dies in the tribulation and some receive the mark of the beast. They will die in God's judgment and burn in the Valley of Hinnom at Jerusalem. This can be seen in Revelation 14:9-11 and Enoch 90:26-27. Enoch refers to them as blinded sheep. Also, Enoch adds that this fiery abyss is next to the Temple. The fire will burn for a long time. Worshippers that come to the Temple in the Millennium to worship the LORD will see the judgement of fire still burning. This is the same thought when Yeshua talked about being a place of judgement where the fire dies not in Mark 9:44-48 when he quoted Isaiah 66:23-24, "And it shall come to pass, that from one new moon to another, and from one Sabbath to another shall all flesh come to worship before me, says the LORD. And they shall go forth and look upon the carcasses of the men that have transgressed against me; for their worm shall not die, neither shall their fire be quenched; and they shall be an abhorring unto all flesh" (Isaiah 66:23-24). We have five different groups of Israel out there. So when we're looking at prophetic scriptures, we have to figure out what group of Israel we are talking about. It's very important to understand that.

We've talked quite a bit about the different judgments coming, the different wars coming, and the people coming against Israel. Now, we're going to talk about the actual revelation of the LORD to Israel and the release of the captivity.

Deuteronomy 30:1-2
"And it shall come to pass, when all these things are come upon thee, the blessing and the curse, which I have set before thee, and thou shalt call them to mind among all the nations, whither the LORD thy God hath driven thee, And shalt return unto the LORD thy God, and shalt obey his voice according to all that I command thee this day, thou and thy children, with all thine heart, and with all thy soul."

Has that happened? No, it has not happened. The gathering of Israel in 1948 was a preliminary gathering for the nation of Israel to exist for God to begin his work so these prophecies will come true. The part where it says "they shall return unto the LORD and obey his voice" has not taken place. Israel for the most part is not obeying the voice of God. It's a small group that tries, but they're not obeying as a whole. Although there are righteous in the land, Israel is a very secular country.

Now don't get me wrong, I love Israel, I support Israel, because God loves them. I don't always agree with what they do, but I'll always agree they have a right to the land, to exist, a right to Jerusalem. Those are God-given promises and no one should go against that or you are poking God in the eye (Zechariah 2:8). That's why I support Israel immensely, and that's why believers support organizations that support Israel. But is Israel today a righteous nation? Not by any means. They have one of the highest abortion rates, and also a very high homosexual rate. Only a small amount of them are what you'd even consider religious. They're mostly secular, atheists, communists—a mixture of all kinds of people. They're not righteous. But because we know who they are in God's eyes, we're not going to beat up the kid that inherits all things. That would be foolish.

So this is why we love and we support Israel because we have read the end of the book. We know how it's going to come out and we don't want to be in the sheep and goats' judgment in the last days. Matthew 25:31-46 says that after the Tribulation, the Lord will gather all the nations for a final judgment. He refers to them as goats and sheep. He'll separate the sheep and goats and he'll say to the goats, "Because you did not feed me when I was hungry, you did not clothe me when I was naked, you did not visit me while I was in prison, off to eternal judgment." The goats will reply back, "Lord, when did we see you hungry? When did we see you naked? When were you in prison? Surely we would have done those things if you would have just told us!" When the Lord said, "Because you did not do it to the least of these, my brethren [Israel], you did not do it unto me." This is not a charitable teaching concept; there are plenty of those in the Bible we should follow. This is a prophetic judgment against the world and how they treated Israel in the tribulation period.

He then said to the sheep, "Because you did clothe me, because you did feed me, because you did visit me in prison, welcome into my kingdom." The sheep will say, "Lord, when did that ever happen? We didn't know these things were happening to you." He said, "Because you did it to the least of these, my brethren [Israel], you did it unto me." This prophetic judgment will be the last judgment before the millennial reign starts. It won't be good to be in this goat group, not at all. Believers probably won't be in either one of the groups, but anybody that's left upon this Earth had better be in the sheep group. When the tribulation starts, everyone and every nation will be focused in on Israel. So that last judgment has everything to do with how they treated Israel. That nation becomes the focus of the world; Israel is the focus of the tribulation and God knows that if a person does not have a heart for Israel, he does not have a heart for God. We want to have a heart for God.

Deuteronomy 30:3
"That then the LORD thy God will turn thy captivity, and have compassion upon thee, and will return and gather thee from all the nations, whither the LORD thy God hath scattered thee."

The first thing that's going to happen is they're going to return to the LORD. What that means is they're going to repent before the LORD, humble themselves before the LORD, and they're going to obey His voice. Then the captivity of Israel will come back. We see this order of events many times in the scriptures. They will return to the LORD; God will then bring their captivity back. It's not the other way around; captivity first then they return to the LORD. They return first, then their captivity is done away with.

Deuteronomy 30:4-8

"If any of thine be driven out unto the outmost parts of heaven, from thence will the LORD thy God gather thee, and from thence will he fetch thee: And the LORD thy God will bring thee into the land which thy fathers possessed, and thou shalt possess it; and he will do thee good, and multiply thee above thy fathers. And the LORD thy God will circumcise thine heart, and the heart of thy seed, to love the LORD thy God with all thine heart, and with all thy soul, that thou mayest live. And the LORD thy God will put all these curses upon thine enemies, and on them that hate thee, which persecuted thee. And thou shalt return and obey the voice of the LORD, and do all his commandments which I command thee this day."

So is Torah valid? Of course Torah is valid; it tells you that right there. In the final regathering, Israel will follow all the commandments of God as given them this day! That's what it's about. This is why Yeshua said not one jot or tittle will go away from the law until all is fulfilled (see Matthew 5:18). More than likely all things won't be completed until the end of the millennial reign, and the Great White Judgment. So Torah is very valid today.

Believers today understand that Yeshua fulfilled some parts of

Torah. Torah has some manifestational changes dealing with sacrifices, circumcision, separation laws, and things like that, but there's no way anybody can say the Ten Commandments are gone. Even if you ignored all the other commandments, you cannot say the Ten Commandments are gone; they are still valid today.

Chapter 10:

Jerusalem Attack and the Escaping Remnant

When Israel is once again led into captivity, there will be many people who will panic and freak out because they didn't think that was supposed to happen. They think what happened in 1948 was supposed to be the final regathering of Israel, but it's not. It's important to understand that, because what can happen here is that people can lose faith. They can suddenly see the nations come against Israel and lead Israel back into captivity and only a remnant remains in Israel, and they're going to think, *Well, we can't believe anything that people told us.* You can if you read the right scriptures.

This is important to understand about what's going to happen to Israel. If anything, it should put a spark in your heart to pray for Israel and to witness to Jewish people if you know these kind of judgments are coming against Israel. It should really break our heart to see these things because we are kindred with Israel. They are our brothers and beloved of the Father, but they're yet unredeemed. So the redeemed Israel (the saints today) should certainly be concerned about the unredeemed Israel that is over there because one day, God will redeem them, but only after a lot of things go bad. During the Tribulation, many Israelis along with Gentiles and Jews will die in the process.

Even today the enemies of Israel are plotting. Recently there were a tremendous amount of terrorist attacks all across Europe, the Mideast, and in Africa. It's like the enemy is becoming bolder and they're getting more and more violent. We are beginning to see an increase in terrorists

107

attacks in our own country of the United States.

Despite the problems lurking everywhere, Israel has been a blessing to the world. Their sciences and medical breakthroughs are amazing. Their agricultural progress is also a benefit to the world. God promised that the descendants of Abraham will bless the world, and the amount of Jews who have received Nobel Peace prizes is stunning. Of course any Jew who uses his God- given abilities to do evil can do great harm such as Karl Marx. But fortunately, they are few and far between. Unfortunately, God requires obedience and the whole world will be caught up with the beast of Revelation thinking he is God and judgment will come to the whole world including Israel.

Zechariah 12:2
"Behold, I will make Jerusalem a cup of trembling unto all the people round about, when they shall be in the siege both against Judah and against Jerusalem."

What we learn from this chapter in Zechariah and the next chapter is that the nations of the world, with the power of the beast in Revelation, will now surround Jerusalem and try to take the city. It's actually God that brings the beast to Israel. Remember, when we talked about Gog and Magog in Ezekiel 38:4, the LORD said, "I will put a hook in your jaws, O Gog and bring you forth." So even though this is a bad guy, it is the LORD's doing. The reason is that He is bringing judgment upon the whole world for their idolatry, sin, and wickedness.

Now don't forget, however, whatever you see happen to Israel will also happen to the world. So don't think that you're over here nice and safe, because you're not. When this happens, it will infect the whole world. Yet God is going to use this incident to show the world that He is indeed the God of Abraham, Isaac, and Jacob and the Father of our Messiah who will come again but this time for war and judgment.

Zechariah 12:3

"And in that day will I make Jerusalem a burdensome stone for all people: all that burden themselves with it shall be cut in pieces, though all the people of the earth be gathered together against it."

That's an amazing statement. God is going to bring all the people of the Earth against Jerusalem. Now, the beast of Revelation will gather the nations to attack Israel. This beast is probably an angel that's taken on the form of a man, but has incredible powers. He will come against Jerusalem and one of his ultimate purposes is to come to the physical rebuilt temple and proclaim himself God there as seen in 2 Thessalonians 2:4:

Who opposeth and exalteth himself above all that is called God, or that is worshipped; so that he as God sitteth in the temple of God shewing himself that he is God.

When he does, the wrath of God will begin and be poured out upon the whole Earth. The beast desires to be worshiped and he's coming down into Israel and Jerusalem.

Zechariah 12:4

"In that day, saith the LORD, I will smite every horse with astonishment, and his rider with madness: and I will open mine eyes upon the house of Judah, and will smite every horse of the people with blindness."

A lot of times when the LORD talks about riders and horses, He's talking about armies. They may or may not be horses, but He's talking about armies coming—whether they be in tanks, trucks, cars, planes, whatever. This is what is happening here. Remember, people of the past didn't know anything about trucks, trains, planes, and cars. When they speak about horses and riders, they're talking about the armies that are coming. It is at this time that God causes Israel to see who the Messiah is, which is what is meant by "open mine eyes upon the house of Judah." God opens Judah's eyes and also causes Israel to see.

Zechariah 12:5

"And the governors of Judah shall say in their heart, The inhabitants of Jerusalem shall be my strength in the LORD of hosts their God."

God has been with Israel in their wars ever since they became a nation in 1948 but this will be different. At this time, God will empower Judah to fight, at least what is remaining of Judah in the land. Most of the rest of Israel was hauled into captivity. But at this point, when the city of Jerusalem is surrounded, He will empower Judah to be able to fight as you see throughout the scriptures. We know that the resurrected saints will come back also with the Messiah. We will fight with Him and we will judge with Him. A remnant of Judah of the house of David will be empowered to fight and they will fight also to defend Jerusalem.

Zechariah 12:6

"In that day will I make the governors of Judah like an hearth of fire among the wood, and like a torch of fire in a sheaf; and they shall devour all the people round about, on the right hand and on the left: and Jerusalem shall be inhabited again in her own place, even in Jerusalem."

The "governors of Judah" refer to the chiefs, the leaders, the princes, and all of those people. This verse says "I'm going to make the princes of Judah like fire against wood and they will devour, burn up, the wood." If you've ever seen a chaff or sheaf or a dried-up cornfield go up in flames, that's quite a fire! If you've ever seen wheat fields on fire— that's quite a fire! This is what God is going to do with Judah; He's going to empower them to fight like fire against wood, against a sheaf. Judah's going to be empowered—this remnant of Judah that's still in the flesh—is going to be empowered because of Jerusalem.

110

Now, one thing you have to remember: who is the new Jerusalem? Those who follow the Messiah, the Lamb of God, Yeshua. The New Jerusalem will be coming down from heaven during the millennium reign of our Messiah and will be the habitation of the saints who called upon His name and served Him. This city will be on top of the mountains and will have no need of the sun because the glory of God will be the light of it. (More is spoken on this in great detail in the Restoration of Israel.) The people of Israel who have survived the days leading up to the Messiah are going to be encouraged because of the New Jerusalem when they see the saints coming back with the Messiah. Then all of a sudden, power comes upon Judah and they will begin to fight the surrounding enemies. The remnant of Judah that comes back from captivity will still be in the flesh and will fight with the raptured saints.

Zechariah 12:7
"The LORD also shall save the tents of Judah first, that the glory of the house of David and the glory of the inhabitants of Jerusalem do not magnify themselves against Judah."

When the LORD comes with his saints, He's going to help Judah first and then He's going to Jerusalem, which is known as the house of David. He is going to empower Judah to fight against their enemies, particularly the surrounding enemy nations mentioned in Psalm 83 that have gathered at Jerusalem. God will allow Judah to recompense against those that have continually been a thorn in their sides. Perhaps this empowered Judah and the saints will together defeat the armies of the beast. Then the Messiah is going to finish the job in Jerusalem. So he will save Judah first so that Jerusalem can't boast against Judah.

Zechariah 12:8
"In that day shall the LORD defend the inhabitants of Jerusalem; and he that is feeble among them at that day shall be as David; and the house of David shall be as God, as the angel of the LORD before them."

The inhabitants of Jerusalem shall fight like David fought and like the angel of the LORD. So is this verse talking about the saints, or is it just talking about Judah that is in the flesh at Jerusalem? We don't know. It is a good possibility that it will be both but they will fight like David fought. If you know the scriptures, David was a pretty good warrior. As a boy, he killed a lion and a bear when he guarded his sheep. He was not afraid of the carnivorous animals that were coming to attack, although many shepherds would run when they saw a wolf come! Not David; he ran to the beasts and slayed them. As a man, he was notorious in his exploits against the enemies of Israel and the people shouted, "Saul killed his thousands but David his tens of thousands." This is what's going to happen in that day. God will empower the inhabitants of Jerusalem to fight against the beast and his armies that will be in Jerusalem at that time.

Zechariah 12:9
"And it shall come to pass in that day, that I will seek to destroy all the nations that come against Jerusalem."

Government leaders don't understand why believers become upset when they see decisions that do harm to Israel. Why do we get upset? Because of scriptures like this. When you come against Jerusalem, which is the capital of Israel, you are poking God in the eye and you are challenging God. Israel may be unredeemed, but they're going to be redeemed eventually. So if you know that Israel is the apple of God's eye, why would you hurt them and poke God in the eye? In the last days, these nations of the world will do exactly that and God will judge them.

Recently I saw on the news where the Pope has made a peace agreement with the state of Palestine. There is no state of Palestine, but he declared a state and signed a peace agreement with them. Unbelievable how fast things are rolling, how quickly things are changing where the little country of Israel is the world's focus. God is slowly drawing the nations to that country.

Every day I ask myself, "What's new today?" I look at the news and see biblical prophecies coming true. Now I don't believe the Pope is the Antichrist, but I do believe it's very possible that he could be a supporter of the Antichrist. It does say that the beast of Revelation will be united with ten kings. Could the Pope, or someone like him, be one of those kings? I don't know, but he is certainly playing into the hands of the enemy right now.

He also declared that global warming was the most serious problem we have facing the Earth today! Never mind about ISIS beheading people and economies crashing and everything else. Global warming is the issue? Those are the words spoken of by the Pope! He's even has an appointed person for the Catholic church to help them understand how to combat global warming, and that person is an atheist!

It's unbelievable what is going on. Recently ISIS attacked Paris and killed many with guns and suicide bombers, then followed that up with a bombing at the Brussels, Belgium, airport which killed more than 30 people and injured dozens. Do you know at the time of the Paris attack, Al Gore was at the Eiffel Tower trying to convince people that global warming was the most critical thing to worry about? Tell that to the families of the victims who were killed at that time. As a believer in the Messiah I know I must trust in the Lord our God. I may not know what the future holds, but I know who holds the future, and He's the One we need to keep our eyes on all the time.

Zechariah 12:10

"And I will pour upon the house of David, and upon the inhabitants of Jerusalem, the spirit of grace and of supplications: and they shall look upon me whom they have pierced, and they shall mourn for him, as one mourneth for his only son, and shall be in bitterness for him, as one that is in bitterness for his firstborn."

The sign of the Son of Man is going to appear. That will begin (as I've talked about before and I'll be talking about it more in the future) the gathering of Israel from the nations, particularly from Assyria to Egypt. They will be coming back into Israel when they see the sign, when they see the ensign as the Old Testament calls it, and the trumpet sounds. They will begin to be gathered back in the land of Israel. I believe this will be the sign of the Son of Man in Matthew 24:30. When the sign appears and a trumpet sounds, they will look up because the heavens will open up and they'll see the Messiah at the throne of God.

It's not going to be one of those things where Yeshua comes down and stands on the Mount of Olives and shouts, *"Here I am!"* That's probably not the way it's going to be. The sky will open up, the sign of the Son of Man will appear, and the captives of Israel will look up and see him. The book of Enoch says when that event takes place. The world will see the Son of Man actually sitting on the throne of God; His Father's throne (Enoch 51:3, 55:4, 61:8). It Zechariah 12:10 it says that they will look unto the One whom they have pierced, and they'll begin to mourn. The mourning will be so deep as the loss of an only son. That's how great the mourning will be.

Now I've experienced that. I lost my first son, and I know what it's like to have a firstborn son die and the great pain you get from that. So I relate with this scripture because I can just see Israel falling apart with the people falling on their knees weeping and crying at the loss of an only son. Israel will mourn because they will now realize that their rejection of the Messiah has caused them so much pain. They will recall all the bad things they have said about Yeshua (Jesus). Even though it was God's plan for Israel as a nation to reject the Messiah up to this point, so that the Gentiles would get saved. But now His attention is on Israel.

Zechariah 12:11

"In that day shall there be a great mourning in Jerusalem, as the mourning of Hadadrimmon in the valley of Megiddon."

This part of Zechariah explains about the great mourning that occurred when the righteous Judean King Josiah was killed by the Egyptians in the valley of Megiddo. He was greatly loved and all Judea mourned for him. Yet when Israel sees who the Messiah is, the mourning will be greater than that of Josiah's death.

Zechariah 12:12-14

"And the land shall mourn, every family apart; the family of the house of David apart, and their wives apart; the family of the house of Nathan apart, and their wives apart; he family of the house of Levi apart, and their wives apart; the family of Shimei apart, and their wives apart; All the families that remain, every family apart, and their wives apart."

What does that all mean, "...and the wives apart"? Have you ever been in such a deep state of mourning you just want to be by yourself? That's what it's going to be. You don't want anybody around you, you don't want any distractions, you don't want anybody talking to you, you don't want anything. The mourning is going to be so great that you're going to find your own little cubbyhole or closet or whatever, and you're just going to mourn and cry.

Now why does Israel mourn and cry? Think about it. They're finally going to come to the revelation who Yeshua is after all these hundreds of years of persecution, of the Holocaust, the Inquisition, the pogroms, and many other persecutions. They're going to realize now why they came upon them.

Did you know that a lot of the orthodox Jews have curse words for

Yeshua? Some won't even mention the name, but they'll say, *And the name that shall not be mentioned. Cursed be his name.* All of a sudden, they're going to realize, *Oh my word, what have I done? What have I said?* When they look up and see Yeshua sitting on the throne of God, they're not going to know what to do. They will just suddenly walk off into somewhere, fall on their faces, and start crying, start weeping, *God forgive me, I did not know, I did not understand.* Some of it's their fault, some of it's not their fault.

Like I said the reason God blinded Israel was so that salvation would come to the gentiles. Once Israel calls on Yeshua by saying, "Blessed is he who comes in the name of the LORD" (Matthew 23:39) in a corporate setting, then Yeshua will be their king. That's why He fled from them in Jerusalem as the Gospel said when they tried to make Him their king. He would not allow them to make Him a king because He had an ultimate goal in mind. He had to save the gentiles, which were a larger number in the world than Israel, then He'd come back for Israel. God loves the whole world and desires for none to perish.

It helps to understand the entire concept of the two goats of Yom Kippur. The first one was known as the goat for the LORD. This goat had the sins of Israel confessed on it and represented Yeshua on the cross. It was on the LORD's altar and it was for the sins right now for those who call upon Yeshua. That goat was offered and the blood was put on the Ark of the Covenant. Leviticus 17:11 says:

> *"For the life of the flesh is in the blood: and I have given it to you upon the altar to make an atonement for your souls: for it is the blood that makes an atonement for the soul."*

And Hebrews 9:23 says,
> *"And almost all things are by the law purged with blood; and without shedding of blood is no remission."*

116

There cannot be forgiveness for sins without the shedding of blood through sacrifice. If your sins are not covered by the blood of Yeshua, you are dead in them.

Yet there was another goat that carried the confessed sins of Israel and it was turned loose in the wilderness, as the Bible says, alive. Why? That goat will be the atonement for Israel when they look up and see the Son of Man sitting on the throne which is the a sign of the Son of Man in heaven. They will be redeemed by just looking up and calling upon Him at that time. All of these things are yet to happen and will come to fruition down the line. This goat was known as the scapegoat. History tells us that this goat was thrown from a cliff and killed but that was not what the scriptures say was supposed to happen. It was to be let loose alive in the wilderness as it says in Leviticus 16:10. Someday, Israel will stop throwing Yeshua off a cliff and will cling to Him.

Zechariah 13:8
"And it shall come to pass, that in all the land, saith the LORD, two parts therein shall be cut off and die; but the third shall be left therein."

That word "cut off" means cut off from the land and it can also mean to perish. It says, "and die" afterwards. It would be proper to say "cut off" would be "led into captivity". So two-thirds of the inhabitants of Israel will be led off into captivity or killed during this time that the beast comes into the land.

Zechariah 13:9
"And I will bring the third part through the fire, and will refine them as silver is refined, and will try them as gold is tried: they shall call on my name, and I will hear them: I will say, It is my people: and they shall say, The LORD is my God."

117

Has this ever happened? No, none of this stuff has ever happened, none of it. There have been partial concepts with Nebuchadnezzar and Assyria, but it's not been complete. This is what we've been talking about when it comes to prophecy having a double-fulfillment of God's Word. You can have a partial fulfillment, but if everything that was said was not fulfilled, then you have to understand that was a shadow fulfillment and that there is coming a complete fulfillment in the future. You have to understand that concept.

Zechariah 14:1
"Behold, the day of the LORD cometh, and thy spoil shall be divided in the midst of thee."

That spoil is actually talking about captivity again. If you look up the word "spoil" in Strong's Concordance (7998 shalal), it can mean captivity, those taken captive. Spoil is taking up humans or beasts or animals. So in this particular case, it is talking about the people in Israel.

Zechariah 14:2
"For I will gather all nations against Jerusalem to battle; and the city shall be taken, and the houses rifled, and the women ravished; and half of the city shall go forth into captivity, and the residue of the people shall not be cut off from the city."

Most, but not all, of Jerusalem will be taken. The houses will be robbed and the enemy will collect all the gold and silver—anything they think is worthwhile—because the beast is coming with hundreds of thousands of people if not millions. Half of Jerusalem will go into captivity. That did not happen before. Now, Nebuchadnezzar took the whole city. The Assyrians didn't take any of it, but here we see half the city, so you know that this has not happened yet. Yet a residue or remnant of the people shall not be cut off from the city. There's a remnant in Jerusalem that will not be captured by the enemy and they're waiting on the LORD.

It remains unknown what half the remnant will be in. It'll be interesting if it's the Temple Mount, but I really kind of doubt it because the beast will proclaim himself God on the Temple Mount in the temple. That tells me he will have control of the Temple Mount. However, somewhere in the city of Jerusalem, a remnant will be gathered and the LORD will protect them at that time. Also, out of this group a remnant of the remnant will be raptured according to Revelation 12:1-5. The woman mentioned is Israel. She gives birth to a man child who will rule the nations. This child is not talking about Yeshua. It is those who will be raptured at the time of the beast of Revelation. (More on that in a moment.)

> **Zechariah 14:3-4**
> *"Then shall the LORD go forth, and fight against those nations, as when he fought in the day of battle. And his feet shall stand in that day upon the mount of Olives, which is before Jerusalem on the east, and the mount of Olives shall cleave in the midst thereof toward the east and toward the west, and there shall be a very great valley; and half of the mountain shall remove toward the north, and half of it toward the south."*

The Mount of Olives is going to split north and south and create a valley that runs east and west right down the middle of it. This is where the remnant in Jerusalem is going to flee—through this valley. I find it very interesting that there's another story in the Bible about King David running from his son, Absalom. When Absalom came and tried to take the kingdom away from his own father, King David gathered his forces. They went over the Mount of Olives, across the Jordan River by the Dead Sea, and headed south toward the river Arnon. Well, believe it or not folks, that's exactly what's going to be happening to this remnant. They're going to repeat that same journey, only more.

Zechariah 14:5
"And ye shall flee to the valley of the mountains; for the valley of the mountains shall reach unto Azal: yea, ye shall flee, like as ye fled from before the earthquake in the days of Uzziah king of Judah: and the LORD my God shall come, and all the saints with thee."

The Valley of the Mountains would be the Dead Sea area. As this remnant flees and takes the same path King David took, they'll be going down across the Jordan River just north of the Dead Sea and into Jordan. That whole area is known as the Valley of the Mountains, and Azal is where they used to take the scapegoat when they threw it off the cliff, when they were really supposed to turn it loose alive. The scriptures don't tell us why they threw the scapegoat off the cliff, but I imagine it's because probably one day that goat that carried the sins of Israel followed them back to Jerusalem. They couldn't allow to have their sin return unto them, so they went out towards the Dead Sea to a cliff (possibly the area known as the wilderness of Tekoa, which is on the cliff line above the Dead Sea) and they threw the goat off the cliff. The goat was nicknamed Azazel, "The Lord of Azal."

Isaiah 16:1-4
"Send ye the lamb to the ruler of the land from Sela [that is Petra] to the wilderness, unto the mount of the daughter of Zion. For it shall be, that, as a wandering bird cast out of the nest, so the daughters of Moab shall be at the fords of Arnon."
"Take counsel, execute judgment; make thy shadow as the night in the midst of the noonday; hide the outcasts; bewray not him that wandereth. Let mine outcasts dwell with thee, Moab; be thou a covert to them from the face of the spoiler: for the extortioner is at an end, the spoiler ceaseth, the oppressors are consumed out of the land."

What are we seeing here? What is taking place? We see some geographic concepts here—Sela, which is Petra, the mount of the daughter of Zion and the fords of Arnon. The Arnon River runs west halfway down the Dead Sea on the Jordanian side, similar to the same direction King David went when he fled Absalom. He crossed over the Mount of Olives (2 Samuel 15:30), crossed the Jordan River (2 Samuel 17:22), and then headed for a place called Mahanaim. This location is not for certain, but it is believed to be in the south Gilead area near the river Jabbok or even further south. Second Samuel 17:26 tells us that Absalom camped in the Gilead area also. David's men defeated Absalom in this area and put down Absalom's rebellion against his dad.

Continuing to look at Isaiah 16, the daughters of Arnon were told to hide the outcasts and to not uncover (bewray) them to the enemy. The people in this area will hide the remnant that will flee from Jerusalem. Remember, there are really three different remnant groups here. There will be one group that is led away into captivity by the Assyrian (Beast). The second remnant group will be the man child of Revelation 12. This group is the raptured group out of Jerusalem. This rapture could include most believers. The third group is the woman of Revelation 12 who flees into the wilderness to escape the beast. God will take care of her for 3.5 years. More will be discussed about this later in the book.

He's saying to the daughters at the Arnon River, "Hide my outcasts! Take care of them. Feed, them, water them as they are on their journey and hide them from the spoiler." So a remnant of Israel is dropping south, they will stop at the river Arnon to rest and the people living in that area are commanded by God to take care of them. Then they continue their journey south to Petra to give a lamb to the ruler of Sela (or Petra). Why are they doing this? So he could take care of them, too, and allow them to at least go through. They're not going to stop and stay for a long time at Petra like so many prophecy writers write. They may stop and rest there, but they won't remain. Where are they headed? They're headed to the mount of the daughters of Zion that we saw in verse 1. What mountain is in the area they would be going to after they leave Jerusalem? It is not the Mount Sinai in Egypt, but the real Mount Sinai in Arabia, which is about a hundred miles to the south of Petra.

This is where the Jerusalem remnant is fleeing from the beast of Revelation and his armies. Revelation 12 says the remnant (the woman with the twelve stars) will flee into the wilderness. Well, this certainly is a wilderness, the same wilderness that the Hebrews spent part of their 40 years of wandering in the wilderness after leaving Egypt. Isaiah 16 is backed up by Revelation 12. The interesting thing about Revelation 12 is that the woman that travails (talking about Israel) finally gives birth. All throughout the Old Testament, we see prophecies of Israel as a woman being in travail and not giving birth. She just can't seem to give birth. But before this woman flees to the wilderness, while in Jerusalem, she gives birth. What is she giving birth to?

Revelation 12:2-6
"And she being with child cried, travailing in birth, and pained to be delivered. And there appeared another wonder in heaven; and behold a great red dragon, having seven heads and ten horns, and seven crowns upon his heads. And his tail drew the third part of the stars of heaven, and did cast them to the earth: and the dragon stood before the woman which was ready to be delivered, for to devour her child as soon as it was born. And she brought forth a man child, who was to rule all nations with a rod of iron: and her child was caught up unto God and his throne. And the woman fled into the wilderness where she has a place prepared of God, that they should feed her there a thousand two hundred and threescore days."

There are several points to understand here. This is not talking about the birth of Yeshua. Why? Because first of all Israel, the woman, did not flee into the wilderness after Yeshua was born. Second, why would

Revelation start with the resurrected glorified Yeshua and then halfway through Revelation speak of His birth. It doesn't make sense. Yes, it is true that Yeshua will rule with a rod of iron and is at the throne of God. However, this is the same promise to believers who overcome. Revelation 2:26-27 tells us that he who overcomes will have power over the nations and will rule them with a rod of iron. Also in Revelation 3:21 we learn that believers who overcome will sit down with Messiah in His and the Father's throne.

Since God refers to Israel as a woman singular, it is understandable that this man child singular is also talking about a larger group. Thus, this concept here in Revelation 12 is about a rapture, this special remnant of Israel that will be raptured up to God's throne. This may be a worldwide rapture that I like to call firstfruits rapture.

The apostle Shaul, or Paul, tells us in 2 Thessalonians 2:3 that that day will not come until there is a falling away and the man of sin is revealed, the son of perdition. The beast of Revelation, Gog, Antichrist, are all this son of perdition. The beast will chase the woman into the wilderness so he will be revealed at that time. Perhaps this woman is also the 144,000 of Revelation 7. However, God protects this woman. Where? Probably as Isaiah 16 says at the mount of the daughters of Zion, or Mount Sinai. God destroys part of the beast's army and keeps the beast away from the remnant as He nourishes them for three and a half years.

Now if the worldwide rapture takes place in Revelation 12, then who does the beast go after if believers are gone. According to Revelation 12:17, the beast is so angry that he lost a large part of his army by the hand of God when he attacked this remnant (Revelation 12:16), he goes after those who keep the commandments of God and have the testimony of Yeshua. This particular group of believers are those who were left behind after the firstfruits rapture occurred. Many will believe after the rapture because they will see it happen. It will not be a secret rapture. Enoch 50:1-3 says "And in those days a change shall take place for the holy and

123

elect, and the light of days shall abide upon them, and glory and honor shall turn to the holy, on the day of affliction on which evil shall have been treasured up against the sinners. And the righteous shall be victorious in the name of the Lord of Spirits: And he will cause the others to witness this that they may repent and forgo the works of their hands. They shall have no honor through the name of the Lord of Spirits, yet through his name shall they be saved." Only those considered worthy will be in the firstfruits rapture. (See Luke 21:36).

Watch you therefore and pray always, that you may be accounted worthy to escape all these things that shall come to pass, and to stand before the Son of Man.

There will be at least two more raptures to come—the martyr rapture and another large one at the second coming of the Messiah. But that is a teaching for another time.

This particular Jerusalem remnant of Israel will finally be born again. That's what the woman being in travail is talking about. Waiting for that birth.

So they're taking this journey and I believe the mount of the daughters of Zion is Mount Sinai. They're going south; what other mountain could it possibly be? They're not going to Mount Seir of the Edomites. They're not going to Mount Hor where Aaron was buried, they're going to Mount Sinai. Revelation 12 says God will take care of them there for three and a half years. So after the beast of Revelation sweeps in and the remnant escapes out of Jerusalem, the remnant will flee to Mount Sinai. However, the beast will chase them. You see that in Revelation also where he chases them and God sends forth a flood and destroys his army in Revelation 12.

What will happen for three and a half years is that God will dwell with them, instruct them, and protect them at Mount Sinai. In other words, they didn't get it right the first time and God's going to give them the opportunity to get it right the second time. There, He will be with a remnant of His people for three and a half years on Mount Sinai. The beast is so angry he couldn't get that remnant and finish off Israel that he will turn his attention to all of those that have the testimony of Yeshua and keep the commandments of God (Revelation 12:17). It's why the apostle Paul said the rapture will not occur until the son of perdition is revealed (2 Thessalonians 2:3). Is this when the "revealing" part takes place? I don't know. Is this when the firstfruits rapture is going to take place? Very possibly, because the martyrs and the ones after tribulation would come later.

So the firstfruits rapture will take place when Yeshua comes and splits the Mount of Olives in two, raptures the child of the woman (Jew and Gentile believers) out of Jerusalem, and delivers the woman (a remnant of Israel) of Revelation 12. Keep in mind, there is already a raptured element in heaven before this happens. It is the first of the firstfruits, the 24 elders who are there and are given white garments before the tribulation begins (Revelation 4:4, 10; 5:8-10). These 24 represent people from all nations. It is a symbolic number. Twenty-four is symbolic of Jew and Gentile being two twelves, and 12 is symbolic of government. These 24 are made unto God kings and priests.

Jeremiah 31:2
"Thus saith the LORD, The people which were left of the sword found grace in the wilderness; even Israel, when I went to cause him to rest."

Here, we have a situation taking place in which a remnant of Israel from Jerusalem will be in the wilderness where they will find the grace of God. There they will dwell with God in the wilderness. Not in the north country, in Turkey or Assyria, or in the south country at Egypt, but in the wilderness, this remnant found grace. This remnant is the woman of Revelation 12:6 who is taken care of in the wilderness for three and a half years. Let me explain a little bit more about this wilderness journey that will take place.

As mentioned before in Zechariah 14, the LORD himself shall descend upon the Mount of Olives and it shall split north to south and make a valley in between so that the remnant in Jerusalem can flee into the wilderness, passing through the Mount of Olives. Where do they go? I believe Isaiah 16 tells us the LORD tells the daughters of Arnon to take care of the outcasts in their journey. They will flee across the Jordan River into the current nation of Jordan today and then they will turn south and camp at the Arnon River for a period of time. In Revelation 12, we realize that the beast starts to chase this woman that is fleeing into the wilderness.

Isaiah goes on to say that they will leave the Arnon River and go to Petra (Selah), and the scripture says for Israel to give a lamb to the ruler of Petra. In other words, appease the guy, let's stay there for a short period of time. But they don't remain there; they're just passing through Petra going south.

Then Isaiah says another interesting thing: "On their way to the mount." So they go to Arnon, they go to Petra, on their way to the mountain. What mountain? There can only be one possible mountain, and that's Mount Sinai which is on the northwestern side of Saudi Arabia, not the Egyptian Sinai Peninsula. Yes, there is a lot of evidence that the real Mount Sinai is in northwestern Saudi Arabia. People who have managed to sneak in the area and get pictures have shown incredible photographs of this mountain that's burned on the top with plains all around it. There is evidence of camps all around it and of graffiti being drawn on the rocks of the same mountain with fire and smoke coming off of it. A quarter of a mile away, a 60-foot monolith rock is split in two. That's the rock of Horeb. Calcium deposits come from that rock and the deposits show that a river once ran from the rock to a low area and formed a lake that is now long dry. There's a cave upon that mountain that people who visited this site call Elijah's cave—the very cave Elijah hid in when he fled to Mount

Horeb. Thus, the evidence is overwhelming that this is the real Mount Sinai in northern Saudi Arabia just across the Jordanian border.

So this remnant that's fleeing into the wilderness will cross the Jordan River, go south, stop at the River Arnon to be taken care of, head to Petra to rest, and then head another 100 miles or so to Mount Sinai. Revelation 12 says that God will take care of them for three and a half years; the last half of the Tribulation period. The beast goes after them, but God destroys the army of the beast that tries to pursue them just like He did with the Amalekites. He takes care of His people a second time as they go to Mount Sinai where He will meet them again. This is where the group finds grace in the wilderness.

At some point, they will come back to Jerusalem.

Zechariah 14:10-12

"All the land shall be turned as a plain from Geba to Rimmon south of Jerusalem: and it shall be lifted up, and inhabited in her place, from Benjamin's gate unto the place of the first gate, unto the corner gate, and from the tower of Hananeel unto the king's winepresses. And men shall dwell in it, and there shall be no more utter destruction; but Jerusalem shall be safely inhabited. And this shall be the plague wherewith the LORD will smite all the people that have fought against Jerusalem; Their flesh shall consume away while they stand upon their feet, and their eyes shall consume away in their holes, and their tongue shall consume away in their mouth."

It appears that the land around Jerusalem will lift and be a plain for many miles around. Perhaps this is what is referred to as a new earth when the Messiah reigns. This is also maybe why God removes the remnant out of Jerusalem. Not only is He going to protect them, He is going to do some landscaping in and around Jerusalem.

The LORD will also judge those who fought against Jerusalem while they're still standing! The fire of the LORD will cause the flesh of these people to be consumed off their bodies before their bones hit the ground. That's a pretty nasty judgment. We're talking about a pretty hot fire, but this has happened before. What happened to Aaron's two sons who burned strange incense to the LORD? They were immediately consumed with the fire of God (Leviticus 10:1-2). Now we're talking about a fire that's probably a million degrees hot, and yet the LORD can control how far He wants it to go. However, this is what it says: it's a plague against those that come against Jerusalem.

Zechariah 14:13

"And it shall come to pass in that day, that a great tumult from the LORD shall be among them; and they shall lay hold every one on the hand of his neighbour, and his hand shall rise up against the hand of his neighbour."

This is talking about the judgment of the nations that come against Jerusalem. The LORD will not only consume them, but He will cause many of them to fight each other. Yeshua talked about this in Matthew 24:7 and 10, Mark 13:8 and 12, and Luke 21:10 and 16. God has done this before; He causes the enemy to fight each other to death. This is seen in 2 Chronicles 20:23 where the armies of Ammon and Moab fought against the Edomites and killed each other when just moments before they were as one coming against Jerusalem. This is also seen when Gideon defeated the Midianites in Judges 7:22.

Zechariah 14:14

"And Judah also shall fight at Jerusalem; and the wealth of all the heathen round about shall be gathered together, gold, and silver, and apparel, in great abundance. And so shall be the plague of the horse, of the mule, of the camel, and of the ass, and of all the beasts that shall be in these tents, as this plague. And it shall come to pass, that every

one that is left of all the nations which came against Jerusalem shall even go up from year to year to worship the King, the LORD of hosts, and to keep the feast of tabernacles."

There we have Judah again, and God empowering Judah to fight. This Judah that fights will most likely be the returning captivity and the remnant that fled into the wilderness that God watched over for three and a half years. They will come back to Jerusalem and fight the enemies in their land.

During the millennial reign, all of the nations that are left alive after the tribulation will be required to honor the Feast of Tabernacles in Jerusalem. Since not everyone from the nations could fit in Jerusalem, they will probably have to send a representative to Jerusalem during this Feast. For those who think the feasts of Leviticus 23 are done away with, think again. Even in Ezekiel 45:21 when describing the millennium reign, tells us that Passover and the Unleavened Bread Feast will be celebrated also. During the millennium reign of the Messiah, every aspect of Torah will be adhered to for those living in the flesh during that time. This is why Yeshua in Matthew 5:18 said, "till heaven and earth pass, not one jot or tittle will depart from Torah until all is complete".

We read a lot about the armies surrounding Jerusalem in Zechariah 12–14. Half the city of Jerusalem will be taken, and the women raped and people murdered. You may say, *Well, that happened in the Babylonian captivity.* Yes, but here we have a parallelism that commands our attention. Did the king of Babylon, Nebuchadnezzar, take the entire city of Jerusalem? Yes. However, in Zechariah 14, we ask, was the entire city of Jerusalem taken by the enemy? No. So you know that there's something else going on. Did the Mount of Olives split in two during the time of Nebuchadnezzar? No. Did the Jerusalem remnant flee and escape into the wilderness during the time of Nebuchadnezzar? No. So you begin to see that yes, Nebuchadnezzar surrounded the city, took the entire city, and burnt the temple. However, in Zechariah 14, only half the city is taken and God protects the other half. That didn't happen. So you see that this is going to repeat itself but with a greater fulfillment because there are items that were not fulfilled through Nebuchadnezzar. It's important to understand this concept because some prophetic commentators say that the Zechariah prophecies were fulfilled when Nebuchadnezzar came. However, he didn't do all that Zechariah said, so parallelism is taking place and that means it's going to happen again. History will repeat itself.

Zechariah 9:8

"And I will encamp about mine house because of the army, because of him that passeth by, and because of him that returneth: and no oppressor shall pass through them any more: for now have I seen with mine eyes."

This is talking about Jerusalem, and the LORD will encamp around it. Basically, Zechariah is saying this bad guy will pass by Israel on his way to destroy Egypt, and on his way back again he'll attack Jerusalem just like the Greek/Syrian King Antiochus Epiphanes did in the second century BC. In the Daniel, chapters 9 and 11, Daniel received visions of things that were in the future. Some of these things were about Antiochus Epiphanes who was a shadow of the Antichrist himself. Again, this was parallelism as not all that Daniel talked about was fulfilled by Antiochus. We do know that Antiochus went to fight Egypt and then returned to fight Jerusalem, very much like what Zechariah 9:8 says. But the promise that "no oppressor" shall pass by Jerusalem anymore was not fulfilled as there have many oppressors since then such as the Romans, Byzantines, Mongols, and Islam which means there is a final fulfillment of this scripture.

Zechariah 9:9

"Rejoice greatly, O daughter of Zion; shout, O daughter of Jerusalem: behold, thy King cometh unto thee: he is just, and having salvation; lowly, and riding upon an ass, and

upon a colt the foal of an ass."

This scripture is very much like Genesis 49:10-11 which says, "The scepter shall not depart from Judah, nor a lawgiver from between his feet, until Shiloh (Messiah) come; and unto him shall the gathering of the people be. Binding his foal unto the vine, and his ass's colt unto the choice vine; he washed his garments in wine, and his clothes in the blood of grapes." And as Zechariah says, Yeshua rode into Jerusalem on the ass. We knew that Yeshua's first coming fulfilled that scripture right there. Genesis 49:11 is a very interesting scripture that can slip right by you. This Shiloh who is none other than Yeshua, will tie his foal to the vine. Foal in Hebrew is ayir. It can also mean a full grown male ass. So this concept most likely means that the LORD at mount Sinai made his covenant with Israel the vine. Yet also we see that the ass' (female) colt (children) ties herself to the choice vine. This female ass (athown) represents the Holy Spirit and makes a covenant with all who are filled with the spirit by believing in Yeshua. This choice or noble vine is the saints. When Yeshua came into Jerusalem the first time, he brought both animals showing the first and second covenant with those who believe in him. He will honor the first covenant he made with Israel's fathers and create a new covenant for all who call on him. This is another good example of the heavenly and physical Zion concept. Genesis 49:10 also says that the scepter will not depart from Judah until Shiloh comes. History tells us that when Herod the Great was appointed king of Israel by the Romans, all authority of the Jewish Sanhedrin was reduced, including the right for capital punishment. That was in 7 AD. Was Shiloh here at that time? Many rabbis mourned because the authority of Judah was taken away and Shiloh had not come. However, He was here as a youth in Nazareth known as Yeshua.

Zechariah 9:10

"And I will cut off the chariot from Ephraim, and the horse from Jerusalem, and the battle bow shall be cut off: and he shall speak peace unto the heathen: and his dominion shall be from sea even to sea, and from the river even to the ends of the earth."

So what is the LORD talking about here? He's going to destroy the enemy that attacked Jerusalem. Shortly after, the swords will be beaten into plowshares and peace will come to the Earth as Isaiah 2:4 tells us.

Yeshua's dominion will go from sea to sea. He will rule. That's why it says in verse 9, "Your king comes to you." Remember, during Yeshua's first coming, there were many who were trying to make Him king, but He refused. Why? He had to be the Lamb of God first to make atonement. Otherwise, we would not have salvation, but He's coming back as king.

Zechariah 9:11
"As for thee also, by the blood of thy covenant I have sent forth thy prisoners out of the pit wherein is no water."

The blood of the covenant—that's what He did on the cross. If you don't have Yeshua in your life, you are a prisoner to Satan and to demonic activity. This is why the scripture says there is liberty in the Lord. Once you have the Lord, you're set free. *"I'm free!"* How many times have you heard that? This is what it's talking about. You were once a slave and a prisoner, and now have been set free by the mercy and grace of God and the blood of the covenant.

Zechariah 9:12
"Turn you to the strong hold, ye prisoners of hope: even to day do I declare that I will render double unto thee..."

The stronghold basically could mean anything that's strong and solid; a fortress. Here it just means turn to the LORD. He is our stronghold, He is our defense, He is our rock. He is all those things. When we turn to Him, He watches after us. Did you know that the word "prisoner" can also be translated as "captive"? So, we're talking about the captivity returning. You can use the word "prisoner" or you can use the word *captive*. Here, King James decided to use "prisoner." However, if you are in captivity, you *are* a prisoner. He's saying turn to the stronghold, turn to the LORD, you prisoners of hope. In other words, there's a calling upon you; there's a direction for you. The LORD has something for you. "Call upon me and I will set you free, I will bring you out of the pit, I will deliver you." This is what he's telling Israel right here.

So the time frame is during Israel's future captivity and the LORD's calling upon them. "Turn to the stronghold you prisoners of hope. Even today I declare that I will render double unto you." What does that mean, "Render double unto you"? That doesn't mean double bad things. Double also means also "second," and render means "I will return unto you." What the scripture is saying is, "I will return your captivity the second time." The LORD is saying, "I am going to bring you back like I did in Egypt the first time. I'm going to bring you back the second time" (Jeremiah 16:14-15).

Chapter 11:

Location of Final Battle of Armageddon

Habakkuk 3:3
"God came from Teman and the Holy One from mount Paran."

God says he is coming from Teman. Where is Teman? It is a city in Edom near the southern area of Israel by the Dead Sea. Paran is also in southern Israel. The Hebrews spent a lot of time in Paran in their wilderness journey. Why is God coming from Teman? It is here that He defeats Gog. This is a place of judgment.

In **Isaiah 63:1** we have a question.
Who is this that comes from Edom, with dyed garments from Bozrah? This that is glorious in his apparel, travelling in the greatness of his strength? I that speak in righteousness mighty to save.

One of the definitions of "dyed" is red. So Isaiah is saying that someone is coming with bloodstained garments.

This is the same as **Revelation 19:13**:
"And he was clothed with a vesture dipped in blood: and his name is called the Word of God."

This is no other than the Messiah. This is Yeshua coming to judge Gog and the rest of the world.

Where is Bozrah? Bozrah is in Edom near the southern area of Israel, not far from Teman.

Teman and Bozrah are not far from the real Mount Sinai in Saudi Arabia. This is where Gog's forces are going to accumulate chasing the remnant of Israel that escapes out of Jerusalem, fleeing to the wilderness, and the beast pursues them. God's going to wipe out a large portion of Gog's army here. This will not occur in northern Israel where they claim the battle of Armageddon will be, but right in here in Edom and the southern Dead Sea area.

Why right there? Revelation 16 tells us that when the sixth vial is poured out, God is going to dry up Euphrates for the kings of the east to come down. Prophecy writers have various opinions of who the "kings of the east" are. Some say that it's China coming to join the battle. Then they try to mix the army of the 200 million of Revelation 9 with the Revelation 16 "kings of the east" and say there must be 200 million Chinese coming.

Stop to think about that for a moment. What are the logistics of trying to push 200 million people from way over there in China all the way over here in Israel? It's impossible; literally impossible! If you're talking about a spiritual army, maybe, but not a physical army. Do you know how difficult it would be to feed and provide fuel and shelter for 200 million people coming across the land from China to Israel? It's not going to happen. You can't take Revelation 9 and compare it to the kings of the east; they are two separate things.

Revelation 9, the 200 million—it tells you what they are. They are the army of the four horsemen of the Apocalypse. This is the spiritual army of Joel 3 that says they don't die, they don't break from their ranks, and they sweep across the world in judgment. This is a judgment of God, of a spiritual army, and these 200 million are needed to cover the whole world. These are not Chinese marching into Israel. Again, my opinion. If you think it's Chinese, God bless you, but I don't see it.

Other prophecy writers say the kings of the east are other Muslim nations east of the Euphrates River. That's a possibility because it seems like it's a Muslim invasion that's going to take place. So if these eastern Moslem nations decide to join Gog where it all starts, they're blocked by the Euphrates River. So God will dry up the Euphrates River to allow the kings of the east to come on in. Turkey has dams on the Euphrates River and they can completely block the flow of the river to allow eastern nations to come over.

We really don't know who or what the kings of the east are. The word "east" quite often in the Bible refers to a judgment of God such as the eastern wind. We know that Yeshua comes from the east. He will enter the eastern gate at Jerusalem. Perhaps the kings of the east are speaking of Yeshua and the saints coming with him. Later we will see scriptures that indicate the Lord and Saints fighting against the enemies of God and the armies of Gog.

If that is the case, why do we need the Euphrates River to dry up? Because if we're already saints in glorified bodies, we'll just fly there. Why do we need to cross the Euphrates River? I've struggled with that for many, many years and could not find an answer to it until it occurred to me one day that we will be in paradise where the Garden of Eden is. Eden is a spiritual place with a river there called Euphrates. Is that Euphrates River a protective boundary that will not allow anybody in or out of paradise without proper escort? If that boundary is removed when we get a call from the Lord to come out of paradise, that would just be like the Euphrates River drying up. Could the saints be the kings of the east and/or perhaps the army of the book of Joel? I don't know. It's not really that important but one thing for sure, we are coming with the Lord when He comes for judgment.

The kings of the east, if you look at it as armies, are going to come down from the east and cross the Euphrates River. Now from the Euphrates River there is an ancient highway that drops right straight down south toward Egypt, known as the King's Highway. This is how they traveled from east to Egypt, on the east side of the Jordan River, coming through what is today Jordan. If these armies are headed toward Teman, Paran, and Bozrah toward the final battle, they most likely will come down the Kings Highway. Now Gog's forces overflowed into Israel. However, a massive amount of the armies are coming right straight down the King's Highway to a great battle that's going to take place not far from the Dead Sea at that time.

Why are they coming there? Revelation says that the beast will gather the nations of the world to make war with the Lamb of God. These people's minds are so messed up, they're coming to fight the Lamb of God. Why? In Islam, they teach that what we call the Lamb of God is really the Antichrist. They are all convinced that when the heavens open up and the Son of Man appears, He must be the Antichrist because they say Yeshua already came with the Moslem Messiah called the Mahdi. Islam claim that Yeshua never died, never rose again, but He'll come with the Mahdi and convince all Christians to be Muslims. This false Moslem Jesus may be the false prophet. Gog will be the beast, the false prophet will be this man they're going to call Jesus, while we look for the real Lamb of God. This is why when Yeshua appears in the heavens, the Muslims will call Him the Antichrist and are convinced that they have to fight Him.

Why will this battle be in Edom or southern Israel? I think when the Messiah comes, He will also head for the real Mount Sinai in Saudi Arabia where a remnant of Israel will gather. This is the woman of Revelation 12 who flees into the wilderness. Zechariah 14:5 tells us that a remnant from Jerusalem will flee through the Mount of Olives and head for the Valley of Azal. No one knows where Azal is. Some speculate that it is the place where the scapegoat of Yom Kippur is killed. The scapegoat is called Azazel so a close tie is possible.

Isaiah 16:1-4 may hold more clues of why the nations are coming to southern Israel and Edom. Although Isaiah 16 was mentioned earlier, it is worth mentioning it again to add clarity.

Isaiah 16:1-4

"Send ye the lamb to the ruler of the land from Sela to the wilderness, unto the mount of the daughter of Zion. For it shall be, that, as a wondering bird cast out of the nest, so the daughters of Moab shall be at the fords of Arnon. Take counsel, execute judgment; make thy shadow as the night in the midst of the noonday; hide the outcasts; bewray not him that wandereth. Let mine outcasts dwell with thee, Moab; be thou a covert to them from the face of the spoiler: for the extortioner is at an end, the spoiler ceaseth, the oppressors are consumed out of the land."

As previously stated, Isaiah 16 tells us that the remnant will flee to the Arnon River, and then to Petra (Selah) on their way to the mount of the daughter of Zion. This most likely is Mount Sinai. The Beast according to Revelation 12 chases this remnant to these areas. They are all in the Dead Sea area or south to Edom. "The extortioner is at an end" is about the Beast's destruction.

Ezekiel 39:4 tells us that the armies of Gog shall fall on the mountains (*har-* which can mean mountain or hill) of Israel. It does appear that this could be any and all mountains of Israel. This army of Gog will fill Israel with its presence. However, even the mountains around the Dead Sea are also part of the mountains of Israel. This can be seen in Numbers 20:22; 23:7; 33:47; Isaiah 42:11; Deuteronomy 2:5; 8:7; Genesis 14:10; 19:17; and many more. Basically the whole ridge of the Dead Sea east and west and south are also referred to as mountains.

Ezekiel 39:6 tells us that God will send fire on Magog. So not only will God destroy Gog and his armies, He's going to send fire upon the land of Magog and probably upon the nations of the world. "Among them that dwell carelessly in the Isles, and they shall know that I am the LORD." So those that think they're out of trouble and not involved in all this, fire will come upon *all* nations. God has always destroyed the nations that have come against Israel even when He was angry with Israel. This should be a warning to all nations.

Ezekiel 39:7

"So will I make my holy name known in the midst of my people Israel; and I will not let them pollute my holy name any more: and the heathen shall know that I am the LORD, the Holy One in Israel."

Ezekiel 39:9 says that Israel will burn all the weapons that they collect. This will take seven years. How can this be? How do you burn metal? This has confused prophecy writers for a long time. Some people write that they must be fighting with weapons of wood and it is wood that is burning for seven years. Why is this? What's taking place here? Is it because at that time the technology has gotten to the point that powerful nations can shut down anything electronic so we revert back to operating with wood and nonmetal items? Who knows? Perhaps we have to go back to things made out of wood to avoid radar- seeking missiles and everything else because they won't go after the wood. That's a possibility. We have to also keep in mind that wars in the not-too-distant future might be by bionic or robots. China is actively creating robotic warriors.

Ezekiel 39:11

"And it shall come to pass in that day, that I will give unto Gog a place there of graves in Israel, the valley of the passengers on the east of the sea: and it shall stop the noses of the passengers: and there shall they bury Gog and all his multitude: and they shall call it The valley of Hamongog."

The east side of the Dead Sea is the King's Highway. God's going to give that area on the east side of the Dead Sea as a place of burial for Gog, and it's called The Valley of Hamon-Gog. It would take seven months to bury the dead. If you look up Hamon-Gog on the internet or a reference book, they all tell you it's the east side of the Dead Sea. This isn't northern Israel; this isn't the Valley of Megiddo which many call the Valley of Armageddon as mentioned in Revelation 16:16. Armageddon means *Har Megiddo,*. *Har* meaning *mountain or hill.* So Armageddon means the mountains or hills of Megiddo. However, you need to translate "Megiddo" also.

A lot of people say there was a Solomon chariot fortress in the Valley of Jezreel called Megiddo, so that must be where Armageddon is. Thousands and thousands of people who go over to Israel every year are being told that this place in the Jezreel Valley in northern Israel is where Armageddon will be. However, Megiddo means "place of gathering." When you translate *Har* and Megiddo together it says, *In the mountains of the place of gathering.* That could be anywhere.

What we see here are the mountains of Israel in Hamon-Gog by the King's Highway on the east side of the Dead Sea and further south. That's where the cities of Teman and Bozrah are and also Edom. As you read in Obadiah, all the judgments that are going to take place in the last days will be in Edom—a big battle. This is probably where Armageddon truly will take place, not northern Israel.

We see this also in **Joel 2:20.**

"But I will remove far off from you the northern army, and will drive him into a land barren and desolate, with his face toward the east sea, and his hinder part toward the utmost sea, and his stink shall come up, and his ill savour shall come up, because he has done great things."

Most commentaries say that the east sea is the Dead Sea which he will face and his back side will face another sea (whether the Mediterranean or the Red Sea I don't know). He'll be facing the Dead Sea when the LORD comes and judges him, which doesn't fit the idea that the final battle is going to be in northern Israel. There's no evidence to indicate it's going to be in what they call the Valley of Megiddo. As we said, the whole translation of the word "Armageddon" is *the mountains of the place of gathering*. That's wherever God decides He wants to gather the nations. There is a mountain range all along the range of the Dead Sea and further south. So the evidence appears that the LORD will destroy this army in this area because it is here that the LORD will afterwards come out of Bozrah and Teman of the land of Edom. He'll come out of Bozrah with his garments dipped in blood where He slaughtered that army when He arrives. This is good evidence that the Dead Sea and southward is where the final battle will take place.

Again, we can't be dogmatic here. It's not that important if Armageddon will happen in the south or in the northern area. But if we put all the scriptures together and look at all the consequences, a picture begins to arrive.

Chapter 12:

The Ensign or the Sign of the Son of Man

Isaiah 11:10

"And in that day there shall be a root of Jesse, which shall stand for an ensign of the people; to it shall the Gentiles seek: and his rest shall be glorious."

Certainly there was much fulfillment of scripture upon Yeshua's first coming, but this is not talking about His first coming; it's talking about His second coming. There will be a root of Jesse as In the scriptures we see that Yeshua is the root or branch of Jesse, a descendant of King David (Isaiah 53:2). Romans 15:12 also speaks of Yeshua being the root of Jesse, the father of King David and Revelation 5:5 and 22:16 speak of Yeshua as the root and offspring of David. What does that mean? Jesse being the father of King David, and Yeshua being of the root of King David—that's the lineage. Isaiah 11:1 also says, "There shall come forth a rod out of the stem of Jesse, and a branch shall grow out of his roots." This rod and branch is Yeshua. Jeremiah 23:5 speaks of a righteous "branch" who will be king and rule in the Earth. Jeremiah 33:15 also speaks of this "branch of righteousness" unto David, and Zechariah 3:8 refers to him as "my servant the Branch." All of this refers to Yeshua the Messiah.

Now back to Isaiah 11:10. "The people" referred to is Israel. There's going to be an ensign which means "sign, signal or standard." So there will be a sign for the people of Israel, but at the same time the gentiles shall seek it also for His rest shall be glorious. It's important to understand this concept here that this sign will most likely be the sign of

143

the Son of Man Yeshua spoke of in Matthew 24:30.

Matthew 24:30
"And then shall appear the sign of the Son of man in heaven: and then shall all the tribes of the earth mourn, and they shall see the Son of man coming in the clouds of heaven with power and great glory. And he shall send his angels with a great sound of a trumpet, and they shall gather together his elect from the four winds, from one end of heaven to the other."

When this sign of the Son of Man appears, Israel will begin to look upon the One they have pierced (Zechariah 12:10) and begin their return to the land. The gentiles will also begin to seek the Son of Man. This sign will be a worldwide event. In Revelation 11:15 we learn that at the seventh trump, the kingdoms of the Earth are now the kingdoms of our Lord and of His Messiah. In verse 19, it says the Temple of God in heaven was opened with all its glory. Now in the book of Enoch 51:3 it says, "And the elect one [Yeshua] shall in those days sit on My [Lord of the Spirits] throne." It is possible the sign that will appear will be Yeshua sitting on the throne of God. Right now He's on the right hand of the Father, but there comes a point where the Father backs off and He completely glorifies His Son. Matthew 24:30 talks about the sign of the Son of Man, although it doesn't tell us what the sign is, but according to Enoch, the world may see Yeshua sitting on the throne. When that happens, that is the beginning of the final judgments of God upon the Earth as Revelation 11:18 says "… your wrath is come." The seven vials will then be poured out on the Earth.

This elect is Israel, the captivity. So when the sign of the Son of Man appears, that will begin the captivity collection. Of course, there has to be a captivity first. Israel is going back into captivity and then regathered. You have to understand how these scriptures work together here. When the false prophet (a false Yeshua) and the beast (the Assyrian Gog) show up on the scene, miracles are going to happen with the power of Satan to deceive the world. So Yeshua's warning us now to not believe those deceiving miracles. He says "You will know when I come; the heavens will open up. The heavens will part like lightning is in the east and to the west (Matthew 24:27). You shall see the Son of Man coming with the clouds which means the host or his heavenly army will be with him (Matthew 24:30)." He's not going to drift in on some little storm cloud.

This is symbolism. The righteous saints are all going to be clothed in white. You put millions of saints in their glorious garments together, they're going to look like a white cloud and they're going to come with the Messiah, along with His angels. That's how you know He's coming. Do not be deceived by any other way because great deception is coming upon the Earth. Matthew 24:26 tells us not to believe anyone who says they are the Messiah that comes out of the desert or is in the secret chambers. Obviously, there will be false Messiahs that will come from those places. For instance, it could be from Mecca or the one who will stand in the Holy of Holies in the future. Remember that the cosmos will introduce the true Messiah. Why do you think they call him the false prophet? He's going to deceive the world and cause people to worship the beast.

We are not a people who are unaware. We are not a people who think of foolish things nor are we a people caught up in signs who suddenly think, "Oh, this is God!" We like signs when it's of God, but many people in the world today are looking for signs. They're going to be tricked; they're going to be caught up in false beliefs when the beast and the false prophet call fire down from heaven and maybe even raise people from the dead. The world will flock to them thinking they're God. We cannot fall prey to that kind of deception that will take place. That's why the Lord warns us in Matthew 16:4 that "a wicked and adulterous generation seeks after a sign." As believers we are shown that signs follow those who believe, but this is coming from believers anointed by the Holy Spirit who show forth fruit of their faith and not from powerful leaders. Be careful.

Isaiah 11:11

"And it shall come to pass in that day, that the LORD shall set his hand again the second time to recover the remnant of his people, which shall be left, from Assyria, and from Egypt, and from Pathros, and from Cush, and from Elam, and from Shinar, and from Hamath, and from the islands of the sea."

This event is the second time of regathering. The first regathering was when the LORD brought them out of Egypt as mentioned before in Jeremiah 16:14-15 where it says people will no longer say great is the LORD who brought His people out of Egypt, but great is the LORD who brought all His people from all the countries where He had scattered them. So in this second event, the whole world is going to see the LORD create a highway between Assyria and Egypt and begin to bring his people back to the land with wonders and miracles greater than what we saw in Egypt. So much so, no one will be talking about Egypt anymore. Every year at Passover, we talk about what happened in Egypt, but there's coming a point where we'll no longer talk about that; we'll be talking about how great is the LORD who brought the people of Israel from all the countries of the world back to Israel. This will be a huge, huge event.

It says, "…which shall be left." I thought those were interesting words, "shall be left." That means many will perish; many will die. Those who are left from Assyria, Egypt, Pathros, Cush, Elom, Sinar, Hammoth, and from the islands of the sea. This regathering will be from all over the Middle East, including the islands of the sea. Usually when you see the words "islands of the sea," it's not talking about Hawaii. It's talking about countries across the ocean. If you look up that word "islands" which is pronounced "iy", the definitions are islands, regions, coastlands, and countries. So it's talking about wherever the second captivity was scattered, God's going to bring them back at that time.

Isaiah 11:12
"And he shall set up an ensign for the nations, and shall assemble the outcasts of Israel, and gather together the dispersed of Judah from the four corners of the earth."

All the nations will see this sign and the LORD will begin to gather the outcasts from all over the Earth. Again, have we seen this cosmo's sign yet? The sign of the Son of Man will be visible to all the Earth.

Isaiah 18:3
"All ye inhabitants of the world, and dwellers on the earth, see ye, when he lifteth up an ensign on the mountains; and when he bloweth a trumpet, hear ye."

Even though this scripture is the beginning of the gathering of the captives of Israel, the LORD is calling to the world and the nations, "Look and see my sign that I'm going to set up in the heavens and hear the trumpet!" When these two events happen, the captivity will begin to return, but also the remaining gentiles who have survived the Tribulation up to that point will seek it also. Probably about two-thirds of the entire world population will be destroyed in the Tribulation, and those who are left are going to see this sign. Also this event of Isaiah 18:3 will include a rapture for the saints of God. Isaiah goes on to describe His glorious apparel after the rapture happens. Isaiah declares He will shine as the luminaries and take His rest. Some translations say "herbs" which doesn't make any sense.

Isaiah 5:26
"And he will lift up an ensign to the nations from far, and will hiss unto them from the end of the earth; and, behold, they shall come with speed swiftly."

This ensign or sign will be visible to all the Earth. The LORD will call His captives and they will come quickly back to the land. The word "hiss" means also to whistle or pipe with an instrument as in a call. Probably the trumpet sound is what is meant.

Isaiah 31:9
"And he shall pass over to his strong hold for fear, and his princes shall be afraid of the ensign, saith the LORD, whose fire is in Zion, and his furnace in Jerusalem."

"He" is the Assyrian, which is the bad guy of the last days. He will come out of the lands of the Parthians, the Meads, Armenia, Georgia, eastern Turkey, northwest Iran, and north Iraq—from the old empire of Assyria. This Assyrian is most likely the beast of Revelation.

This Assyrian who will lead Israel into captivity and his army are also going to see the sign and they're going to be scared. They're going to look up and see the heavens open up, and they're going to see the sign of the Son of Man. The princes are going to abandon their leader and head back to their land. Verse 8 says the Assyrian will fall and his young men will be discomfited or forced into servanthood that are not killed. They will not be able to escape. Even the bad guys are going to see this sign and they're going to be fearful.

In Islamic doctrine, the Moslems believe that when this event occurs, they must fight the one who is coming. Moslems say that the one the Christians are looking for is really the Antichrist and they must join together and fight him. This is why the book of Revelation says they will make war against the Lamb of God. They are demonically brainwashed. How else can you explain their actions to make war against the Lamb of God who is coming with the powers of heaven.

Matthew 24:31
"And he shall send his angels with a great sound of a

trumpet. And they shall gather together his elect from the four winds from one end of heaven to the other."

When Matthew speaks of the elect, that can conjure up debates of all sorts, but this elect is talking about Israel. The church can be called the elect, but Israel is also called the elect, so you have to look at it in the context of which "elect" he's talking about. When elect is used prophetically it is almost always Israel. But this gathering of the elect will not happen until Israel calls upon the Messiah and it will be Yeshua Ha Mashiach as Zechariah 12:10 says: "They shall look upon me whom they have pierced, and they shall mourn for him, as one mourns for his only son, and shall be in bitterness for him, as one that is in bitterness for his firstborn."

The Church in general is called either saints or the righteous. I find it interesting that the book of Enoch mentions that the elect and righteous shall dwell together. "And the righteous and elect shall be without number before Him for ever and ever. And all the righteous and elect before Him shall be strong as fiery lights" (Enoch 39:6-7). Both the righteous and elect (Israel) will have glorious garments and dwell in the heavenly Zion together. Yet somehow even the heavenly Zion and the earthly Zion will be tied together for the remnant of Israel that were not caught up in the rapture. This topic will be discussed at length later, but there will be a heavenly Zion or New Jerusalem and a physical earthly Zion in Jerusalem.

Matthew 23:39

"You shall not see me henceforth till you say blessed is he that comes in the name of the Lord."

What does that mean? This scripture took place when Yeshua was at Jerusalem. Many scholars refer to it as the Jerusalem Discourse, as Yeshua was praying over the city. How He would have loved to take the city under His arms and under His wings, but they rejected Him. So He spoke prophetically to the city of Jerusalem and said, "Oh Jerusalem,

Jerusalem! You will not see me again until you say 'Blessed is he who comes in the name of The Lord.'" Yeshua was quoting Psalm 118:26, a Messianic call. So until Israel corporately says *Blessed is he who comes in the name of the LORD,* Yeshua won't come. That's one of the many trigger points for the Messiah to come. Israel corporately has to call out to Him, and it begins to occur when the sign of the Son of Man shows up in heaven. When the sign shows up, the whole world will see it.

Now it is interesting to learn what the book of Enoch says: "And on that day Mine Elect One shall sit on the throne of glory" (Enoch 45:3). Also, in Enoch 62:1-5:

"And thus the Lord commanded the kings and the mighty and the exalted, and those who dwell on the earth, and said: 'Open your eyes and lift up your horns if ye are able to recognize the Elect One.' And the Lord of the Spirits seated him on the throne of His glory...and they [the world and the captivity] shall see and recognize how he sits on the throne of his glory...then shall pain come upon them as on a woman in travail...and they shall be terrified."

Enoch 51:3 also says, "And the Elect One shall in those days sit on My throne." If you didn't already know, the Elect One is the Messiah and that is Yeshua. The Lord of the Spirits is the Father God.

Basically, it says that the sign will be showing Yeshua sitting on the throne of God. Right now He's at the right hand of the Father as an intercessor, but there's going to come a point, in Revelation 11:15, when the kingdoms of this world become the kingdoms of our Lord and He sits on the throne of God. Throughout scriptures God and the Lamb are shown sitting on the throne together (see Matthew 25:31; Acts 2:30; Hebrews 1:8; Revelation 7:17; 22:1, 3). According to the book of Enoch, the heavens will open up and the whole world will see Him sitting on that throne. At that time, Israel will look upon the One whom they have pierced and call upon Him, and they will be delivered and become saved at that point. As

Romans 11:26 says, "so all Israel shall be saved" once the Deliverer comes. The rest of the world will flee in panic when they see this sign. This is why many will hide in caves and say, "Rocks, fall on us! Protect us from the one who is coming!" (Revelation 6:16). They're terrified because they'll know it's too late for them and if they've been treating Israel harshly, it's really too late for them. They will begin to see that.

Chapter 13:

Return of the Messiah

Prior to Yeshua's return, He is at the throne of God interceding for all those that call upon Him on the Earth. He is at the right hand of the Father. His grace and mercy are for all who call upon Him for forgiveness of their sins. However, when He leaves the throne of God, grace is over. He is coming now to judge the Earth. One cannot suddenly say they believe and expect to be forgiven when they see the heavens roll back. It's too late.

When talking about the return of the Messiah, one has to understand that this is not talking about the rapture or raptures that have already occurred except for possibly the final rapture at His coming. (See 1 Corinthians 15 for a quick explanation of several raptures.) "But every man in his own order" indicates more than one rapture. There will be another at Yeshua's physical coming to Earth.

Yeshua will briefly appear on the Mount of Olives as stated in Zechariah 14:4 when He splits the Mount of Olives to allow a remnant in Jerusalem to escape. This most likely will coincide with the firstfruits rapture of Revelations 12 with the woman's child.

His main coming will be for judgment toward the wicked and to deliver Israel. When Israel calls for Him, as mentioned before, He will come to deliver them. As Romans 11:26 says, "And so all Israel shall be saved: as it is written, 'There shall come out of Sion the Deliverer, and shall turn away ungodliness from Jacob.'" Keep in mind Israel needs

Yeshua to be saved. Then and only then when Israel calls on Yeshua will they be saved. When they call on Him, He will respond quickly and begin gathering them and defeating their enemies.

Matthew 24:26

"Wherefore if they shall say unto you, Behold, he is in the desert; go not forth: behold, he is in the secret chambers; believe it not."

Yeshua says in Matthew 24:26 that there are appointed individuals who are going to come—particularly the false prophet and maybe even the beast—who claim to be the Messiah or God. Yeshua's telling us, "Believe it not. Don't be tricked." It says if possible, even the very elect will be fooled. Don't be tricked, Yeshua's telling us right now. Two places are mentioned here—the desert and in the secret chambers. It is possible that the desert is a reference to Mecca and the secret chamber is the Holy of Holies in Jerusalem where Paul references the Son of Perdition as sitting in the Temple showing himself as God (2 Thessalonians 2:4). Islam believes that Yeshua never died and was never the son of God. However, there one is coming who will proclaim himself the Moslem messiah or the Mahdi and will destroy the world. This is the one Yeshua was talking about. Don't believe it. When the LORD comes, all the heavens and universe will announce it.

Matthew 24:27

"For as the lightning cometh out of the east, and shineth even unto the west; so shall also the coming of the Son of man be."

When the Messiah comes, all of the cosmos will introduce Him. Don't be fooled into believing that the beast of Revelation is the Messiah or God.

Once the sign of the Son of Man appears the whole world begins to cry out. They know what is getting ready to happen. Yeshua will send the angels to gather the elect as He comes to execute judgment on the Earth (Matthew 24:30).

Chapter 14:

Return of the Captivity

Ezekiel 39:25

"Therefore thus saith the Lord God; Now will I bring again the captivity of Jacob, and have mercy upon the whole house of Israel, and will be jealous for my holy name."

This is the return of the captivity, after the Gog-Magog War. It hasn't already happened; we haven't had a Gog-Magog War. Have we ever had a war where weapons are burned for seven years and the dead are buried for seven months and they swept into Israel and all the nations of the world? No, that's never happened. Which tells you right here in verse 25, God is going to release the captivity of Gog and the iniquity of Jacob will be purged. He will have mercy on the whole house of Israel and they will be jealous for His holy name. No longer will they shame God's name or His Messiah. They will actively pursue and serve Him and be obedient to Him.

Ezekiel 39:26

"After that they have borne their shame, and all their trespasses whereby they have trespassed against me, when they dwelt safely in their land, and none made them afraid."

When this regathering begins to take place, Israel will mourn over their sins and rejection of the Messiah. This can be also seen in Zechariah 12:10: "They shall look upon me whom they have pierced, and they shall mourn for him, as one mourns for his only son, and shall be in bitterness for him, as one that is in bitterness for his firstborn." Israel will go into great sorrow but with the mercy of God their sorrow will turn to joy. They shall never be afraid of anyone or anything and neither will there be any more contentious fighting over the land like is happening today. *Oh, you can't build in Jerusalem in this area, that's Palestinian area. You can't do this, you can't do that...* It's always about the land. That's why scriptures say that one of the things that's going to start the tribulation period is the "controversy over Zion" (see Isaiah 34:8). So shortly after the Gog-Magog war there will be peace and no more controversy over the land, Jerusalem, or the Temple Mount. It is interesting that even today the United States still won't recognize that Jerusalem is the capital of Israel.

Ezekiel 39:27-29
"When I have brought them again from the people, and gathered them out of their enemies' lands, and am sanctified in them in the sight of many nations; Then shall they know that I am the LORD their God, which caused them to be led into captivity among the heathen: but I have gathered them unto their own land, and have left none of them any more there. Neither will I hide my face any more from them: for I have poured out my spirit upon the house of Israel, saith the Lord God."

After God gathers them from their enemies, and Israel calls upon the name of the LORD for their sanctification, then they will know the LORD with His Spirit being poured out on them (see Joel 2:28). This is why **Romans 11:26-27** says,

"And so all Israel shall be saved: as it is written, There shall come out of Zion the Deliverer, and shall turn away ungodliness from Jacob: For this is my covenant unto them, when I shall take away their sins."

It is important to understand the role of Israel here. This does not mean that everyone who calls themselves Jews or Israel today will be saved. Many Israelites and Jews around the world will die in the Tribulation period. Many will receive the mark of the beast and be judged severely. Of course this applies even more so to the gentiles and nations of the world. Billions of people will die. However, when the Messiah or Deliverer comes, then will Israel corporately be saved. Afterwards, the world will see the final completion of Joel 2:28 concerning the pouring out of the Spirit of God upon Israel.

What happened on Shavuot (Pentecost), is a small thing compared to the outpouring of the Spirit that is coming. Joel tells us that there's coming a day when God's Spirit will be poured upon all flesh, including on the whole house of Israel and Judah. At that time, God's Spirit will come all over Israel and they will not sin anymore against God. They will not have idols anymore against God, and they will no longer trespass against God. That did not happen in 1948, this is yet to come.

Isaiah 11:15-16
"And the LORD shall utterly destroy the tongue of the Egyptian sea; and with his mighty wind shall he shake his hand over the river, and shall smite it in the seven streams, and make men go over dryshod. And there shall be an highway for the remnant of his people, which shall be left, from Assyria; like as it was to Israel in the day that he came up out of the land of Egypt."

After a great judgment on Egypt, the LORD will dry up the Nile for His captive people. This has not happened yet; the LORD is going to do this in the future. It will be one of the great miracles in the last days. The final promises of the LORD to Israel will begin to manifest themselves.

God will make a highway between Assyria and Egypt, and will

159

cause people to come down that highway. Even the very stones will be removed out of the highway so they don't stumble as mentioned in Isaiah 62:10: "Go through, go through the gates; prepare ye the way of the people; cast up, cast up the highway; gather out the stones; lift up a standard for the people." So a highway will be made, stones removed, and a sign will appear for the people traveling the highway.

If God has to dry up a huge river like the Nile River, if He has to dry up the Euphrates River—whatever He has to do, He is going to make it happen so His people can come back to the land.

What kind of highway did the LORD make for the Hebrews when they came out of Egypt? He led them with a pillar of fire and a cloud, split open the Red Sea made a smooth walk across. Nothing will stop the second gathering of Israel coming in the land. The LORD Himself will lead them and make sure He brings them into the land by a highway He creates.

So the second time the LORD's going to recover His people, it will be similar to what happened in Egypt, but the highway will begin out of Assyria, connecting to Egypt, and going through Israel. God will ensure this highway will be built

Jeremiah 16:14-15

"Therefore, behold, the days come, says the LORD, that it shall no more be said, the LORD lives, that brought up the children of Israel out of the land of Egypt; But, the LORD lives that brought up the children of Israel from the land of the north, and from all the lands whither he had driven them: and I will bring them again into their land that I gave unto their fathers."

The world does not say great is the LORD who brought Israel back in 1948. Those who study scriptures were amazed and gave glory to God, but it wasn't anything like what happened in the Exodus of Egypt. It will be greater than what happened at Passover, greater than what happened when all those miracles and judgments came upon Egypt. Did anything like that happen in 1948? No. It's coming. Yet, at the same time, many are going to die, many are going to perish, but this is why we pray. This is why we tell people to prepare their hearts and get ready. There are many things that have to happen yet.

This is one of those scriptures you need to mark in your Bible, highlight, make notes about it, and remember it. It's a very key scripture about what's going to happen in the last days. During Passover celebrations every year, we talk about God's deliverance of the Hebrews from Egypt. That's a big story; every year we tell that story. Every year we celebrate it at the Passover Seder. We talk about God's great deliverance, all the plagues, the parting of the Red Sea, the pillar of fire and the cloud that was leading them. It's a great story of promise and deliverance by God.

Yet something is coming that's going to be greater than that. Can you say what happened in 1948 was greater than God's deliverance out of Egypt? No! It says, "No longer will they say the LORD lives that brought the Hebrews out of Egypt, but that the LORD lives and brings them from the rest of the countries where he had scattered them." People don't say today *The LORD lives in 1948!* Some believers may say that, but most of the world doesn't. Matter of fact, the world curses it. So there is going to be another incredible deliverance for the children of Israel greater than what happened in Egypt that we have not seen yet. This second regathering will be incredible. The whole world will be astonished at it. Jeremiah 16:14-15 are very, very important scriptures that fit in a return of captivity pattern with all the other ones we're talking about.

Jeremiah 30:8
"For it shall come to pass in that day, saith the LORD of hosts, that I will break his yoke from off thy neck, and will

burst thy bonds, and strangers shall no more serve
themselves of him:"

In other words, "I'm going to break this yoke, I'm going to break
his bonds, says the LORD. And no longer shall foreigners and strangers
oppress you." Peace shall come upon the land. Has that ever happened?
No! This is yet in the future.

Zechariah 10:6-7
"And I will strengthen the house of Judah, and I will save
the house of Joseph, and I will bring them again to place
them; for I have mercy upon them: and they shall be as
though I had not cast them off: for I am the LORD their
God, and will hear them. And they of Ephraim shall be like
a mighty man, and their heart shall rejoice as through
wine: yea, their children shall see it, and be glad; their
heart shall rejoice in the LORD."

When the Bible speaks of Ephraim, it's almost always speaking of
the ten northern tribes of Israel. Ephraim is also known as the house of
Joseph.

Isaiah 11:13
"The envy also of Ephraim shall depart, and the
adversaries of Judah shall be cut off: Ephraim shall not
envy Judah, and Judah shall not vex Ephraim."

Know that "Ephraim" is just another word for the ten lost tribes of
Israel. When this regathering takes place, Ephraim and Judah will no
longer be enemies but will return to the land as one. Unfortunately, an
awful lot of bad doctrine is being passed around today that says the church
is Ephraim. You have the Ephraim Movement that says the church is
Ephraim, so Judah and the church are going to get along. Well, the
problem here (and you can find other scriptures that deal with this) is that

Ephraim will come back to their land (Ezekiel 37:19-21). Like I said earlier, when did the church ever get taken out of its land of Israel? The church was not appointed any land in Israel, so how can it be Ephraim? That Ephraim Movement is another false doctrinal movement that really hampers Messianic congregations. Many Messianics are adhering to that false doctrine. Believers in Yeshua are not Ephraim, and those that adhere to this doctrine try to justify it by saying Joseph had a gentile wife and produced sons called Ephraim and Manasseh. Certainly, Joseph was a shadow type of the Messiah but that doesn't make Ephraim the church. Why don't those in this movement consider themselves Manasseh?

Many scriptures are also very negative concerning Ephraim. Why doesn't the church consider those? It makes for a nice story, but when you look at all the scriptures about Ephraim, it's really talking about the ten tribes of Israel. Judah and Israel were always fighting each other and did not get along until the Assyrians finally hauled Israel off into captivity. That's not the church.

Be careful not to get caught up in these kinds of things. It's a lustful concept in our spirit that we want to somehow or other find ourselves as being part of Israel in the flesh. Well, the church can be called Israel in the spirit. Gentiles have been grafted in and adopted into the household of faith. No longer are they separated from God. The middle wall of partition is torn down that kept gentiles away. In Messiah, Jew and gentile are one.

If you could go back and trace your spiritual history to its roots (it's impossible, but if you could), you will find that most of you came into salvation because of one of the twelve apostles. The twelve apostles went out and began to spread the word. If you could follow every spiritual lineage that happened there, you'd eventually be able to track your salvation to one of those apostles. Perhaps in the kingdom every believer will find that out when we begin to know all things in our next life. Most of us have a spiritual seed in one of the apostles.

Zechariah 10:8
"I will hiss for them, and gather them; for I have redeemed them: and they shall increase as they have increased."

Another way to say that is, "I will call for them through an instrument of some sort." To hiss could mean to whistle. Can this be that great trumpet?

Zechariah 10:9-10
"And I will sow them among the people: and they shall remember me in far countries; and they shall live with their children, and turn again. I will bring them again also out of the land of Egypt, and gather them out of Assyria; and I will bring them into the land of Gilead and Lebanon; and place shall not be found for them."

Israel will return to the LORD and will come back to the land. "A place shall not be found for them." That means there are going to be so many of them, it will be hard to find a spot for them all. It doesn't mean the land is gone, it just means it's going to be hard to place all these people coming in the land of Israel at this time. Currently, there are about seven million who live in Israel. Not all are Jews but it is estimated that there are at least 14 million Jews in the world. So if all Jews came back to Israel today, the inhabitants of Israel will double rather fast of Jews alone.

Zechariah 10:11-12
"And he shall pass through the sea with affliction, and shall smite the waves in the sea, and all the deeps of the river shall dry up: and the pride of Assyria shall be brought down, and the sceptre of Egypt shall depart away. And I will strengthen them in the LORD; and they shall walk up and down in his name, saith the LORD."

They'll walk up and down in the name of Yeshua. They'll walk up and down the land proclaiming the name of Yeshua and knowledge of Him and belief in Him. That has not happened yet but is coming upon the whole world very soon. Remember what I said before— what happens in Israel also will happen in the world. So just because it's specifically speaking of Israel here, and even Assyria and Egypt, affliction will happen all over the world. So one cannot sit even in the United States and say, *Well, I'm glad I'm not over there!* It will overflow over here, too— guarantee it. That's why it's so important to be walking with the LORD; so important to be walking in righteousness. In the final chapter of Revelation, the Bible says those who kept the commandment of God have the right to enter into the holy city—the new Jerusalem. You must be obedient to the commandments of God as they apply today.

Certain ceremonial/sacrificial laws have been fulfilled through Yeshua but certainly the ethical laws and moral laws of the LORD have not been eliminated through Him. The rest of those moral laws are mentioned in the gospels many times, particularly in Galatians and Ephesians. They talk about almost every one of the ten commandments in those two gospel books. So if the law was gone, why would Paul mention it in Ephesians and Galatians? It's not gone. That's why Yeshua said, "If you love me, keep my commandments" (John 14:15).

In Revelation, those who keep the commandments of God get to enter the new Jerusalem. If you don't keep them, you still might have eternal life, but you don't get to enter the city. How sad would that be to come this far then miss it because you can't give up your sins that beset you! That's why He said of the churches of Revelation, "To them that overcome will I write my name on their forehead, my father's name on their forehead, and the name of the new city." That's your ticket to get you in the spiritual Zion, otherwise known as the New Jerusalem which represents the kingdom of God. The Father's name, the Son's name, and the city's name will be written on your foreheads if you are an overcomer.

God is not mocked, you know. We can't just say "I believe" and keep operating in sin. It's a bad thing. I know we all struggle with sin and yes, I know there are certain things we fight with, but become overcomers! Change your mind, redirect your mind and your thoughts and become overcomers. Love the Lord God with all your heart, all your soul, and all your mind, and love your neighbor as yourself.

Isaiah 49:22-23

"Thus saith the Lord GOD, Behold, I will lift up mine hand to the Gentiles, and set up my standard to the people: and they shall bring thy sons in their arms, and thy daughters shall be carried upon their shoulders. And kings shall be thy nursing fathers, and their queens thy nursing mothers: they shall bow down to thee with their face toward the earth, and lick up the dust of thy feet; and thou shalt know that I am the LORD: for they shall not be ashamed that wait for me."

When the Lord God lifts up this standard, the gentiles will come to assist Israel. By the way, the word "standard" is the same as ensign or sign. When this sign appears, the people who are in the Earth at that time will bring Israel's children on their shoulders to the land. This is not talking about the saints who come back with Him. The saints are caught up to Him earlier. Only those who love His appearing will be caught up in a rapture. If you're not loving His appearing, you're not part of that group. What do I mean by "loving His appearing"? If suddenly somebody came in and said, "The heavens are rolling back right now and I see Yeshua!" and you shout, "Yeah! I've been waiting!", that's loving His appearance. If you say, "I'm not ready for this; I got a few things I have to fix first. I got to do this, I got to do that," that's not loving His appearing and you will not be going to Him or coming back with Him at that time.

This is important to understand! Today is the day of salvation!

166

Today is the day to be included in that first fruits rapture! Today is the day to be joined together with the Messiah! Yes, you may have a chance at salvation afterwards, but you will not be rewarded with rewards and the concepts of the kingdom of God. You can call Him Lord after the fact and you may, in fact, be saved, but you will not have a high position in the kingdom or perhaps not even allowed in a kingdom which is ruled by the priests and the kings that are determined worthy through Yeshua. If you love him, you're going to be a king and a priest. That's what the kingdom of God is all about; you're going to be kings and priests before the LORD. You'll come back and you'll rule with Him the nations of the world in the holy heavenly city of the New Jerusalem as promised in Revelation 2:26-27 and train and judge the world as they repopulate for the next thousand years.

Now, where are you going to be ruling and reigning? Your headquarters are going to be in the New Jerusalem, the heavenly Zion, and also the physical Jerusalem and Zion on Earth. This heavenly Zion most likely will dwell above the physical Jerusalem. One must understand that the heavenly Zion or New Jerusalem will come down during the millennium reign and not after. Why would Yeshua keep His bride away for a thousand years. That holy city will come soon after Yeshua begins to reign on Earth. All we know is we will be with Him and that day is coming. But when the sign does appear, the gentiles who are left on the Earth at that time will suddenly realize, "I am going with the Jews because I know God is with them!" Not now, but then. Suddenly God will pour out His spirit upon them, and He'll pour out his spirit upon all flesh as the final fulfillment of Joel 2:28-29. The gentiles will run and take hold of the *tzitzit* (garment tassels) of a Jew's garment and say, "I'm going to be with you because I heard God is with you."

Psalm 14:7
"Oh that the salvation of Israel were come out of Zion! when the LORD bringeth back the captivity of his people, Jacob shall rejoice, and Israel shall be glad."

The words "Oh that" means *to show, to send, to deliver.* The word "salvation" is Yeshua. Another way to say it is, "Show us Yeshua out of Zion!" We know Yeshua is our salvation; Yeshua means salvation, and He will come out of Zion, the heavenly Zion. It's almost like Israel is calling for Him, "Blessed is he who comes in the name of the LORD!" The LORD will not come back until they say that. So they must first return to the LORD. Yeshua said in Matthew 23:39, when speaking of the Messianic phrase from Psalm 118, "You will not see me again Jerusalem until you say, 'blessed is he who comes in the name of the LORD!'" In Hebrew, Israel must say "Baruch haba B'Shem Adonai." So Israel will see the sign of the Son of Man, and they will call for Him! They will say Baruch haba B'Shem Adonai. Psalm 14:7 is basically saying the same thing in a different way: "Send Yeshua out of Zion when the LORD brings back the captivity of his people." This is what's getting ready to happen.

Psalm 126:1
"When the LORD turned again the captivity of Zion, we were like them that dream."

We were like them that dreamed when the captivity is going to be released in the last days. Those that understood prophecy were really excited in 1948 but this final event is going to be unbelievable.

Jeremiah 29:14
"And I will be found of you, saith the LORD: and I will turn away your captivity, and I will gather you from all the nations, and from all the places whither I have driven you, saith the LORD; and I will bring you again into the place whence I caused you to be carried away captive."

In other words, "You will call upon me and I will hear. You will be found of me, says the LORD, and I will turn away your captivity and I will gather you from all nations and from the places I drove you to bring you again into the place where I caused you to be carried away captive." So first, they have to call on the LORD, then the LORD will return the captivity. Jeremiah is loaded with many scriptures about this.

Jeremiah 30:3
"For, lo, the days come, saith the LORD, that I will bring again the captivity of my people Israel and Judah, saith the LORD: and I will cause them to return to the land that I gave to their fathers, and they shall possess it."

Jeremiah 30:6
"Ask ye now, and see whether a man doth travail with child? wherefore do I see every man with his hands on his loins, as a woman in travail, and all faces are turned into paleness?"

Israel travailing is a major theme in the Bible. If you ever want to do a study, study the travailing of Israel—Israel getting ready to give birth. You can read this in Revelation 12 where the woman who represents Israel is in labor and she is travailing. The beast of Revelation is trying to destroy her. Suddenly she gives birth to a man-child (as it says in King James). The word actually is a reference to a son, and the Lord catches him up to heaven. Israel is waiting to be birthed of the Lord. One concept to be considered here in Revelation 12 is that this birth of a son is a rapture of one of the remnants of Israel. Consider that the woman is in singular form and the son is singular also. So if the woman represents Israel as a whole, then the son is most likely speaking of many also. This group will be a special group that will be known as sons of God. They will be caught up forever to be with God.

Now, many prophecy writers will turn around and say, *Well, the man-child of the woman is Jesus.* There's a problem with that. Why, at the beginning of Revelation, when he says, "I am the Alpha and Omega" (that He was dead and rose alive), do we suddenly find halfway through

Revelation that the subject of His birth is mentioned. It doesn't make any sense. More than likely this occurs in Jerusalem when the beast has the city surrounded. The beast wasn't chasing the woman when Yeshua was being born. In Revelation 12:6, it tells us that the beast chases the woman and she flees into the wilderness to be taken care of by God. That did not happen with Yeshua. That man-child of the woman was caught up to the Lord in some kind of rapture.

As mentioned before, the rapture of the saints will not happen until the son of perdition is revealed as Paul said in 2 Thessalonians 2:3. There is no better explanation then when the beast comes into Jerusalem to declare at that point that he is God, then the son of perdition is revealed. This may be the rapture of saints and the elect together. The book of Enoch gives us several clues. In chapter 39, verse 1, it says "And it shall come to pass in those days that elect [Israel]) and holy children [saints] will descend from the high heaven." Before they can descend, they must have gone up first. Verse 7 of the same chapter says that "the righteous and elect before him shall be as fiery lights." This elect remnant and the saints both will be given white glorious dazzling garments.

In chapter 50, verse 1, it says, "And in those days a change shall take place for the holy and the elect, and the light of days shall abide upon them." Based on what Enoch says, the rapture will include the saints and the elect. So the holy, being the saints that have been raptured, now this remnant of the elect will also be raptured and the two shall be glorified and come back together. This is the travailing concept. Israel is waiting to give birth to a remnant that will be born again. Basically, Revelation 12 and the woman giving birth is talking about a born-again experience and being caught up to God.

Isaiah 11:11
"And it shall come to pass in that day, that the LORD shall set his hand again the second time to recover the remnant of his people, which shall be left, from Assyria, and from

Egypt, and from Pathros, and from Cush, and from Elam, and from Shinar, and from Hamath, and from the islands of the sea."

So in every place where Israel is scattered, the LORD is going to bring them back. If that scripture stood by itself, you could say that was probably something that happened in 1948 because we did have a partial fulfillment of that, but not a complete fulfillment.

Jeremiah 31:8-9

"Behold, I will bring them from the north country, and gather them from the coasts of the earth, and with them the blind and the lame, the woman with child and her that travaileth with child together: a great company shall return thither. They shall come with weeping, and with supplications will I lead them: I will cause them to walk by the rivers of waters in a straight way, wherein they shall not stumble: for I am a father to Israel, and Ephraim is my firstborn."

The LORD will lead them just like He did out of Egypt! He led them with a pillar of fire and a cloud! He led them out of that land, and this is going to happen again in the last days. The LORD is going to lead them. Ephraim (any time you see Ephraim, he's referring to Israel) is one of the tribes in the land of Israel, but throughout scriptures of certain prophets, Ephraim is used instead of Israel. What it is not, and I have mentioned this before but it is important, Ephraim is not the church. There is a movement called the Ephramite Movement that believes the prophecies about Ephraim pertain to the church. Not so!

Why do I say that? The scriptures say that the LORD is going to bring Ephraim back into the land, a land that they lost and will no longer be removed from. When was the church ever given land? When was the church ever removed from the land? It's not a good way to interpret scripture. The Ephramite Movement, as well as the British Movement, the Kingdom Now, and several other movements have led to confusion among believers. Many of these movements are off-base scripture wise; they're no more than people wanting to believe that somehow or another, they are of the lost tribes of Israel.

Even though most of Israel was led away into captivity by Assyria, many of Israel fled to Judah when Jeroboam began his idolatry (2 Chronicles 11:13-16). Many other Israelites joined with Judah that were not taken into captivity to celebrate Passover (2 Chronicles 30:1-6 and 2 Chronicles 35:17-18). So today, it is possible that many Jews really are a mixture of all tribes of Israel. There are some remote tribes still being discovered but it seems that many Jews today represent all tribes.

Jeremiah 31:5-7

"Thou shalt yet plant vines upon the mountains of Samaria: the planters shall plant, and shall eat them as common things. For there shall be a day, that the watchmen upon the mount Ephraim shall cry, Arise ye, and let us go up to Zion unto the LORD our God. For thus saith the LORD; Sing with gladness for Jacob, and shout among the chief of the nations: publish ye, praise ye, and say, O LORD, save thy people, the remnant of Israel."

Who's he talking to here? Whoever this is, it says, "Publish you and praise you" and they're asking the LORD to save the people of Israel and the tents of Jacob. The watchmen on Mount Ephraim in the past are those who guarded and announced feast times and new moons. Today, this would be believers who love God's Word, love Israel, and pray for Israel. These are those that call upon his name. So the LORD is actually telling us that we need to publish and praise God and say, "LORD, save your people; the remnant of Israel!" Those who call upon the name of the LORD give the LORD no rest until he makes Jerusalem a praise in the Earth, as Isaiah 62:7 says. We as believers and those who call upon the name of the LORD are to have Israel continually on our hearts and in our prayers at all times.

Thursday nights in our congregation is our night of prayer, and the main topic we start off with is Israel and the Jewish people because of scriptures like this that say, "Publish you, praise you." When you stop and think about it, what is the percentage of the world that prays for Israel? Probably less than 1 percent, maybe half of 1 percent. It's a tiny, tiny number, but God does amazing things with small numbers. That's why He chose little Israel among all the big nations because He takes the small things to show how great He is. It's a very small fraction of people who pray for Israel and the Jewish people. So if you're one of those, you're in great company and God is with you.

Jeremiah 31:10
"Hear the word of the LORD, O ye nations, and declare it in the isles afar off, and say, He that scattered Israel will gather him, and keep him, as a shepherd doth his flock."

I mentioned the word "isles" before. It has several meanings. It can mean "island," a coastland, or it could just mean countries. It doesn't necessarily mean we're talking about isles out there in the ocean somewhere. It's really talking about anybody across the sea, including the United States. When this begins to occur, the nations of the world will begin to see the awesomeness of God. They're going to see God bringing the captivity back out of captivity and all the nations that didn't perish in the Tribulation will begin to declare the glory of God! This is what's going to happen when they see this taking place.

Jeremiah 31:11-12
"For the LORD hath redeemed Jacob, and ransomed him from the hand of him that was stronger than he. Therefore they shall come and sing in the height of Zion, and shall flow together to the goodness of the LORD, for wheat, and

*for wine, and for oil, and for the young of the flock and of
the herd: and their soul shall be as a watered garden; and
they shall not sorrow any more at all."*

To be ransomed means you were in captivity and are now released.
There will be no more sorrow. Does Israel still sorrow today? Yes, of
course they do. Did Israel have sorrow in the last three major wars, in
1948, in 1967 and 1973, the Yom Kippur War? They were successful in
those wars but many Israelis died. They had a lot of sorrow. They were
almost taken over in the 1973 war. Israel has been constantly harassed
from suicide bombers to the Lebanese Hezbollah guerrillas, the Hamas—
all these people. There's lots of sorrow. Not a family in Israel exists that
hasn't been affected one way or another by those sorrows. Yet, they remain
a happy people for the most part. So this verse says they will have no
sorrow anymore at all. That has not happened; this is a future promise that
it's going to take place in the not-too-distant future.

Jeremiah 31:23

*"Thus saith the LORD of hosts, the God of Israel; As yet
they shall use this speech in the land of Judah and in the
cities thereof, when I shall bring again their captivity; The
LORD bless thee, O habitation of justice, and mountain of
holiness."*

The people in Israel are getting ready to say this statement. The
LORD commanded them in this scripture to say this statement, and they
will say it when they come back into the land. When Israel starts coming
back in the land, they're going to say, "LORD, bless you, O habitation of
justice and mountain of holiness!" That phrase has a deeper meaning. Let
me explain it.

The word "justice" is *righteous*; it's *tzaddek*. Saying "justice" is not
a good way to use that word in this context; it's righteous. A better way to
say it might be, "O habitation of righteousness," or "O sanctuary, those

who dwell in righteousness," or "those who live in righteousness." "Mountain of holiness" can be translated "mountain of the holy." So when Israel comes back in the land and start saying, "LORD bless you O habitation of the righteous and mountain of the holy," they're not blessing God, they're blessing this habitation and his mountain.

Who and what is the LORD talking about? Who comes back with the Messiah? The holy and righteous saints come back with Him who walk in righteousness and love the LORD's appearing. The LORD will take the saints in that firstfruits rapture; they are coming back with him. The saints—or more specific, the Heavenly Zion—is the mountain of the holy! The saints are the ones dwelling in the habitation of righteousness! They will be there in the Holy Zion, the New Jerusalem, with the Messiah ruling with him with thrones and crowns! The captivity of Israel is going to say, "LORD, bless them!" because finally they're going to realize who the Messiah is, and they're going to honor the believers that have been praying for them. The saints will come with the Messiah and even make war with the beast. They will help deliver Israel. What an honor! An honor we don't deserve, but Yeshua gives it to us because of His grace and mercy in our lives and because of our love for Him. Can you imagine that? The captivity of Israel coming back to Jerusalem and seeing the saints will cry out "LORD, bless them!" They're going to feel so indebted because of our prayers and our actions and fighting with the Messiah to deliver them.

When we pray for Israel, it's good to say, "LORD, guard Israel; protect Israel. Bring them into their salvation, LORD!" We must understand we are brothers with Israel. Whether you're a Jew or gentile, if you have the Messiah, you are brothers with Israel. You are redeemed; they're not yet, but they will be. What a great honor we have, but at the same time what a great responsibility we have to Israel.

Jeremiah 33:7

"And I will cause the captivity of Judah and the captivity of Israel to return, and will build them, as at the first."

When the LORD first brought His children out of Egypt and gave them all the cities of the Canaanites, the land began to be fruitful and multiply. This will happen again after the captivity returns;, they will prosper. Now, we know Israel is prospering today, so we see part of that fulfillment even today, but it will be even greater because Israel will go back into ruin again at the captivity. The enemies that are coming against Israel will burn everything, and in God's judgment there'll be a great earthquake (see Revelation 16:18-19) that will level every city on Earth, and that includes every town and city in Israel. All those cities are going to be leveled when the seventh vial is poured out in the book of Revelation. But God is going to bless Israel when they come back and they will rebuild the waste cities. The land will begin to be fruitful again.

Remember the army of Joel? The land in front of them will be like the Garden of Eden and the land behind them as a wilderness because they will devour everything like fire in front of them and burn it to the ground. That's a supernatural army because it says they don't die, that God is going to unleash out upon the Earth a terrible army. We all sing that wonderful song, "Blow the trumpet in Zion, Zion. Sound the alarm on My holy mountain!" This song is about that destructive army. It gives you a little different sense when you sing that song, doesn't it? But that is what is coming upon the whole world.

Jeremiah 33:8
"And I will cleanse them from all their iniquity, whereby they have sinned against me; and I will pardon all their iniquities, whereby they have sinned, and whereby they have transgressed against me."

Has that happened yet? No!

Jeremiah 33:11
"The voice of joy, and the voice of gladness, the voice of the

bridegroom, and the voice of the bride, the voice of them that shall say, Praise the LORD of hosts: for the LORD is good; for his mercy endureth for ever: and of them that shall bring the sacrifice of praise into the house of the LORD. For I will cause to return the captivity of the land, as at the first, saith the LORD."

That's not happened yet. The people of Israel are not praising the LORD corporately. And neither are they bringing the sacrifice of praise into the house of the LORD. There currently is no physical house of the LORD. There are so many things that haven't happened yet.

Jeremiah 33:25-26

"Thus saith the LORD; If my covenant be not with day and night, and if I have not appointed the ordinances of heaven and earth; Then will I cast away the seed of Jacob and David my servant, so that I will not take any of his seed to be rulers over the seed of Abraham, Isaac, and Jacob: for I will cause their captivity to return, and have mercy on them."

The LORD just said "If I have not appointed the ordinances of heaven and of earth…" In other words, "If I did not put the stars in the heavens, if I did not put the sun up there, if I did not put the moon up there, if I have not caused the Earth to rotate and have seasons, if I didn't do that, then will I cast off Israel." So basically what the LORD is saying, "I have set those things in motion; I have set those things to be an everlasting ordinance, so forever My heart and mind is upon Israel and I will not cast them out."

Jeremiah 31:31-34

"Behold, the days come, saith the LORD, that I will make a new covenant with the house of Israel, and with the house of Judah: Not according to the covenant that I made with

177

their fathers in the day that I took them by the hand to bring them out of the land of Egypt; which my covenant they brake, although I was an husband unto them, saith the LORD: But this shall be the covenant that I will make with the house of Israel; After those days, saith the LORD, I will put my law in their inward parts, and write it in their hearts; and will be their God, and they shall be my people. And they shall teach no more every man his neighbour, and every man his brother, saying, Know the LORD: for they shall all know me, from the least of them unto the greatest of them, saith the LORD: for I will forgive their iniquity, and I will remember their sin no more."

No longer will anybody say, "Do you know the LORD?" When this day arrives, all will know the LORD but it does not mean all inhabitants of the Earth will be obedient.

Jeremiah 31:35-37

"Thus saith the LORD, which giveth the sun for a light by day, and the ordinances of the moon and of the stars for a light by night, which divideth the sea when the waves thereof roar; The LORD of hosts is his name: If those ordinances depart from before me, saith the LORD, then the seed of Israel also shall cease from being a nation before me for ever. Thus saith the LORD; If heaven above can be measured, and the foundations of the earth searched out beneath, I will also cast off all the seed of Israel for all that they have done, saith the LORD."

Wow! Have the foundations of the Earth been searched out? No. Has the moon ceased to be in the heavens? Has the sun ceased to shine? Have the stars ceased to shine? No! They're up there for an everlasting ordinance. So every time you go outside and see the sun, the moon, or the stars, remember the covenant of God. His promises are sure and amen.

That's important to everyone who trusts in the LORD. If God will hold His word, what He said He would do for Israel and base it off the ordinances of the heavens and the Earth, so shall He also keep His promises to all who trust in Him. He will not cast us off if we trust in Him and believe in Him. When God says something, it's sure. It doesn't change. We can count and rely on those promises that God has us in the palm of His hand at all times. We love Him and we serve Him. We were never promised that we won't have problems. We were never promised that we won't suffer sorrow. We were never promised that we won't shed a tear and have heartaches. Those are never part of the promise. The promise is that He will bear our iniquities for us, He will cleanse us, and He will not forget us. These are promises we can go to the bank with—the bank of God. Those ordinances will not depart and neither will the promises of God toward Israel or toward anybody who calls upon his name.

Jeremiah 46:27
"But fear not thou, O my servant Jacob, and be not dismayed, O Israel: for, behold, I will save thee from afar off, and thy seed from the land of their captivity; and Jacob shall return, and be in rest and at ease, and none shall make him afraid."

The first thing that happens is God is going to save them. The order of events that we have alluded to appears to be this: Israel will go back into captivity, then the sign of the Son of Man will appear and the trumpet will blow. They shall look unto the One whom they have pierced. When they look up and see that sign of the Son of Man, they're going to know Yeshua is the Messiah. They'll look unto the one they have pierced. This isn't one of those popular concepts where Yeshua comes down and stands over the Mount of Olives, and the rabbis come up to him and say, "Well, is this your first or second coming?" That's silliness; it won't happen that way. The sign of the Son of Man appears in the midst of the captivity. They go to captivity first, then the sign of the Son of Man appears. They will look unto it and they will call upon Him, "Baruch haba

B'Shem Adonai; blessed is he who comes in the name of the LORD!" Then they will become believers at that point. Once they become believers, they shall come out of their captivity. "And none shall make him afraid." That's the order of events and how it will happen, but none of those things have happened yet.

Jeremiah 46:28
"Fear thou not, O Jacob my servant, saith the LORD: for I am with thee; for I will make a full end of all the nations whither I have driven thee: but I will not make a full end of thee, but correct thee in measure; yet will I not leave thee wholly unpunished."

This scripture repeats what we learned earlier in Jeremiah 30. The LORD's reminding Jacob that He will deliver you, but you're not going to come out of this fully unscathed because of your wickedness and your sins. Remember, Israel is not a righteous nation any more than the United States is. Although Israel is a wonderful nation and has righteous individuals living in it, they are far from the righteousness God desires. Our righteousness must be according to God's standard and not in comparison to other nations.

Israel has a high rate of homosexuality and also a high per capita abortion rate. Many of them don't believe in God. They are secularists, atheists, and communists, but nonetheless God will not forget Israel. The unrighteous ones will perish in the Tribulation. Believe it or not, folks, many even in Israel will be deceived by the beast. They will receive the mark of the beast and will perish by the hands of the LORD. But those who trust in the LORD are not a people who dwell in darkness. We are a people who dwell in light and we shall not be deceived. Yeshua said, "Don't believe it when they say I am in the wilderness. Don't believe it when it says I am in the holy place."

That's what the beast is going to do. Although the Beast will come out of the old Assyrian Empire, he probably will go to Mecca to proclaim himself the Moslem Messiah. Mecca is part of the wilderness. The beast will also proclaim himself God in the temple in Jerusalem—the holy place where Yeshua is saying, "Don't believe that's me. You will know when I come. My coming shall be as lightning from east to the west." The heavens will roll back like a scroll and you shall see the Son of Man coming in His glory with His host, also known as His clouds (the saints) coming with him. Just because somebody can call fire down from heaven and work miracles and say that they're God or the Messiah, don't believe it! You will not be deceived if you understand the scriptures, but a large part of the world will be deceived because they don't know the scriptures. Remember, you are children of light and not of darkness.

Ezekiel 39:25-29

"Therefore thus saith the Lord God; Now will I bring again the captivity of Jacob, and have mercy upon the whole house of Israel, and will be jealous for my holy name; After that they have borne their shame, and all their trespasses whereby they have trespassed against me, when they dwelt safely in their land, and none made them afraid. When I have brought them again from the people, and gathered them out of their enemies' lands, and am sanctified in them in the sight of many nations; Then shall they know that I am the LORD their God, which caused them to be led into captivity among the heathen: but I have gathered them unto their own land, and have left none of them any more there. Neither will I hide my face any more from them: for I have poured out my spirit upon the house of Israel, saith the Lord God."

As we read in Joel, the Lord's going to pour out his spirit upon all flesh which is the ultimate fulfillment of Pentecost. What happened on the Day of Pentecost or Shavuot was just partial fulfillment of the outpouring of the Holy Spirit. There's going to be a total fulfillment of that promise in

Joel and the Spirit of God will be poured out upon all flesh, but it happens at the end of the Tribulation. So the people who are left on the Earth will get to reap that benefit, but many will perish before then. Some say as many as two-thirds or more of the people on Earth will perish in the Tribulation.

Obadiah 1:20

"And the captivity of this host of the children of Israel shall possess that of the Canaanites, even unto Zarephath; and the captivity of Jerusalem, which is in Sepharad, shall possess the cities of the south."

Some people say that Sepharad is in Assyria, some say it is in Media, some say it was in Asian Minor (modern-day Turkey). Yet others suggest it might even be Spain but Spain doesn't make any sense at all. So nobody knows where Sepharad is. I find it interesting that Sepharad also means "separated," indicating a place of exile. But the children of Israel and some of the captivity of Jerusalem will be taken there. Remember, only some of the inhabitants will be led into captivity and another group will escape into the wilderness.

Because the book of Obadiah is about the judgment of Edom, Sepharad is probably in Edom or northern Arabia. This Jerusalem remnant will possess the southern areas of Israel and Edom (southern Jordan today) and probably northern Arabia after the release of the captivity.

On the other hand, the captivity of Israel will possess the land of the Canaanites and Zarephath which is in today's Lebanon. None of this has happened at this time.

Obadiah 1:21

"And saviours shall come up on mount Zion to judge the mount of Esau; and the kingdom shall be the LORD's."

Who do you think those saviors are? Most likely, they are the saints as the saints of Jews and gentiles will come back to help fight the enemies of Israel with the Messiah. The word for "come up" is alah and it also means come, rise, rouse, meet and depart. These saviours will come from the heavenly Zion and perhaps come to the physical Zion in Jerusalem to begin their judgment against Edom. The mount of Esau is just a concept, an idiom, that could possibly mean the world, but it is certainly talking about the enemies of Israel, and could also be talking about the Arab nations south of Israel.

The land of Edom, which was settled by Esau, is in southern Israel to the southeast, but it extends from there all the way to the Arabian Peninsula. So when they're talking about the mount of Esau, they could be talking about that whole area from the southern Dead Sea area to where Mecca and Medina are, and more. These Muslim countries are going to be part of this in the war against Israel, but saviors are going to come up on Mount Zion. Why? Because that's where Yeshua will be. Most likely this is the heavenly city of Zion. It could also be in the Mount Zion of physical Jerusalem; however, the holy and elect will be with Him either place.

We're going from there to destroy the enemies of Israel. That's why Israel says, "The LORD bless you!" in Jeremiah 31:23 when speaking of this group coming with the Messiah. The saints are going to have a hand in it. I don't know how this will happen, I don't know how the saints will make war against the enemies of Israel, but scripture says that there's none to help Israel but the LORD (Isaiah 63:4-6). But because we are with the Messiah, we are counted in that group and we will help Israel.

If you are a kingdom person, you may be saying, *Oh, well, I don't think I like that. I'm not a violent person. I'm not sure I can do stuff like that.* You won't have a choice. God will empower you and you'll have a righteous indignation taking place in your spirit and in your heart, and you're going to be chomping at the bit to help get this done out of love for the Messiah and Israel! Will we be waving swords, or will we be speaking the words and things happen? Who knows? It'll be interesting to see how this is all going to take place.

Again, one must understand that word "Zion" can be understood in two ways. There is the physical Zion within the physical Jerusalem at the Temple mount and there will be the heavenly Zion where the saints will dwell. This heavenly Zion is also known as the New Jerusalem. It will hover just above the land and probably centered over the physical Jerusalem. The saints will be in resurrected bodies and will have their own habitation in this holy city that puts the sun to shame in its glory. (See the last two chapters of Revelation.) This city will come down at the beginning of the millennium period of the reign of Messiah and not afterwards. The whole world will see this heavenly city of Zion. It will be here during the millennial period and beyond. Saints will travel back and forth from the heavenly to physical Zion in Jerusalem. The bridegroom is not going to wait a thousand years to present His bride to the world. If the saints are going to rule with Messiah, then most likely, they will be nearby.

Hebrews 12:22
"But ye are come unto mount Sion, and unto the city of the living God, the heavenly Jerusalem, and to an innumerable company of angels, to the general assembly and church of the firstborn, which are written heaven, and to God the Judge of all,, and to the spirits of just men made perfect, and to Jesus the mediator of the new covenant, and to the blood of sprinkling that speaketh better things that that of Abel."

Abraham looked for a city built by the hands of God and not by the hands of man. This city is the New Jerusalem of Revelation 21—the place where Yeshua said He would go and prepare a place for us so we will be with Him forever. It is the habitation of the saints. (More will be said on this later.)

Chapter 15:

God's Judgment and the Remnant at War

Zechariah 10:3
"Mine anger was kindled against the shepherds, and I punished the goats: for the LORD of hosts hath visited his flock the house of Judah, and hath made them as his goodly horse in the battle."

More than likely the shepherds are the ones that the book of Enoch refers to that who are to watch over Israel. They are probably angels. These shepherds can also be rulers and teachers who did not guide with righteousness. Whether they are angels or men, God will judge them severely. But God is going to cause that remnant in Israel to rise up and they will also go to battle. Why? Because they also believe in Yeshua by this time. The sign has already appeared, Israel is coming back into the land, and this time they're coming into the land all knowing the Lord, the Messiah Yeshua.

This final battle is going to take place against all of the nations that came against Israel, including all of the Ezekiel 38 and 39 nations of Gog, Magog, Assyria, Ethiopia, Libya, Turkey, Iran, Armenia, Georgia, Iraq and possibly Russia as well as many other nations mentioned in Psalm 83. The nations of the world that come against Jerusalem and Judah will be destroyed. The Messiah, the saints, Judah, and Israel will rise up and fight also at this time.

The goats could be the judgment against the goats in the story of the sheep and goats. They were those that did not help Israel as seen in

Matthew 24:31-46. The least of these my brethren is speaking of Israel. The judgment is all about the nations' treatment of Israel. Even though the armies of the beast will be destroyed and judgment falls all over the world, each living individual will also be judged on how they treated Israel. Did they feed them, visit them in prison, clothe them? Unfortunately, there will be a lot of goats that will be destroyed.

Zechariah 10:4
"Out of him came forth the corner, out of him the nail, out of him the battle bow, out of him every oppressor together."

This is talking about Yeshua's army of Israel and saints. Corner is a metaphor for corner stone or a chieftain or prince of the people. The nail indicates one who drives. It can also be a metaphor for a leader who is tough. Oppressor is one who is a ruler or taskmaster. This army of Yeshua's will be very serious to rid the land of her enemies.

Zechariah 10:5
"And they shall be as mighty men, which tread down their enemies in the mire of the streets in the battle: and they shall fight, because the LORD is with them, and the riders on horses shall be confounded."

Isaiah 11:14
"But they shall fly upon the shoulders of the Philistines toward the west; they shall spoil them of the east together: they shall lay their hand upon Edom and Moab; and the children of Ammon shall obey them."

After the sign appears as mentioned in Isaiah 11:11, God will begin to gather this captivity and bring them into the land, and the LORD will be with them. He will empower them and they will fight the surrounding nations when they come. This isn't going to be a nice, little peaceful event for the world. God will empower the remnant of the captivity to gain power and fight with great strength, and they will begin to reclaim their land from those who took the land when they went into captivity. They're going to chase the enemy out. Israel is not just going to come back in and go "LORD, help us get our land back!" The LORD's going to say to them, "I'm going to empower you and you're going to take your land back." It says they'll fly upon the shoulders of the Philistines toward the west; they shall spoil them of the east together: they shall lay their hand upon Edom and Moab; and the children of Ammon shall obey them.

Israel will begin to fight against her enemies and destroy them. The Messiah Himself will destroy the beast of Revelation and his armies, but Israel will fight the surrounding enemies of their country. These neighboring nations will join together with the beast to come against Israel, but God will empower the Israelites to fight and they will defeat these enemies. They will fly upon the shoulders of the Philistines (Gaza today) toward the west. Edom, Moab, and Ammon is today's country of Jordan.

Is Ammon obeying them today? No. This is future stuff. As a matter of fact, Zechariah 12:8 also says, "In that day shall the LORD defend the inhabitants of Jerusalem; and he that is feeble among them at that day shall be as David; and the house of David shall be as God, as the angel of the LORD before them." In defending Jerusalem, the house of David will fight like the angel of the LORD, which is the Messiah Himself.

God is going to inspire the children of Judah to be mighty men.

As mentioned before, the sign must appear, then the regathering will occur. When the sign of the Son of Man shall appear in heaven, then will He begin to gather the outcasts to the land. That hasn't happened yet. In 1948 God was certainly involved in the creation of the State of Israel, because Israel had to be reestablished before all the nations could challenge them. This is so the nations will know that he is the LORD God.

So Israel had to be reestablished, and His hand was on that. He sent out His angels to make sure it was going to happen. You have probably seen shows, movies, and stories about all the angels defending Israel during their wars and the miraculous things that happened. Yes, God's hand is on Israel because He was going to make sure that they became a nation again, but it's only the beginning of the things He's going to do. No one can deny that Israel can fight valiantly but not as the Angel of the LORD yet.

So, what is happening here in Isaiah 11? It begins with the sign of the Son of Man who will appear. At that time the gathering of His captivity from the four corners of the Earth will begin and then He will empower them to fight against their enemies. We can see a little bit of that today with Israel. They do a pretty good job of fighting their enemies, but it'll be even more so. They will destroy all their enemies with the help of God. Many people don't understand that when the final regathering happens and God begins to bring them back in the land, they will fight with awesome power and the house of David will fight like David fought. They will have supernatural power and they will fall upon the shoulders of the enemies because the LORD will be over them. Now, the believer's position may be the same. Believers in the Messiah will come back with the LORD and help Israel. They are coming back as kings and priest and will sit in judgment. That's our calling because we are going to be like Messiah. We will sit with Him on thrones; we're going to rule with Him. (More on that in the Restoration.)

Zechariah 9:13
"When I have bent Judah for me, filled the bow with Ephraim, and raised up thy sons, O Zion, against thy sons, O Greece, and made thee as the sword of a mighty man."

Basically what this is saying is, "I am going to take Judah and Ephraim and fight against these enemies, and I'm going to use them like bows and arrows to fight their enemies." God is going to empower them to fight the enemies. Who they're going to attack are named specifically here.

Poor Greece. That isn't completely correct. That word Greece is really not there.

The areas of Turkey, Armenia, Georgia, Northern Iraq, and Western Iran is where it's all going to start and come down to attack Israel. These massive armies will be led by the beast of Revelation. We see some of this today. ISIS is in these areas and the fight against them will possibly draw in the nations. Perhaps this fight is the beginning of the Gog war. It will spread out in all directions until the whole world is involved. Somewhere, the beast is going to build or occupy a city that he will probably rule out of. It is very possible that the end-times Babylon may be Mecca as it is a city in the wilderness as Revelation says. No other city that is considered is in the wilderness. Mecca is the center of Islam and the beast will use it for his advantage. This is why Babylon rides the beast but eventually the beast destroys Babylon once he is done using her.

Let's get back to Greece. The word "Greece" is really *Yavan*—the son of Japheth, one of the sons of Noah. He settled in modern Turkey and eventually spread out, even over to modern Greece. Yavan is the area where it all starts.

Thus, Zechariah 9:13 is saying to Israel that their sons will fight the sons of Yavan and destroy them. It fits the other scriptures that Israel is going to be empowered to destroy all those people who came against them, but not until after the sign of the Son of Man appears and God begins to bring them home and Israel says, "Baruch haba B'Shem Adonai; blessed is he who comes in the name of the LORD." That is when they finally see who Yeshua is—when they look up to the heavens, see the One whom they have pierced (Zechariah 12:10), and finally realize that Yeshua is Messiah. They will repent, they will honor God, and God will fill them with the spirit (also with the spirit of the warrior David), and Israel will defeat Yavan and others.

Another concept to be aware of is in Zachariah 9:13 where it says that Israel will fight and at the same time the LORD will raise up the sons of Zion to fight. There could be a twofold meaning here. First, this could be talking about those from Jerusalem. Second, it could be the resurrected saints who are also known as Zion.

I talked about this earlier about how God was going to empower Judah and Ephraim to fight. Ephraim, when speaking prophetically, is a word for Israel. It's one of the tribes of Israel and quite often in the Bible, God will say Ephraim instead of Israel. So he's going to empower Judah and Ephraim to fight and fill the bow or archers with Ephraim. They're going to be warriors. But that next phrase is important also: "and raise up your sons O Zion." I don't know how many times I've read this, just went right by it and didn't think much about it, but it's bigger than I imagined. Judah and Ephraim are going to fight their enemies, and at the same time, God is going to raise up the sons of Zion. What did he mean by that? That word is the same Hebrew word *uwr* that is used in so many other scriptures, particularly Isaiah 52:1 where it says, "Awake [*uwr*], Awake [*uwr*])! Put on your strength, O Zion, put on your beautiful garments!"

This is a rapture scripture. It's talking about the saints rising up and putting on new resurrected garments where they will shine like the sun, like the luminaries! That's what that the word *uwr* means! We see in verse 13 that He's going to raise up the sons of Zion. What He's talking about here is a resurrection of a remnant of Israel, the elect, who are going to dwell in the heavenly Zion along with the saints that come back with Yeshua. We are going to rule and reign with the remnant of Israel in the holy city Zion in other words, the New Jerusalem!

So it appears that Zechariah 9:13 is saying that when the LORD empowers Judah and Ephraim to fight, the rapture will have occurred for the saints and the elect and they will come back with the Messiah.

It is possible that physical Israel and the resurrected saints who come back with the Messiah will fight these enemies.

192

Remember the scripture "Whatsoever a man sows, that shall he also reap" (Galatians 6:7). That is like a physics principle with God. So all those nations that came against Israel, God is going to allow Israel to take them out. Now Yeshua Himself will take out the beast, along with all the bad angels that are going to come in the land of Parthians and the Medes that Enoch talks about (Enoch 56:5-8). These angels are all coming back and they will stir the nations and gather them in the attack against Israel. As a matter of fact, they may be stirring up trouble in the Middle East at this moment and we can't see them. Now, Yeshua and His saints will take care of the angels as well as the beast. They will join in with Israel to fight the armies in the flesh that the angels bring together as they gather the nations and make war against Israel, and particularly against Jerusalem. God will empower His people to come back out of captivity and to fight them.

Zechariah 9:14
"And the LORD shall be seen over them, and his arrow shall go forth as the lightning: and the LORD God shall blow the trumpet, and shall go with whirlwinds of the south."

With Judah and Ephraim, the LORD is going to be over them and they are going to destroy these enemies. What you sow is what you reap! So these nations that came against Israel and did harm to Israel, God is going to empower Israel to execute judgment against them. Many of these battles will take place in the southern part of Israel.

By the way, that word south is "Teman"—whether they're actually talking about the city of Teman, or just from the south direction. But southeast of Israel in the land of Edom is also where the city of Teman is located. The Lord will begin in this area and sweep over the armies of the beast with the gathering of His people. They'll just keep moving upward and destroy or bring some of them into captivity. Israel will get all their

193

promised borders back.

The scriptures say that God came from Teman, and the Holy One from mount Paran (Habakkuk 3:3) and the Lord will "send a fire upon Teman, which shall devour the palaces of Bozrah" (Amos 1:12). Teman, Paran, and Bozrah are all in southern Israel/Jordan area. They are places of ancient Edom.

By the way, do you know what the actual God-promised boundaries of the land of Israel are that was promised to Abraham, Isaac, and Jacob? That border starts at the Red Sea, comes out across all the way to the Euphrates River, and back again. Most of Syria, Lebanon, and Jordan will all become part of the land of Israel. That includes Damascus, Syria and Amman, Jordan. That's probably quadruple the size of the land they have right now. That's the land God promised them through Abraham, Isaac and Jacob. They're going to get that land back. During the millennial reign, all of that land will belong to Israel and they will not have any enemies to fight them over it as today. All the enemies of the Psalm 83 war will be destroyed. More than likely, this war will be part of the Gog-Magog war. I believe it's all part of that same time when God empowers Israel to take all their promised land and destroy their enemies.

Zechariah 9:15-16
"The LORD of hosts shall defend them; and they shall devour, and subdue with sling stones; and they shall drink, and make a noise as through wine; and they shall be filled like bowls, and as the corners of the altar. And the LORD their God shall save them in that day as the flock of his people: for they shall be as the stones of a crown, lifted up as an ensign upon his land."

One of the things we're going to see take place here is that Judah and Ephraim will be empowered, and at the same time, God is going to raise up His sons of Zion to dwell in the heavenly Zion. Most of the time when we say "Zion" we think that's probably just another word for Jerusalem. It is in a sense, but not totally. There is a slight difference between Jerusalem and Zion. Jerusalem is the city; Zion is where God dwells in the city. Whether it be the Temple Mount or the place God prepares for His saints and elect, that's Zion. That's where the presence of God is. That's where He sits, that's where He dwells. That's the inner court of Moses' tabernacle, and it's very possible—using the concept of Moses' Tabernacle—the city of Jerusalem could be the outer court. Or maybe outside the walls of Jerusalem is the outer court, it could be either way. But being in Zion is the inner court.

All believers should strive to be in the inner court. To get to the inner court, a person must pass the brazen altar for blood atonement for the forgiveness of sins. This would be the cross of Yeshua. Then you have to go through the brazen laver which represents repentance and being filled with the Holy Spirit before you come inside the inner court. No one who does not wash at the brazen laver can enter the inner court where God dwells. Inside the inner court is the menorah, the table of showbread, the golden altar, and the ark of the covenant where the LORD sits and dwells. This inner court of Moses' tabernacle is symbolic of the heavenly Zion. It's an important concept to understand.

Throughout the Bible, trumpets are blown. When the LORD appeared on Mount Sinai, that was after a trumpet sound. Isaiah 27:13 says, "A great trumpet shall be blown and they shall come which are ready to perish in the land of Assyria and the outcasts in land of Egypt shall worship the LORD in the holy mount at Jerusalem." So when that trumpet blows, it brings the captivity back, and at the same time raises up the sons of Zion. That's why when we talk about the rapture, it comes at the last trump before the seven vials are poured out on the Earth. Revelation 11:15 says at the seventh or last trump, "the kingdoms of this world are now become the kingdoms of our Lord and of his Messiah." Verse 18 is talking about how it is the time of giving rewards to the saints, prophets, and those that fear his name. This happens after the rapture. As mentioned earlier,

Revelation 12 is a follow up of Revelation 11 and is about the rapture when the firstfruits (man-child) are caught up to heaven. 1 Corinthians 15:52 also says, "In a moment, in the twinkling of an eye, at the last trump: for the trumpet shall sound, and the dead shall be raised incorruptible, and we shall be changed." Isaiah 27:13 says, "they shall worship the LORD in the holy mount of Jerusalem." That's followed by the Hebrew letter *bet* which means "in, on or at." So the word could mean, "Worship the LORD in the holy mount, on the holy mount, or at the holy mount." It could be any one of those. It is doubtful they will be allowed in the Holy Place, so most likely it will be at or near the mount.

I always found this interesting. Israel's going to fight with sling-stones? I don't think so. This is one of the concepts you can probably say is symbolism by using a metaphor of sling-stones. Israel is going to have weapons of some sort which may actually be slings. But who knows? David was pretty powerful with his sling and stones. That word "noise" is a roar. Like you see in movies where somebody's going to attack somebody else; they're all shouting as they're running for battle. That's exactly what we're talking about here. Israel is not going to be whispering coming after the enemy. They're going to be shouting, and they shall be filled like bowls at the corners of the altar.

When we're talking about the altar, we're talking about the recessed areas in the corner of the altar where they pour the blood of sacrifices. What he's saying is that Israel will be filled with the spirit of God. They're going to be mighty warriors in the spirit of God like King David was as they begin to fight against their enemies. Their bowls will be filled with blood by the sacrifice of the enemy. Isaiah 34:6 tells us that the LORD has a great sacrifice in Bozrah and a great slaughter in the land of Idumea. The Messiah, saints, and Israel in the flesh will destroy these armies.

Jeremiah 30:8
"For it shall come to pass in that day, saith the LORD of hosts, that I will break his yoke from off thy neck, and will

burst thy bonds, and strangers shall no more serve themselves of him:"

In other words, "I'm going to break this yoke, I'm going to break his bonds, says the LORD. And no longer shall foreigners and strangers oppress you." The person spoken of here is the Assyrian, Gog, which will be known as the beast of Revelation. The beast and false prophet will be thrown into the Lake of Fire (Revelation 19:20) after their armies are destroyed. Satan himself—who was the root cause of all of this—will be locked up for a thousand years (Revelation 20:2). Peace shall come upon the land. Has that ever happened? No! This is yet in the future.

Jeremiah 30:10

"Therefore fear thou not, O my servant Jacob, saith the LORD; neither be dismayed, O Israel: for, lo, I will save thee from afar, and thy seed from the land of their captivity; and Jacob shall return, and shall be in rest, and be quiet, and none shall make him afraid. For I am with thee, saith the LORD, to save thee: though I make a full end of all nations whither I have scattered thee, yet I will not make a full end of thee: but I will correct thee in measure, and will not leave thee altogether unpunished."

The writer says, "I will bring to an end of all the nations where they were scattered." He will not bring a full end of Jacob, but he says that I will punish you. Israel doesn't escape. When the beast of Revelation, i.e. the Assyrian or Gog, sweeps into the land and brings them into captivity, many will perish, many will die. Even in the city of Jerusalem when half the city is taken, many will perish, many will die. So when this attack occurs on the land of Israel, Israel will definitely be punished. Romans 11:26 says, "And so all Israel shall be saved: as it is written, 'There shall come out of Sion the Deliverer, and shall turn away ungodliness from Jacob.'"

I've heard many times that we "don't worry about Israel; they have their own covenant." Not true. They need Yeshua just as much as anybody else. When He comes, and only then, shall all of Israel be saved. But up to that point, many will perish, many will die. A lot of these prophecy writers seem to think that we don't have to worry about Israel; they're going to be saved. No! The apostle Paul said, "I'm a Jew to a Jew that I might save some of them." Israel still needs Yeshua today and when He comes, then will the remainder be saved. Paul understood that. "And unto the Jews I became as a Jew, that I might gain the Jews; to them that are under the law, as under the law, that I might gain them that are under the law" (1 Corinthians 9:20). Many rabbis today in Israel say that Israel can be saved corporately only by revelation when the Messiah comes as it was at Mount Sinai. Well, they are right as far as the end result. The apostle Paul knew that many will perish and he did his best to save some. Israel will be saved corporately but many will perish between now and then. Teach the gospel to save some now and this goes for the world also.

To understand this concept is very important. That's why we need to not only reach the nations, but we have to reach the Jewish people, we have to reach Israel. Many of them are going to die and perish! So many believers keep hands-off of Israel because they think they have a separate covenant, but it's not true. Some people say, "Israel is the wife of the LORD, the believers are the bride of Christ." Well, that's interesting. Are we going to have a wife and a bride in heaven, two separate married groups? No! There will be one bride and that will be of Messiah and it will consist of Jews and gentiles that come to know the Messiah. God has a covenant with Israel and it will come to fruition with Yeshua.

Israel must come to terms with Yeshua to be forgiven of their sins. This is why we must tell people of the things that are coming upon the Earth because many will perish. We don't fear; we know our position as believers. But Yeshua said He's coming with great reward to all of those who love Him, those who serve Him, and do righteous works in His name. We are called to righteous works. Dead works don't accomplish anything, but righteous works accomplish a lot and our reward is based on that.

As Daniel 12:3 says, some will shine as the luminaries (he's talking about the sun and the stars) and some will be shameful to look at. What does that mean? In the resurrection, the body you get, the clothing you get, the white garments you get, their degree of intensity of light depends on your rewards of things you did for the LORD. How bright you're going to shine! Now, don't get me wrong; those that are shameful to look at will not shine like others. They could be naked or much dimmer. They're going to still be happy, but it's like comparing a ten-watt light bulb to a million-watt light bulb. One is shameful to look at compared to others who shine with the glory of the LORD.

It's important for us, as the apostle Paul said, to seek the mark of the high calling, to run the race. Seek the incorruptible crown! Paul is trying to warn us that there are rewards. Seek those things, don't sit back on your laurels and think, "I've got it made with salvation. That's all I need to worry about." That might get you in, and some people may just get in and smell like smoke because they were so close to that other door. But let it not be so among the saints; let us strive for the things God wants us to strive for, serve Him, love Him, and be obedient to His ways.

The righteous works we do are important. Even Yeshua said that anyone who gives a cup of water to these little ones in my name or the name of a disciple shall no wise lose their reward (Matthew 10:42, Mark 9:41). That was a righteous work. If you're sweeping floors in the congregation, that's a righteous work. If you're helping someone who comes to your door, that's a righteous work. These are the kind of things God is talking about—to love God and our neighbor. He's not talking about works of our own inventions; those are dead works. It just breaks my heart to see people whipping themselves and causing blood to come out of themselves thinking they're doing a work for God. God didn't call us to do something like that. That's dead works; they will not be honored for doing that. Or, people who climb up many flights of steps on their knees until their knees are bloody in front of a big temple or cathedral somewhere, thinking they did a marvelous thing for God. Not! Those are the works of man; they are not works of God. It's works of God that we must accomplish. You can wear a tefillin and it will get you nowhere if it is not done by love for God or your neighbor.

This is why James said, "You show me your faith without your works, and I'll show you my faith by my works" (James 2:18). That's why Paul says, "Strive for the mark of the high calling" (Philippians 3:14), and also in 1 Corinthians 3:11-15 that we have a foundation which is in Yeshua. That's your foundation! That's where you get your salvation, by the faith and grace and mercy of God do you establish a foundation. That's how you get saved! "LORD, come unto me. Save me, LORD! I believe in You. Wash away my sins. I trust in You." That's establishing that foundation.

But Paul goes on to say, "What do you build on that foundation?" Some people will build upon it wood, hay, and stubble and when they stand before the judgment seat of Messiah and that judgment fire comes and burns their works made out of wood, hay, and stubble, their works are consumed. There's nothing left but ashes. But Paul goes on to say "Yet you still have the foundation so thus you are still saved, you just have nothing to show for it." You're going to be what I like to refer to as "a naked believer." You will have nothing to show for your works. When we're sitting around the heavenly campfires at night, and we're talking about the wonderful acts and works of God, what are you going to talk about? What will you say if you're a naked believer? *Well, I believed.* So did we. What else did you do? *I guess that was about it.*

It's important that we do things for God, but we don't do those things just for reward. We do them because we love Him and they come automatically. This is an area you have to be very careful about; we don't do works because we think of getting rewards, but because our heart is toward God and our fellowman. That's the difference and God knows the difference. One is dead works; one is righteous works. These are important concepts to get in our hearts and our minds. It is important to build on that foundation gold, silver and precious stones. This is not talking about wealth but the precious things of God and His Kingdom.

If you've been paying attention to the news of what's going on in the Middle East, you are beginning to see the nations rising up against Israel. The UN is rising up against Israel. Many things are happening across the world. The UN, of course, represents the nations—nations, particularly Iran, that want to destroy Israel. The plan is taking place. Satan is sifting these nations and getting them to do his will against Israel. All of those nations that attack and scatter Israel will come to an end. So pray for your nation to be a blessing to Israel. I pray for my nation, the United States, to maintain biblical concepts, especially with Israel. We don't want to be counted among these nations that will be brought to a full end because of what they've done to Israel.

In Jeremiah 51:49, the LORD says, "As Babylon has caused the slain of Israel to fall, so at Babylon shall fall the slain of all the earth." A nation doesn't have to be part of an army that attacks Israel. If they've caused the slain of Israel to fall—either by holding back weapons or tying their hands or whatever—God will bring those nations to an end also. No nation is going to be able to say, "Well, I didn't fire a bullet." Yeah, but you provided the bullets. You caused the slain of Israel to fall. No nation will be found innocent that has caused the slain of Israel to fall.

RESTORATION

Except for a small remnant, surviving Israel will go in the millennial reign in the flesh. So all of Israel that survive the Tribulation will live in the land and will be ruling out of Jerusalem in the flesh. During the millennium reign sacrifices will come back. Why do sacrifices come back? Why don't we have them today? Number one, there's no temple, and number two, Yeshua was the final sacrifice for those who believe today. Why? We don't see Him, we're relying on the grace and mercy of our God through Yeshua as He appropriates His sacrifice for us. Angels do not have the mercy of God. Why? They're with Him, they see Him and everything about Him. So when they go against God, they're doomed. There is no mercy for them.

It's the same concept when Messiah is ruling out of Jerusalem. People will see Him, they will know Him, they will know who He is. The age of grace is over when that happens. All who are living in the flesh at that time will be required to follow the law. Torah will come into full effect again. This is what Isaiah 2:3 is talking about when it says, "for out of Zion shall go forth the law [Torah], and the word of the LORD from Jerusalem."

The Torah of God will come back in full force for that thousand-year period, and the sacrifices will come back for those who are living in the flesh in Jerusalem at the temple. For those that believe in Messiah today, that doesn't apply. Our job is done. His work is finished in us. We will dwell and rule with Him in the heavenly Zion, the New Jerusalem. Ezekiel, chapters 40–48, describe the events of the temple during the millennium reign. The Aaronic Priesthood and many of the moedim (feasts) will be restored such as Passover, Unleavened Bread and Tabernacles (Ezekiel 45:25 and Zechariah 14:16). It is interesting that Shavuot (Pentecost), Yom Teruah (Day of Shouting or also known as Feast of Trumpets) and Yom Kippur (Day of Atonement) are not mentioned.

And of course, sacrifices will come back.

This doesn't apply to believers in Messiah when He comes back since they have resurrected bodies and are sealed into eternity living in the heavenly Zion. However, believers might minister at the physical Jerusalem, instructing and making sure the law of God is followed. Torah will become honored completely during this thousand-year reign. It's like God is saying, "You didn't get it right the first time. I'm going to have you do it again a second time and see if we can get this right."

Remember, Yeshua said in Matthew 5 that not one jot or tittle will ever go away from the law (Torah) until all be complete. Has everything been completed? No, not until after the millennial reign when death and hell are destroyed and the final judgment takes place. Then will all be complete.

The truth is, God's word is sure and true. His prophetic utterances will all fit into the pattern or total picture correctly if you understand it correctly.

Chapter 16:

Time of Rebuilding

Jeremiah 30:18
"Thus saith the LORD; Behold, I will bring again the captivity of Jacob's tents, and have mercy on his dwellingplaces; and the city shall be builded upon her own heap, and the palace shall remain after the manner thereof."

The LORD is talking about how He's going to rebuild Israel. The cities are going to be rebuilt and the palace will remain. We don't know exactly what the palace is. It could be a reference to the temple, or it could be a reference to a government or king's palace. A palace where rulers will rule is most likely what it is. From verse 17, it is understood that the city is Zion, the physical Jerusalem. It is important to understand the concept of the physical and heavenly Zion. Both will exist during the millennium reign of the Messiah. Sometimes it is difficult to tell which one the scriptures may be talking about. The saints of Messiah will be housed and rule from the heavenly Zion which shall be hovering above the Earth. I believe it will be hovering above the physical Zion or the Temple Mount of Jerusalem. The size of this heavenly city will stretch from Egypt to Assyria. It will be awesome.

The rebuilding of Israel is one of the promises in the scriptures. Since Israel came into existence after World War II, the Israelis have done an incredible job of rebuilding their land. Swamps were drained, cities were built and rebuilt. The land of Israel is a wonderful place to be. However, cities will once again be destroyed by the beast, Gog, the

Assyrian, and the armies of Joel as well as the judgments of God. After the return of the captivity, the rebuilding will commence again.

Amos 9:14

"And I will bring again the captivity of my people of Israel, and they shall build the waste cities, and inhabit them; and they shall plant vineyards, and drink the wine thereof; they shall also make gardens and eat the fruit of them."

Now many will say, this has happened already and still is going on. You are right; however, there is more to the story. Amos is not totally fulfilled yet. There are other promises the LORD says He will do that hasn't happened that lead us to understand this is still a future promise of rebuilding. Amos 9 includes other scriptures that were not fulfilled. The first part of Amos 9 talks about God judging the house of Israel and will scatter them. This certainly looks like a past fulfillment. Let's continue.

Verse 11 says that the LORD will raise up the tabernacle of David and raise up his ruins. I'm not sure if we can say that is complete, but the rebuilding of Jerusalem could be a fulfillment of that prophecy. Verse 12 says Israel will possess the remnant of Edom. This has not happened.

In verse 13 we see the prosperity of the mountains dropping sweet wine and the hills shall melt. This could be a reference to wonderful agricultural concepts as Israel produces crops the land yields to them even today.

Amos 9:15

"And I will plant them upon their land, and they shall no more be pulled up out of their land which I have given them, saith the LORD thy God."

We know this is a last day's promise. What's happening to Israel today? They're constantly fighting over the land. They're constantly being asked to give up land that they obtained by being attacked first. When the political pressure increases, the Israeli government has and will bulldoze Israeli settlements in these areas. Even today Israel has no peace over the land and the fighting continues. The pressure of giving up more land is constant.

This has not had final fulfillment. Israel doesn't have all their land promised to Abraham from the River of Egypt to the Euphrates River. They are still fighting for it. The controversy of Zion or the Temple Mount is still a hot potato today. Gaza, Golan Heights, and the West Bank (Judea and Samaria) are all part of the land promised to them—and more—by God. Yet these areas are greatly contested today and full of violence. I conclude that Amos 9:15 has not seen its final fulfillment.

Not only are the enemy armies going to destroy everything—and, in particular, that army of Joel—but that great earthquake in Revelation at the seventh vial will destroy all the cities on Earth. Now we know Israel began to rebuild waste places even before 1948. In the early 1900s when the Zionist movement began, Jews came and drained the malaria infested swamps and planted the fields which provided jobs for migrants even Arab migrants.

When Israel first started coming in the land in the late 1800s and the early 1900s, it was totally barren. If you go into Israel today, you see farm lands everywhere and fruit growing. They help feed the world. They are the largest exporter of flowers, even more than Holland. In fact, they sell a lot of their flowers to Holland. The land responds to the promised owners. But we see this as only a shadow of what's going to happen when they come back out of their captivity when the LORD will completely bless their land.

Hosea 6:11

"Also, O Judah, he hath set an harvest for thee, when I returned the captivity of my people."

What did he mean by "a harvest for you"? It's an agricultural term, but he's not talking about a lot of wheat, a lot of barley, a lot of pomegranates, figs, and grapes. That's not what he's talking about. So many people have died in the Tribulation period at this point that God is going to cause Israel to prosper as far as giving birth to children. Their dwellings will be very fertile, and all of a sudden they'll start giving birth to repopulate the land again. During this thousand-year millennial reign, an old man will not die that hasn't seen his days and a child shall die at 100 years old. In other words, when one dies at 100 years old, he/she will still be considered a child. Never again will there be an infant of days (Isaiah 65:20).

Can you imagine how fast the population's going to increase on the Earth during the millennial reign in that thousand-year period? We're up to 7 billion now, and a majority of those are going to perish in the Tribulation period. But during the thousand-year tribulation reign, the Earth will begin to repopulate. There will be no sickness, no wars, no dying early. What keeps the population in a slow increase today is because we die young because of drugs, sickness, wars, accidents, abortions, and other things that keep the population growth on a slow increase for sure in Israel and Jerusalem and perhaps on the Earth. Most of these promises are for those in Israel and Jerusalem and not necessarily for the world. You erase all those things, the population is going to increase rapidly. So at the end of the thousand-year period, there are going to be a lot of people again on planet Earth.

Isaiah 51:3

"For the LORD shall comfort Zion: he will comfort all her waste places; and he will make her wilderness like Eden, and her desert like the garden of the LORD; joy and gladness shall be found therein, thanksgiving, and the voice of melody."

In this case, to comfort Zion would mean God's comfort to the land of Israel and Jerusalem. The LORD will have compassion on

Jerusalem and all her waste places. He will cause the land to become like the Garden of Eden and the desert like a garden. Israel is trying to do this now but it will not be like anything that will happen after the captivity.

Chapter 17:

Nations Gather to Worship the LORD

Zechariah 9:16

"And the LORD their God shall save them in that day as the flock of his people: for they shall be as the stones of a crown, lifted up as an ensign upon his land."

They're going to be lifted up like stones that go on a crown; they're going to sparkle and shine. Isaiah 62:3 says that Zion will be a "crown of glory in the hand of the LORD, and a royal diadem in the hand of your God." Did you know that God may have jewels for the saints' crowns? We learn in Revelation 11:18, when the seventh trumpet blows, Yeshua begins to hand out rewards to the saints. And when He comes back to the Earth in Revelation 22:12, His reward is also with Him but this reward is not the same as Revelation 11:18. This reward is for the sinners on the Earth, which for the most part will be death. However, the saints are coming back to the Earth with their Messiah-given rewards for their work for the kingdom. If you look at all the scriptures dealing with rewards, it's really awesome but it's also very sobering because He talks about man being rewarded according to what they have done. Some saints will receive outstanding rewards, some lesser rewards, and some no rewards at all. Yeshua is a rewarder of those who love Him. Saints will have their own wonderful rewards of thrones, crowns, jewels, garments of light and many other things, yet sinners will be judged severely and it won't be pretty.

Zechariah 14:9

"And the LORD shall be king over all the earth: in that day

211

shall there be one LORD, and his name one."

After the LORD delivers Jerusalem, He will be king over all the Earth. This has not happened yet.

Zechariah 8:20-21

"Thus saith the LORD of hosts; It shall yet come to pass, that there shall come people, and the inhabitants of many cities: And the inhabitants of one city shall go to another, saying, Let us go speedily to pray before the LORD, and to seek the LORD of hosts: I will go also."

This is after the Tribulation is over and the millennial reign of the Messiah is happening. The people of the nations of the world will come to Jerusalem to worship the Messiah.

Zechariah 8:22

"Yea, many people and strong nations shall come to seek the LORD of hosts in Jerusalem, and to pray before the LORD."

There will be a gathering of the nations that have survived the tribulation. The goat and sheep judgments, the Psalm 83 judgments, and the Gog-Magog judgments are over. They're now going to come to Jerusalem to worship the Lord God.

Zechariah 8:23

"Thus saith the LORD of hosts; In those days it shall come to pass, that ten men shall take hold out of all languages of the nations, even shall take hold of the skirt of him that is a Jew, saying, We will go with you: for we have heard that God is with you."

Now that's interesting, isn't it? Again, we're talking about the gentile nations left over from the Tribulation. They survived the final judgments or failed to be raptured. They are not part of the firstfruits nor an inhabitant of the New Jerusalem. They will take hold of the *tzitzit* (tassels sown onto the four corners of Jewish garments and worn by Jews as commanded in scripture) of the garment of the Jew, saying, "I'm hanging on to you because we heard that God is with you." They're in the flesh, too. They're going to hang on to a Jewish person who's now had a revelation of God, the Messiah, and are filled with the Holy Spirit. It's the Joel 2 concept fulfillment.

The first Pentecost or Shavuot was just a shadow of the final fulfillment of Joel 2 where the spirit of God is poured out on them mightily. So the gentiles of the world who are in the flesh are going to hang on to a Jewish person and say, "I'm going with you because God is with you." A believer may be thinking, *I'm going to be there; why won't they hang on to me?* Well, they may be scared of saints, and they're probably not going to relate with them very well. The saints will have a glorified resurrected body; they will shine like the sun. This is why the Holy Zion or New Jerusalem will outshine the sun. However, it is possible that the saints (holy and elect) will be able to turn on and turn off their glory to be able to minister to the people. Ezekiel 42:15-19 gives us a clue on how this might happen. When ministering before God in the inner court, the priest must have on their holy garments and when they go to the outer court they must take off the holy garments first to minister to those in the outer court. Keep in mind that Yeshua was able to turn his light on and off when he transfigured before Peter, John and James (Matthew 17). When the people come to Jerusalem or even Israel, they're not going to grab a saint's *tzitzit*, they're going to grab the *tzitzit* of the garment of a Jew who's living in the flesh in the millennial period at that time.

This skirt concept is very similar to the *tzitzit* (Deuteronomy 22:12; Numbers 15:38) to remind the Jewish person to obey the commandments of God. The *tzitzit* has knots in it to represent 613 laws of Torah as determined by Jewish sages.

The Gentiles alive at that time in the flesh will be Israel's nursing fathers and mothers and they shall bow down with their face toward the Earth and lick up the dust (Isaiah 49:23). That's the kind of honor Israel's going to get, but don't you know they will do it also to the saints who will be the spiritual Israel? The people left alive in the Earth will not only bow down to the physical Israel coming back to the land, they will bow down and will be terrified of the saints because they will have their resurrected bodies and the glory of God will shine on them. The saints will be kings and priests and they will rule and judge the world.

Don't forget that a remnant of Jews that were raptured will be also in the New Jerusalem. The majority of Jews that survive the Tribulation will be in the land and at the physical Jerusalem and will have great honor beyond compare to the rest of the physical earth. God is going to cause the nations of the world to honor Israel. The twelve tribes of Israel at this point will also be ruled and judged by the 12 disciples (Matthew 19:28 and Luke 22:30).

Scripture says that Israel was blinded from the Messiah two thousand years ago so that salvation will come to the gentiles. Why? There are a lot more gentiles than there are Jewish people. Yeshua needed to become a lamb for spiritual salvation before He would become a king over the physical world. However, as He said, when "the times of the gentiles are fulfilled" (Luke 21:24), then God's full attention will go to Israel. So for many millennials, Israel has been trying to seek the LORD God and to have a personal relationship with Him. Except for a few cases, they corporately have not found Him. This now redeemed Israel are those who truly try to seek the Lord and keep His commandments. I'm not talking about atheist Jews, disobedient Jews, or secular -Jews, I'm talking about those who have been trying to seek the Lord and can't seem to find Him. Of course, God will not blind anyone who individually truly seeks Him. That's why there are many Messianics today.

One day, God is going to turn Israel's attention to Him and they're going to suddenly look upon Him, particularly when the sign of the Son of Man appears. They're going to look up and see the One whom they pierced and perhaps say, "Oh no, that is Yeshua!" Then they're going to remember all the things they said that were bad, all the times they rebelled against Yeshua, and all the name calling and curse words they said against Yeshua. All of a sudden, as it says in Zechariah 12:10, they will mourn as one who lost an only son. They're going to be fearful, too, and will most likely say, "He is the Messiah, what have I done?" Yet God's going to show them mercy.

But wait a minute, is He leaving his throne? How can mercy apply if He's leaving His throne? It doesn't apply to anybody else, so how can it apply to Israel at that point? The two goats of Yom Kippur both had the sins of Israel confessed on them. One was sacrificed, the other one was supposed to be let loose alive in the wilderness, but they threw it off a cliff as Leviticus 16:10 and 22 says, "To be presented alive before the LORD." Although the scapegoat represents the resurrected Yeshua, it is also symbolic that Yeshua took the sins of Israel even now for atonement so that when He comes back, they have their atonement through Him when they call upon Him.

It's the same principle today. Yeshua died for our sins, but you still have to call upon Him. It's also the same with Israel. He had already died for their sins. So once He leaves the mercy seat of God's throne and comes as the King of kings and the Lord of lords, Israel will call upon Him in their captivity. He will deliver them because Yeshua is both goats of Yom Kippur. Although it could be argued that when the sign of the Son of Man appears, Yeshua is still on the throne and so grace could be granted to many others until He actually leaves the throne. Remember, the throne is the mercy seat of the heavenly ark of the covenant where Yeshua intercedes today.

Jeremiah 30:9

"But they shall serve the LORD their God, and David their king, whom I will raise up unto them."

This is an interesting scripture. Most of the time, prophetically speaking, when a verse speaks of David, it's talking about Yeshua. The Bible says that there will always be a descendant of David upon the throne. When Yeshua came, He was like the final descendant of David to be on the throne. So it's always in reference to the Messiah. He sits on the throne of David. This also can be seen in Isaiah 9:7. Jeremiah 23:5 says "Behold, the days come, saith the LORD, that I will raise unto David a righteous Branch." This branch is Yeshua. Jeremiah 33:17 tells us that "David shall never want a man to sit on the throne of the house of Israel." If this is not about Yeshua, then this prophecy failed. This is talking about the Messiah. So when you see scriptures prophetically speaking about David, it's almost always talking about the Messiah.

Now, I said "almost." Some scholars think that verse 9 of Jeremiah chapter 30 is not talking about the Messiah. It says, "They will serve the LORD their God and David their king, whom I will raise up unto them." Some say that David may actually rule in Jerusalem as a prince. It's an interesting concept, something to stick in the back in the cobwebs of your brain and consider when you're reading.

Chapter 18:

Prosperity and Joy

Isaiah 51:11

"Therefore the redeemed of the LORD shall return, and come with singing unto Zion; and everlasting joy shall be upon their head: they shall obtain gladness and joy; and sorrow and mourning shall flee away."

The LORD is saying that this redeemed of the LORD, shall return from their captivity and come singing unto Zion and everlasting joy shall be upon their head. They shall obtain gladness and joy, and sadness and mourning shall flee away. Joy and great happiness shall be upon their heads! There will be no mourning or sorrow. God knows Israel's been through enough of that, but when they are redeemed by the Messiah, it's going to be awesome when they come back into the land. This is why the gentiles alive on the Earth at that time will grab hold of a Jew and say, "I'm going with you for the LORD is with you!" (Zechariah 8:23). It also says the gentiles will take the returning captives children and carry their sons and daughters back into the land (Isaiah 49:22). The ships of Tarshish shall bring them first to the land (Isaiah 60:9). Isaiah 51:11 has not been fulfilled yet and it could have a double fulfillment concerning both the heavenly and earthly Zion of the saints and the remnant of Israel. There will be no crying in both Zions but that's not a promise for the rest of the world.

Isaiah 60:9

"Surely the isles shall wait for me, and the ships of Tarshish

first, to bring thy sons from far, their silver and their gold with them, unto the name of the LORD thy God, and to the Holy One of Israel, because he hath glorified thee."

We don't know what or who Tarshish is. Some people say it's Spain, others say it was the whole west coast of Europe, including England. So when you stop and think about it, whoever this country of Tarshish is, they have the honor of first bringing the children of Israel and the Israelites back to the land. Who are they? Well, if Tarshish is indeed Spain and/or the Europeans and England, which countries founded the United States? Can the United States be the sons of Tarshish? Could be. Because of their love and support of Israel all these years, despite our wicked condition now, nonetheless God doesn't forget the wonderful things they have done for Israel.

Will the USA have the first honor to bring the overseas captivity back using their ships? The ships of Tarshish are going to bring the captivity of Israel to the land first, which means many other nations will follow suit afterwards. Tarshish will bring them first across the seas and oceans but not over the land. God Himself will lead the land excursions between Assyria and Egypt.

Isaiah 52:6-8

"Therefore my people shall know my name: therefore they shall know in that day that I am he that doth speak: behold, it is I. How beautiful upon the mountains are the feet of him that bringeth good tidings, that publisheth peace; that bringeth good tidings of good, that publisheth salvation; that saith unto Zion, Thy God reigneth! Thy watchmen shall lift up the voice; with the voice together shall they sing: for they shall see eye to eye, when the LORD shall bring again Zion."

When the LORD restores the physical Zion in Jerusalem, there will be great joy. The heavenly Zion will be above it. Both the heavenly Zion and the restored physical Zion will see eye-to-eye. The watchmen in this case is most likely the saints of the heavenly Zion. Watchmen can mean to behold, watch, view, but can also mean prophets, to shine, and to be bright. This description of watchmen could be talking about the saints.

There is a concept here that is hard to grasp, but I will attempt to explain as I see it. Let's look at several scriptures from the book of Enoch.

Enoch 39:4-7b

"And there I saw another vision, the dwelling places of the holy and the resting places of the righteous. Here mine eyes saw their dwelling with His righteous angels, and their resting places with the holy. And they petitioned and interceded and prayed for the children of men. And righteousness flowed before them as water. And mercy like dew upon the earth. Thus it is among them for ever and ever. And in that place mine eyes saw the Elect One (Yeshua) of righteousness and of faith. And I saw his dwelling place under the wings of the Lord of Spirits (Father God). And righteousness shall prevail in his days. And the righteous and elect shall be without number before him for ever and ever. And all the righteous (saints) and elect (certain elect of Israel) before him shall be strong fiery lights."

Enoch 41:2

"And then I saw the mansions of the elect and the mansions of the holy."

Trying to define holy, righteous and elect is not easy. The righteous appears to be the saints consisting of Jews and Gentiles who trusted Yeshua. The holy can mean the same thing or the holy angels. The elect appears to be speaking of Israel. Yet it doesn't refer to all of Israel but only the raptured group. All of these particular groups will be as fiery lights.

Enoch 38:2

"And when the Righteous One shall appear before the eyes of the righteous, whose elect works hang upon the Lord of Spirits, and light shall appear to the righteous and the elect who dwell on the earth."

This seems to say that when the appearing of Yeshua occurs he will clothe the righteous with light and also a remnant of the elect who will still dwell on the earth. That is most likely at the physical Jerusalem. So this seems to indicate a rapture.

Enoch 38:4-5

"From that time those that possess the earth shall no longer be powerful and exalted. And they shall not be able to behold the face of the holy, for the Lord of Spirits has caused His light to appear on the face of the holy, righteous, and elect. Then shall the kings and the mighty perish and be given into the hands of the righteous and the holy."

In this book, I speak several times according to the biblical scriptures that Israel and the saints will fight against the evil armies on the earth when powered by the LORD. So we see in Enoch the righteous, and holy (saints) and the elect (remnant of Israel) being able to dwell close at hand, 'eye-to-eye' as Isaiah says.

It appears that both groups (saints and raptured elect) will be given garments of light. This raptured elect Israel will also dwell in the physical Zion to rule as promised by God's word. Remember that even the Apostles were promised to rule the twelve tribes of Israel. This elect will also dwell in the heavenly Zion with the saints. There will also be the non-raptured elect remnant who God chooses to reign in the physical Zion. Perhaps it is the woman of Revelation 12 or the 144,000 of Revelation 7. The righteous will be those who believe in Yeshua before the sign of the son of man appears. They comprise of gentiles and Jews who believed in Yeshua by faith. The elect come into their calling due to the promises given to them by the LORD. It is not by faith. This is why they are called the **elect**. They will also believe in Yeshua. I suppose that the righteous can travel between the heavenly and physical Zions as well as the raptured elect. The rest of the elect cannot go to both Zions and only to the physical Zion, yet they can see eye to eye. Remember, all we can do is put the puzzle pieces together as we see it now. The LORD will probably reveal more as we get close to his coming.

So the remnant of Israel that was raptured will look eye-to-eye with the saints; in other words, they will join with the saints. I find it interesting that in the book of Enoch it says when talking about the final gathering of the holy and elect, "the righteous and the elect shall be without number before Him for ever and ever. And all the righteous and elect before Him shall be strong as fiery lights" (Enoch 39:6-7). In other words the righteous will dwell with the elect—being the raptured remnant of Israel. The saints who believed in Him before His return are the righteous and they will dwell with each other in their glorious garments given to them after the rapture. Those who are still in bodies of flesh and blood on the Earth through the millennial reign will see the righteous and elect in the holy city of Zion. Remember, there will be a physical Zion and a heavenly Zion.

Isaiah 52:9-10

"Break forth into joy, sing together, ye waste places of Jerusalem: for the LORD hath comforted his people, he hath redeemed Jerusalem. The LORD hath made bare his holy arm in the eyes of all the nations; and all the ends of the earth shall see the salvation of our God."

When you see the term "holy arm," that is just another description of the Messiah who is the LORD's holy arm. Yeshua sits at His right hand at the throne before He actually will sit on the LORD's throne. The LORD will bare, in other words reveal His holy arm in the eyes of all the nations.

Yeshua will be revealed to the nations and all the ends of the Earth shall see the salvation of our God when the sign of the Son of Man appears revealing or baring His holy arm!

Isaiah 52:11

"Depart ye, depart ye, go ye out from thence, touch no unclean thing; go ye out of the midst of her; be ye clean, that bear the vessels of the LORD."

More than likely this is talking about the scripture in Revelation 18:4 that says, "Come out of her [Babylon], my people." But this can have multiple meanings. For sure, the LORD wants us to come out of the world and sin as represented by Babylon. It could be a call for the captivity to come out of the land of Assyria or Babylon back to Jerusalem. It is a call for those who will carry the vessels of the LORD. Yet there is also another possible interpretation. Isaiah 52:1 tells us of the subject of this chapter. It is the heavenly Zion.

"Awake, awake; put on thy strength, O Zion; put on thy beautiful garments, O Jerusalem, the holy city: for henceforth there shall no more come unto thee the uncircumcised and the unclean." This scripture is talking about a rapture. The raptured inhabitants of this city will be clothed in dazzling white shining garments and will light the city where there is no need of the sun. The saints will be clothed with power and strength. This Zion has been made clean by the blood of the Messiah. The saints are being referred to as Zion in verse 1. They are the Temple of the LORD (1 Corinthians 3:16-19; 6:19) who also carry the vessels of the LORD within them. All of the vessels of the Tabernacle of Moses and their symbolism and meaning should be manifested in every believer's life. The saints will be removed from the Earth and will dwell in the New Jerusalem or the heavenly Zion. The word "depart" in 52:11 is *cuwr* and it also means "take away, remove, take off, withdraw, and escape," which could all have symbolisms of the rapture.

There is a good chance that Isaiah 52 in general operates as parallelism in the calling of the physical and heavenly Zion at the same time.

Isaiah 52:12

"For ye shall not go out with haste, nor go by flight: for the LORD will go before you; and the God of Israel will be your reward."

In other words, the captivity is not going to come out of the captivity running a marathon. They're going to come out easy, just like they did coming out of Egypt. Every aged person and every child are going to come out of their captivity, particularly from the north and the south (Assyria and Egypt) and they're going to come back into the land at God's pace as He will lead them. God will be with them and no enemy is going to be able to do a sneak attack on them like the Amalekites did to the Hebrews coming out of Egypt. Nobody will be able to do that to them.

Isaiah 52:13-14

"Behold, my servant shall deal prudently, he shall be exalted and extolled, and be very high. As many were astonied at thee; his visage was so marred more than any man, and his form more than the sons of men."

That's prophetic, talking about how marred Yeshua was when he went to the cross and the people were astonished.

Isaiah 52:15

"So shall he sprinkle many nations; the kings shall shut their mouths at him: for that which had not been told them shall they see; and that which they had not heard shall they consider."

At that time, the whole world will begin to see that Yeshua is the

Messiah and they will believe in Him. All shall know the LORD at that time, but at a huge cost—a huge price. That's why today is the day of salvation. No one should let it go by. There will be a rapture; actually there will be a series of raptures, but there will be initially a firstfruits rapture and those that are in the firstfruits rapture will miss the wrath of God and the pouring out of the vials of His wrath.

You don't want to have to go through the Tribulation. If you do not love His appearing, you will be left behind. If you're not obedient to His commandments, you will be left behind. Seven churches are mentioned in Revelation, and I believe those seven churches represents every believer today. We all fall into one or a mixture of those categories and we should take heed to the warnings given to them. Only one of those churches, the church of Philadelphia, was promised, "I will keep you from the hour of temptation that's coming upon the Earth to test mankind" (Revelation 3:10). The other six were not promised that. Philadelphia represents the firstfruits rapture for those who will escape. When will that take place? After the beast of Revelation shows up. We're never promised to escape the wrath of men and bad angels; we're just promised to escape the wrath of God. You would not want to be here during that time.

Amos 5:18 says, "Woe unto you that desire the day of the LORD! To what end is it for you? The day of the LORD is darkness and not light." Why would anyone desire to be here on the day of the LORD? It's foolishness. I actually had an individual tell me one time, "I want to be here for the Tribulation. I want to be able to lead people to the Lord." That's just foolish talk. He was a young man. He had a lot of zeal for God and wanted to do a lot of things for God, but he just made a dumb statement. I appreciate his zeal and his love of the Lord, but nobody, nobody, should ever desire to be here at that time.

Daniel 12:1 says that when Michael the archangel stands up, there will be a tribulation that will comes upon the Earth, the unlikes of anything that has ever happened before. Think of all the terrible things that

224

man has done to man! We can't even imagine the horrors that will occur, yet people ignore the signs and blow it off. It's going to be sad. When that firstfruits rapture occurs, even Enoch 49:1-3 says that the whole world will see it and many will turn to the Lord, but they still will go through the Tribulation. Those who believe will be raptured later but will receive no honor, and now they're going to suffer for it. We want to be ready, for the Lord will come as a thief in the night. He will catch us unawares; He'll catch us off-guard. Walk in righteousness, walk in holiness, and be ready for Him. If the heavens start rolling back and people come in the door saying, "The heavens are rolling back! There's lightning from east to west —the sign of the Son of Man has appeared! He's coming!" If you say, *Oh, I'm not ready for this,* you're in trouble. But if you say, *I'm ready!,* then you are loving His appearing as 2 Timothy 4:8 says. The spirit and the bride says "Come!" Remember to come out of her, O my people.

Chapter 19:

Jerusalem and Zion

When looking at prophetic scriptures about Jerusalem and Zion, one must understand that there is a physical Jerusalem and a heavenly Jerusalem as well as a physical Zion and a heavenly Zion. The New Jerusalem of Revelation is also the heavenly Zion. God's promises to Israel include the physical Jerusalem and Zion. Sacrifices are coming back during the millennium and they will be conducted in the physical Jerusalem. Most of the feasts of Leviticus 23 will be celebrated in Jerusalem during the millennium except for perhaps the firstfruit feasts of barley and wheat which includes Shavuot (Pentecost). Also, Yom Teruah (Day of Shouting or Feast of Trumpets) and Yom Kippur (Day of Atonement) are not mentioned either. Certainly, Passover, Unleavened Bread, and Tabernacles will be conducted. See Ezekiel 45:25 and Zechariah 14:16. The eternal concepts mostly deal with the heavenly Zion.

Hebrews 12:21
"But ye are come unto mount Sion, and unto the city of the living God, the heavenly Jerusalem, and to an innumerable company of angels, to the general assembly and church of the firstborn, which are written in heaven, and to God the judge of all, and to the spirits of just men made perfect."

The writer of Hebrews tells us that those who have Yeshua are going to be inhabitants of this heavenly Jerusalem with the angels of God. It is the habitation of the firstborn, also known as firstfruits. These are they who are looking for the LORD and love His appearing. They are overcomers which is what every church in Revelation was told to be—an overcomer. This is the concept of the heavenly inner court of the Tabernacle of God. Those in this city will be kings and priests and will rule with the Messiah. It can be difficult sometimes when studying scripture to delineate which Zion or Jerusalem the LORD is speaking about. To Him, they are linked together. The physical world and the heavenly world need each other. Zion is where God has His throne. In the physical world it will be at the Temple Mount in Jerusalem. Ezekiel, chapters 40–48, describe the earthly temple, the land, procedures, sacrifices, and priesthood during the millennium on Earth. The New Jerusalem will coexist with the physical temple during that thousand-year period.

The heavenly realm is where His born-again, saved people are. When the raptures are complete, that firstfruits group will dwell in the heavenly Zion. They are His temple, which is why Revelation says there is no physical temple in the New Jerusalem. The people are the temple. Revelation 21:22 also says the Lord God and the Lamb are the temple in the New Jerusalem. The New Jerusalem is the bride of the Messiah and has no need of the sun.

Zechariah 1:14

"So the angel that communed with me said unto me, Cry thou, saying, Thus saith the LORD of hosts; I am jealous for Jerusalem and for Zion with a great jealousy."

The LORD says, "I am jealous for Jerusalem, and for Zion with a great jealousy." So you can see the LORD is actually differentiating between Jerusalem and Zion. In this case the LORD mixes Jerusalem and the physical Zion as one. On the other hand, why does He have a great jealousy for Zion? This Zion has two concepts. There is the physical earthly, the temple mount Zion where the priest of the LORD will conduct services during the millennium. We also have the heavenly Zion that will hover above the mountains, over the land of Israel and more. This Zion is the holy Zion, a city built by the hand of God. It is the New Jerusalem. His saints and certain elect are there, those who called upon His name; those who obeyed Him; and those that were born again. Whether they be Jew or gentile, Zion the holy city consists of believers and the LORD has a great jealousy for them. He is also jealous for the physical Jerusalem with the physical Zion. He's coming to deliver both, but the heavenly Zion is His great love. This city on a hill, not built by the hands of man, but built by the hands of God; that's the heavenly Zion!

God has a great jealousy for this, and He says that He will yet comfort Zion, and yet choose Jerusalem (Zechariah 1:17). In other words, He will comfort Zion; He will have compassion on Zion, because He made promises to the elect. Here we see the mercy of God at work, to have compassion on Zion, and also to fulfill the promises to the patriarchs, He will choose Jerusalem again (Zechariah 2:12). Messiah will have a throne in the physical Zion and yet dwell with the saints in the heavenly Zion. This is a place where all the promises of the millennium will become fulfilled; where the wolf, lion, snake, and the children can play together and nobody gets hurt; where the sun is ashamed because of the light coming out of the heavenly Zion. Note that sinners will still be present. Sin will not be eliminated yet. Toward the end of the millennium period, Satan is let out of his prison and will gather the nations again to attack Jerusalem. This is also why it says in Revelation 22:15 "For without are dogs, and sorcerers and whoremongers and murderers, and idolaters, and whosoever loves and makes a lie." So sinners cannot enter Zion (heavenly or physical) but will dwell outside and will be brought forth before God's great white throne at the second resurrection at the end of the millennium to either eternal life or the second death of the lake of fire.

The brilliance in the heavenly city of Zion is so bright you can't even see the sun. If you do, it'll look like a dim light! Only those with resurrected bodies can tolerate that kind of light. Anybody on the outside would be consumed if they tried to come in that light. You're talking about a brilliance of light that's just not imaginable and there'll be no need of the sun. Isaiah 30:26 also says "the sun shall be sevenfold as the light of seven days." I don't think it really means the sun has turned seven times brighter because that will destroy everything on Earth. But in the heavenly Zion, with resurrected bodies, the saints can handle that kind of light. So sinners cannot enter Zion (heavenly or physical) but will dwell outside and will be brought forth at the 2nd resurrection at the end of the millennium to either eternal life or the second death of the lake of fire.

Many places in the scriptures talk about the brightness of the garments of those that follow Yeshua. Daniel 12:3 says, "And they that be wise shall shine as the brightness of the firmament; and they that turn many to righteousness as the stars for ever and ever." Each believer will shine with their own glory as the apostle Shaul (Paul) says in 1 Corinthians 15:40-42. He says there are different glories for each person at the resurrection. The degree of one's glory will depend on their faithfulness, obedience, and service to the LORD. The light from the heavenly Zion of the saints and elect will light the physical Jerusalem. Heavenly Zion is our goal. Zion is where we want to be!

Zechariah 8:4-5
"Thus saith the LORD of hosts; There shall yet old men and old women dwell in the streets of Jerusalem, and every man with his staff in his hand for very age. And the streets of the city shall be full of boys and girls playing in the streets thereof."

Wonderful peaceful events will occur during the millennium. None shall be afraid. Complete peace will rule.

Isaiah 65:20
"There shall be no more thence an infant of days, nor an old man that hath not filled his days: for the child shall die an hundred years old; but the sinner being an hundred years old shall be accursed."

Even in Jerusalem nobody will die early. Isaiah 65:20 says an infant of days will not die until he is a hundred years old. An old man shall not die until he is old. So even in Jerusalem itself, everybody that's still in flesh and blood will live to be very, very old indeed. How old, I don't know. Some commentators even suggested that they will not die until the millennial is over with; that would be a thousand years. I don't know if they'll live a thousand years, but how long did they live in the first epoch of creation? Many of them lived to 700 to 900 years or more!

So maybe it'll be like that again, but we know death is not destroyed yet so they will have to die eventually. Death is not destroyed until the Great White Throne Judgment in Revelation 20:14 when death and hell are thrown into the lake of fire. Death is the last enemy to be destroyed, as Paul said in 1 Corinthian 15:26. However, for those in the heavenly Zion, it's already destroyed. If you're in the New Jerusalem, you will not die. That means you're a born-again, obedient believer who has been raptured and dwells in the heavenly city of Zion. You've already overcome death by your faith in the Messiah who first overcame death. Although death is the last enemy to be destroyed, it doesn't apply to those in the New Jerusalem. If you are born again and living in the city of Zion, you have already overcome death and passed on to eternal life. But those still in the flesh and blood who missed the rapture and the first resurrection, they will still die, but they'll be resurrected in the Great White Throne judgment and be brought forth at that time.

To make things plain, the heavenly Zion is the new Jerusalem. This city will come down shortly after Yeshua completes His judgments and is established as King of the Earth. The last two chapters of Revelation is a description of the millennium reign. These chapters are not in chronological order with Revelation 20. (More on that later in the book.)

Zechariah 8:8
"And I will bring them, and they shall dwell in the midst of

Jerusalem: and they shall be my people, and I will be their God, in truth and in righteousness."

Zechariah 8:22
"Yea, many people and strong nations shall come to seek the LORD of hosts in Jerusalem, and to pray before the LORD."

When the trumpet blows and the captivity comes back from the four corners of the Earth, they'll come back in the land of Israel and they'll come back into Jerusalem. Boys and girls will play in the streets and old men and women will dwell in the city to a very old age. The nations of gentiles will begin to follow suit. They will come to honor and worship the LORD in Jerusalem and see what is taking place. I imagine when the heavenly Zion comes into its own place, the light will be so brilliant that the whole land or even the world will see the light. So the gentile nations will come and say, "What is that? We've got to see what's happening."

It's going to be like a beacon. That's why the Bible likes to use the word "ensign" instead of just "sign." "Ensign" is like a beacon or a banner or a message. They're going to flood into Jerusalem to see this marvelous thing that is taking place. Scripture says they shall all know the LORD (Jeremiah 31:34) at that time. What a promise! There are rabbis in Israel who also believe in this holy city that will come down. Some say there will be a light that connects the holy Zion with the physical city; sort of a Jacob's ladder concept.

Zechariah 12:8
"In that day shall the LORD defend the inhabitants of Jerusalem; and he that is feeble among them at that day shall be as David; and the house of David shall be as God, as the angel of the LORD before them."

So all of a sudden, the inhabitants of Jerusalem are empowered and they'll fight like David fought. If you know the story of David, he killed Goliath with a sling, and as a shepherd, he ripped open a lion's mouth protecting his sheep. He was a really a tough fella! The inhabitants of Jerusalem will fight like David fought. God will empower them, and they will go against their enemies and fight. However, it then goes on to say, "The house of David [that word 'house' is 'bayith,' It can mean house, household, or temple] shall be as God as the angel of the LORD before them." In other words, those who are now of Zion will fight like God. They will fight like the angel of God before them.

The inhabitants of Zion will have supernatural abilities to destroy the enemy. These can be inhabitants of both Zions. It could be the saints and the remnant of Israel that will be empowered to fight. Can you imagine that? Saints are suddenly going to have power like God and the angel of the LORD to fight and help Israel at that time. Now is that a cool promise or what? Are you ready for that? God is going to empower not only the inhabitants of Jerusalem with flesh and blood, but the inhabitants of the heavenly Zion will fight like God and like the angel of the LORD before them.

The saints will be in resurrected bodies; nobody can hurt them, nobody can do anything to them, and woe be to the nations that try. I don't know how the saints will fight. Maybe fire will come out of their mouths. I don't know how it's going to happen, but the righteous and the elect are going to put the beast and his armies into sheer panic because of the fire that's in Zion and the furnace that's in Jerusalem. **Isaiah 31:9** says, "And he (Assyrian) shall pass over to his strong hold for fear, and his princes shall be afraid of the ensign, says the LORD, whose fire is in Zion, and his furnace in Jerusalem." It goes out from there and starts destroying the wicked upon the whole Earth at that time. Of course we can't forget the holy angels, too, that will be there to destroy the wicked.

Psalm 14:7

"Oh that the salvation of Israel were come out of Zion!

233

*when the LORD bringeth back the captivity of his people,
Jacob shall rejoice, and Israel shall be glad."*

The word "salvation" is *Yeshua*. He will come out of the heavenly
Zion with His saints. Jacob and Israel will be glad. Most of surviving
Jacob and Israel will still be in the flesh, and they're going to be really
thrilled when they see the LORD and all of heavenly Zion and its
inhabitants destroy the enemies of the world. Israel will fight also. With
their enemies destroyed, Israel will now live in peace with Yeshua
reigning as their king.

Psalm 48:2

*"Beautiful for situation, the joy of the whole earth, is mount Zion,
on the sides of the north, the city of the great King."*

That word "situation" means *heights; elevation.* So it's basically
saying, "Beautiful is the heights, the joy of the whole earth is mount
Zion." This heavenly Mount Zion or New Jerusalem is going to be lifted
up basically above the whole Earth in that sense. Isaiah says that the
mountain of the LORD's house will be established in the tops of the
mountains (Isaiah 2:2). This house is the heavenly Zion that comes to the
Earth. Beautiful is the height of Mount Zion!

When you're talking about the tabernacle of Moses and in the inner
court, what's on the side of the north? It is the table of showbread where
the priests gather. The table of showbread is symbolic of the fellowship of
the saints; a gathering and assembly of the saints to eat the bread that is on
the table. It is possible this is where the wedding feast will take place,
where they show love toward one another, and where they help one
another. So basically Psalm 48:2 could be saying, "Beautiful for the
height, the joy of the whole Earth is mount Zion! And at the table of
showbread, the city of the great king." How beautiful will be the city of
Zion as it reigns at the top of the mountains.

Psalm 48:11

"Let mount Zion rejoice, let the daughters of Judah be glad, because of thy judgments."

Whose judgments? God's, but we can't forget Zion's judgments, too. The LORD and Zion, let them rejoice and let the daughters of Judah be glad about your judgments. Not only be glad about the judgments of God, but the judgments of the people in Zion, also. The Bible says the saints along with the elect will come back to rule and reign with Messiah and they will judge. That's one of their jobs, judging the nations. Jacob will be glad that Zion the saints are doing it right. There will be no more false judgments that look upon the appearance of men or judgments of bribery or anything else. For the LORD and His righteous shall judge appropriately and Jacob and the world shall be glad that this is taking place. Remember that in Revelation 2:26, those who overcome will rule the nations with the Messiah.

Psalm 50:2

"Out of Zion, the perfection of beauty, God hath shined."

There's something in Zion that is a perfection of beauty and God will be magnified because of it. This is how the LORD will view his saints, perfect! These are the inhabitants of the heavenly Zion. Because of their glory and their shining in there, God will be glorified. This is not because of our own righteousness, but because of the mercy and grace of our LORD when we are washed clean by Messiah's blood as a perpetual atonement. This substitutionary sacrifice has made a way for all to come to Zion who follow the Lamb and are obedient to Him.

Psalm 87:2

"The LORD loveth the gates of Zion more than all the dwellings of Jacob."

Remember what He said even about Jerusalem? He said, "I have a jealousy for Jerusalem but I have a great jealousy for Zion." So it says here the LORD loves the gates of Zion more than all the dwellings of Jacob. The saints will be His bride so as a husband loves his bride so will the LORD love Zion. The gates of a city is where justice is conducted and where elders or judges sit. God will love Zion above all things.

Psalm 87:5

"And of Zion it shall be said, This and that man was born in her: and the highest himself shall establish her."

Notice the reference to "her." This can only be talking about the Bride of Messiah. The highest himself is "Elyon," the most high God, and shall establish her, or another way to say it, "prepare her" or "provide" or "set her up" or "appoint her." So basically it's saying, "Of Zion this should be said, of this and that man was born in her." You're talking about someone being born in Zion. It's not talking about a normal birth here; it's talking about those who are born again and who will be of Zion. The scripture says, you cannot enter the kingdom of God unless you are born again. There is a difference between salvation/eternal life and kingdom principles. You could be saved and have eternal life, but you can't be in Zion unless you are born again. Zion is the inner court concept of Moses' tabernacle. When you are born again, you are born unto Zion.

Psalm 102:13

"Thou shalt arise, and have mercy upon Zion: for the time to favour her, yea, the set time, is come."

This scripture is speaking of the LORD. "For the LORD shall arise and have mercy upon Zion: for the time to favor her." In other words, the time to show grace and mercy and favor and acceptability for her. That word "set time" is "moed," the word used for the appointed feast times. When will that happen? We don't know but I feel it is close. There are things that must still happen.

236

This particular scripture is very dear to my heart because one time I was helping a pastor start a church and he asked me to help him. I said, "Well, I need to know where you stand. How do you stand about Israel?" He replied, "Oh yeah, you've got to be with Israel." He kept saying all the things that he needed to say, so I said, "All right, I'll help you." We brought the church up to about seventy people and one Wednesday night he stood up, gave a message, and said, "Anybody who says that the Jews are the chosen people is calling God a racist." I said, "What?" I literally got up and walked out, and he chased me down in the parking lot during the service. He said, "I know you're not going to be back, but I want to thank you for all the work you've done."

I looked at him and said, "I'm not so sure I did a good thing." I got in the car and drove off. On the way home, my heart was sad and I was wondering, "Lord, what are you doing? What am I supposed to do? What's going on here?" I did one of those silly things—I like doing silly things sometimes, you know—I pulled my Bible out, set it on the seat, flipped it open, put my finger on a scripture. I waited until I got to the next stoplight, picked that Bible up, and used the light at the intersection to see where my finger was. Right there was Psalm 102:13: "You will arise, and have mercy on Zion." I said, "Okay, I got the message, Lord!"

That began my move toward what would eventually allow me to start a Messianic congregation. To favor Zion could be two things. First, to favor the work in Jerusalem and second, to desire to seek the mark of the high calling that the apostle Shaul (Paul) talked about. Seeking the inner court, seeking God with all my heart, and to overcome and to dwell with the LORD at his throne should be our goal.

Psalm 102:16
"When the LORD shall build up Zion, he shall appear in his glory."

In other words, when that rapture occurs, and all who are going to be raptured at that point have been raptured, the LORD will come back to the Earth. This scripture seems to indicate when the last person who will be saved and be part of the kingdom which is the heavenly Zion, then shall the Messiah come. Keep in mind that prior to this, the physical tribulation temple will be built in which will be defiled by the Beast of Revelation and will be a trigger point for the coming of the Messiah. After the Messiah destroys the sinners out of the land, then the new physical Zion and new temple will be established in Jerusalem for the millennium. The heavenly and physical Zion will co-exist during the millennium.

Psalm 125:1

"They that trust in the LORD shall be as mount Zion, which cannot be removed, but abideth for ever."

"Those that trust in the LORD" is speaking of those who believe in the LORD and are committed to Him. That's what "believe" really means in the scriptures when speaking of salvation. It is to trust in what the LORD has said and what He will do. To "believe" is saying "I have head knowledge about something." Head knowledge doesn't get you saved, it's trust that gets you saved. When scriptures say, "Whosoever believes in him [Yeshua] shall not perish but have eternal life" (John 3:16), the word "believe" is really about trust. Whoever trusts in Him shall not perish is a better way to say it—that you believe in God's Word, you're trusting in God's word. It's not head knowledge that God existed! Even the devils know that He exists and you know what their future's going to be. To know that somebody exists isn't going to get you salvation, it's trust. Psalm 125:1 says, "Those that trust in the LORD shall be as mount Zion, which cannot be removed, but abides forever." If you are born again, you will abide forever. You have overcome death, and you shall always be part of mount Zion. You shall always be of the heavenly city of Zion, which is also the New Jerusalem that will come down at the beginning of the millennium reign of Yeshua. To live in the New Jerusalem is to live forever.

Psalm 126:1

"When the LORD turned again the captivity of Zion, we were like them that dream."

The word "turn again" is from the Hebrew word *shuwb* which means return again, return, restore, and bring. In other words, when the LORD brings the captivity then we will be like them that dream. However, the word for captivity is *shiybah* which is used only once in the Bible, here in Psalm 126:1. It really means "those who return" or "restoration." So another way to say that is, "When the LORD brings the restoration of Zion, we were like them that dreamed." We were inspired, we were recovered, we become strong, we become robust. Those are all the definitions of the word "dream."

There are two ways to look at this. One way is the restoration of the Temple Mount in Jerusalem and the return of the captivity of Israel, and second, it is the coming of the holy city of Zion to the Earth. The restoration or those who return of Zion could be the returning of the saints after the rapture. Perhaps it will be both concepts working together. That day is coming when He's going to restore Zion—both the heavenly city and the physical in Jerusalem.

Isaiah 30:19

"For the people shall dwell in Zion at Jerusalem: thou shalt weep no more: he will be very gracious unto thee at the voice of thy cry; when he shall hear it, he will answer thee."

There'll be no weeping in Zion; no more tears! We are not talking about the entire world; we're talking about Zion. Revelation 21:4 tells us that there will be no tears in the New Jerusalem. It is not a promise anywhere else other than Zion, both the heavenly and earthly. So when the

LORD says that those who have been thrown out in the outer darkness will have weeping and gnashing of teeth, people say how can they be weeping if they're not supposed to be? There's no weeping in Zion! There's no promise of that outside those walls. This is why it's important to understand the concept here. That's why when people are thrown into outer darkness, there's weeping and gnashing of teeth. Outer darkness does not refer to hell or a particular place of judgment. It means you are cast out away from Zion, maybe even outside of Jerusalem. So there's weeping and gnashing of teeth because you know what could have been, what should have been, "If I had only" concepts. That's why there's weeping and gnashing of teeth.

Who are the people who get thrown into outer darkness according to scripture? The man who tried to sneak into the wedding without a wedding garment in Matthew 22. The servant with the one talent in Matthew 25 who buried it because he was fearful of the Lord was thrown into outer darkness where there is weeping and gnashing of teeth. Those people weren't thrown into hell. The five foolish virgins in Matthew 25 were left out of the wedding feast for not having oil in their lamps. A virgin in this case is someone who believed in the LORD and were made pure but the five foolish virgins fell away. They were not thrown into hell, but they lost their position in the kingdom to what could have been and what should have been. They didn't lose their salvation. They lost their position, they are no longer now inhabitants of Zion because they're outside in outer darkness. All outer darkness means is away from that brilliant bright light of Zion. That's what outer darkness is, it's not a place of punishment like hell. To be removed from the light, that's what outer darkness is.

In comparison, if the light in Zion is so bright that it shames the sun, and you're outside of Zion, it's going to seem like outer darkness, but it's not hell. Unfortunately, a lot of biblical commentators refer to outer darkness as hell. It's not hell, because what does it take to get eternal life? To believe, to call upon the name of the LORD, to trust in Him, to trust in

His atonement for you. Just because you didn't use your talent like you were supposed to, because you didn't have your lamp full of oil like you were supposed to, how would that guarantee that suddenly you're going to hell? That would fly in the face of the redemptive scriptures of grace and mercy. But you can lose position in the kingdom or even fail to enter the kingdom. That's why there's weeping and gnashing of teeth in the outer darkness. Remember that there are no tears in Zion.

What is the location of outer darkness? No one knows, but it is not Zion. There are some ideas about it. It could be outside the walls of Zion or New Jerusalem. It could be a suburb of Zion away from the heavenly light of the city, or it could refer to parts of the outer court where people are saved but have no honor to enter the inner court or Zion. It could also be in the physical Earth where one is seen by the inhabitants of the Earth as having no honor to be in the city of Zion. We don't know but we know that outer darkness exists.

Matthew 8:12 says, "But the children of the kingdom shall be cast out into the outer darkness: there shall be weeping and gnashing of teeth." What does this mean? Israel was promised to be that kingdom at one time (Exodus 19:6) but it has been taken from them and given to those who are born again of Jews and Gentiles. God will fulfill His promises to the Jews as a nation but they will not be part of the kingdom of God. So in this case, again, outer darkness seems to be away from Zion whether it is in the land of Israel or the world. This elect will still be in the flesh and will not have the light of the glory of God on them. That's why they weep and gnash teeth when they realize what could have been.

Isaiah 33:5

"The LORD is exalted; for he dwelleth on high: he hath filled Zion with judgment and righteousness."

The saints and a remnant of Israel will be in the heavenly Zion and will have the ability to judge properly and with righteous judgments.

That's the power of the Holy Spirit God's going to give them. No judgment will occur because of bad motives or anything like that. Righteous judgments will take place because the judges who are in Zion at that time will be filled with wisdom and not judge by the hearing of their ears or by the sight of their eyes. The saints and remnant will judge according to the will of the LORD. Isaiah 11:3 says, "And shall make him of quick understanding in the fear of the LORD: and he shall not judge after the sight of his eyes, neither reprove after the hearing of his ears." All judgments will be sure and true.

Isaiah 66:8

"Who hath heard such a thing? who hath seen such things? Shall the earth be made to bring forth in one day? or shall a nation be born at once? for as soon as Zion travailed, she brought forth her children."

That scripture's been used a lot talking about Israel becoming a nation in 1948, using the "Israel being born in a day" concept. Although Israel did become a nation rather rapidly, it doesn't appear that this scripture is talking about 1948. It's talking about when that rapture occurs and the raptured believers are filling this city of Zion—that is, the nation being born all at once. When Zion has travailed, she has brought forth her children. Did you know throughout scriptures you often see the concept about Israel being in travail? You see it over and over again. That word means labor pains. She's having labor pains, constant labor pains, waiting to bring forth what she can't seem to bring forth. It's like thousands of years of labor pains. Not very pleasant for you ladies who have experienced labor before. But that's what happened to poor Israel. They've been waiting to bring forth and just can't seem to bring forth. I understand that in 1948, Israel had just come out of the holocaust and some refer to that as travailing. I don't see that. The holocaust was not about giving birth. It was a horrible thing against many people, especially Israel, but it was not about giving birth.

I'm going to talk about something here that you may or may not agree with. All I can say is, search it out with your heart, think about it, and see if what I'm saying is true. Revelation 12 gives us a better understanding of the giving birth concept.

Revelation 12:1

"And there appeared a great wonder in heaven; a woman clothed with the sun, and the moon under her feet, and upon her head a crown of twelve stars."

This woman represents Israel. It comes from the dream Joseph had of his dad, his mom (sun and moon), and his brothers being represented by the 11 stars. Including Joseph that would be 12 stars (Genesis 37:9). That's how we know it's Israel. It has nothing to do with Mary. For those of you who might be taught that in Catholicism, it's about Israel.

Revelation 12:2

"And she being with child cried, travailing in birth, and pained to be delivered."

There's that concept again—travailing—and this is going on at the seventh trump, the last trump. First Corinthians 15:52 tells us that the rapture will occur, "In a moment, in the twinkling of an eye, at the last trump: for the trumpet shall sound, and the dead shall be raised incorruptible, and we shall be changed." This rapture will not occur until the last trump. It very well may be the last of the seven trumpets of Revelation. The last trump is blown in Revelation 11:15 and chapter 12 follows immediately.

Revelation 12:3-5

"And there appeared another wonder in heaven; and behold a great red dragon, having seven heads and ten horns, and seven crowns upon his heads. And his tail drew the third part of the stars of heaven, and did cast them to

the earth: and the dragon stood before the woman which was ready to be delivered, for to devour her child as soon as it was born. And she brought forth a man child, who was to rule all nations with a rod of iron: and her child was caught up unto God, and to his throne."

Who was this child? If you read all the commentaries, they'll tell you that it was Yeshua, but that doesn't make any sense. Why at the beginning of Revelation do you have the Alpha and Omega in His glory who died and rose again, beginning to talk to John, and all of a sudden by chapter 12 we're going back to talk about His birth? That doesn't make any sense! The woman here, which is Israel, flees into the wilderness. Israel did not flee into the wilderness after the birth of Yeshua.

Now you can speculate and say maybe it's about the two witnesses of Revelation or maybe this, maybe that... No, this is talking about the word "child" in here. It could mean also "children" or "son." Since the woman (singular) represents all of Israel, it is certainly plausible that the child singular could mean plural also. The concept here is that Israel has been prepared to give birth to a remnant that is going to be part of the heavenly city of Zion. She finally gives birth to this remnant and runs and flees into the wilderness. The beast chases her into the wilderness after the child is caught up to God. God protects Israel from the beast for three and a half years in the wilderness at that time.

So the beast turns its attention to those who have the testimony of Yeshua—those who were left behind in that rapture and were not overcomers. The beast is after them, and the left-behind believers and new believers must go through that furnace of fire for not being ready when the Lord comes as a thief in the night. What is being seen here in Revelation 12 is the birth of the sons of Zion out of Israel. They will rule the nations with a rod of iron, along with others who were raptured at the same time. This is a promise to those who overcome as stated in Revelation 2:27 to the church at Thyatira. Those who overcome will have power over the

244

nations and will rule them through Yeshua.

Obadiah 1:21

"And saviours shall come up on mount Zion to judge the mount of Esau; and the kingdom shall be the LORD's."

In Revelation 11:15 at the seventh trumpet, Yeshua receives His kingdom. He gets His kingdom authority just after the rapture. So the rapture of the saints and the rapture of that special remnant, the child of that woman, will take place, and believing Jews and gentiles will be the sons and daughters of Zion at that time. When the LORD has built up Zion, then He will appear in his glory (Psalm 102:16). The word "saviours" refers to those saved. These are the saints in Zion and they will judge the Mount of Esau which could be a reference to Edom or the entire Saudi peninsula. Also, it is possible this is a reference of Mount Zion versus Mount Esau. Those saved versus those not, those saved versus the world.

Isaiah 61:1-2

"The Spirit of the Lord God is upon me; because the LORD hath anointed me to preach good tidings unto the meek; he hath sent me to bind up the brokenhearted, to proclaim liberty to the captives, and the opening of the prison to them that are bound; To proclaim the acceptable year of the LORD, and the day of vengeance of our God; to comfort all that mourn."

This may sound familiar to some of you. This is what Yeshua declared when He came into the synagogue in Luke 4:18-19. Yeshua didn't quite quote all of it. He stopped at, "To proclaim the acceptable year of the LORD," then He closed the Torah and didn't say anything more until He said, "This day is fulfilled before your eyes now." Then they wanted to stone Him!

I thought it was very interesting that He left off "the day of the vengeance of our God." What He was doing here was talking about Himself, but He left off "the day of the vengeance of our God" because that's not what He came for the first time. The first time was to set the captives free from death and sin.

If you believe in Yeshua, you are free from death and sin. Even though this corruptible body will decay, it will be renewed in an incorruptible body. You will have victory over death. That's why the apostle Paul said, "O death, where is your sting" (1 Corinthians 15:55). He knew that death would not have hold of him, that even if his body was to go away, he would be resurrected in a new, incorruptible body. Thus, those who believe in the Messiah will be resurrected. This is what Yeshua was talking about. He's fulfilling what Isaiah 61:1 was talking about. In verse 2, "the acceptable year of the LORD" is the year the Messiah came—30 A.D. However, the day of the vengeance of our God is yet to occur, which is about the second coming of Yeshua when He will be ready for vengeance. Yeshua didn't come to execute vengeance on His first coming. That will be reserved for the second coming.

Corporately, Israel rejected Him because he didn't come and execute vengeance against the enemies of Israel, particularly Rome. So they said, "He cannot be the Messiah; He didn't execute vengeance against our enemies!" Well, they didn't understand. First, He came to give us victory in the spirit. The second time, He's going to come with physical victory against the enemies of Israel and eventually completely destroy death altogether.

Israel failed to see this because an imparted blindness from God came over them so that the gospel can go out to the gentiles. Did you not know that God deliberately blinded Israel so the gentiles can be saved (Romans 11)? If Israel would have accepted Him as King and as Lord, then He would have had to fulfill the promises He gave to Israel and gentiles would have been left out. But God's plan all along was to make sure Israel rejected Him so that He can reach the gentiles which are far more in numbers than Israel. Remember, the scriptures say that God so loved the world. He cares about Jews and Gentiles. However, a time is coming when the fullness of the gentiles will be complete, then His full attention will be upon Israel. We're really fast approaching that time when God will take the veil off of Israel and they will look unto the One whom they have pierced. As Isaiah says, He will comfort all who mourn when He establishes His kingdom.

Isaiah 61:3
"To appoint unto them that mourn in Zion, to give unto them beauty for ashes, the oil of joy for mourning, the garment of praise for the spirit of heaviness; that they might be called trees of righteousness, the planting of the LORD, that he might be glorified."

Following Isaiah 61:2 concerning the "day of vengeance of our God," we now have a promise concerning Zion and those who are living in Zion. This is the heavenly Zion or New Jerusalem and I believe it includes a certain Jerusalem remnant residing at the physical Zion on Earth who will be conducting the LORD's business for Israel and the nations that come to it. The inhabitants of both Zions will be appointed garments of praise and they're going to be lifted up. They will be trees of righteousness, the planting of the LORD.

This is the city that is promised during the millennial reign, the city of Zion. But it's not just a physical or heavenly city, it's the people who are in these cities. They'll be glorified, they'll have garments of praise. They'll shine. They'll be brilliant and so much so that the sun will be ashamed. Isaiah 24:23 says, "Then the moon shall be confounded, and the sun ashamed, when the LORD of hosts shall reign in mount Zion, and in Jerusalem, and before his ancients gloriously." It's speaking of the city of Zion and Jerusalem, and includes the saints and remnants of Israel. The saints are going to shine with a great shining, with great glory. Each believer will have a different intensity of that light based on the reward they receive from the Messiah. This is why saints must run the race, seek the incorruptible crown, seek the mark of the high calling, and overcome. There's a lot at stake here.

As I mentioned before in 1 Corinthians 3, to believe and have faith in God is the foundation of salvation. What do you build on that foundation? First Corinthians 3:12 says some will build upon this foundation gold and silver, precious stones, others will build upon it with wood, hay, and stubble, but all of us must come before the judgment seat of Messiah and He will judge our works with fire (1 Corinthians 3:13-15; 2 Corinthians 5:10). All our works that were of the quality of wood, hay, and stubble will be burnt up. If you've done wonderful things for the kingdom of God, that's the gold, silver, and precious stones and it remains. So, even if all your works are burned up, you're still saved as the scripture says. You'll still have that foundation. It just says you won't have a whole lot to show for it.

Now what do I mean by "works unto the kingdom"? We're talking about righteous works; we are not talking about dead works. These are things you do in obedience to God. It's loving one another, loving God, serving God, helping others. Even Yeshua said, "Anyone who gives a cup of cold water to one of these little ones in the name of a disciple shall no wise lose his reward" (Matthew 10:42). That's like a little piece of gold when you give a cup of water to someone who believes in Yeshua because they're thirsty. Those are the things we do to receive the righteous rewards God has for each and every one of us. When we do it for the kingdom, we do it out of love of God. Not dead works. Dead works is when you're out there trying to impress God by suffering through self-affliction or religious rituals. That won't do it. As I mentioned before, there are groups today that will whip themselves with whips and say, "LORD, did I not scar my back for you?" He's going to shake His head and say, "Why? Why did you do that?" Other people will bloody their knees going up steps to certain churches and think they're going to get some great reward. Not! Those are dead works.

God never asked you to do those things, but He did say to love one another and to love the LORD God with all your heart, all your soul, all your strength, and all your might. These are righteous works, things you do to show love. It doesn't necessarily mean something you do in a congregation. What are you doing out there? What are you doing with people? What are you saying to people? Surely, Daniel 12:3 tells us that, "And they that be wise shall shine as the brightness of the firmament; and they that turn many to righteousness as the stars for ever and ever." Those who lead many to righteousness' sake shall shine as the sun.

So you really want to get to the heart of God? Tell people about Him! Get them to repent; get them to follow God! Then, great is your reward because that really goes to God's heart. When you stand against persecution and against ridicule, and you still proclaim the name of the LORD and tell them that they need to repent, that they need to follow God, that God loves them, and He will be with them if they just turn their hearts to Him, that's huge to God! Great are the rewards for those who do such things. The rewards can be to shine like the luminaries as Daniel 12:1-3 says. All of us know how bright the sun is. Could you imagine shining brighter than that? That will be really something to shine brighter than the sun itself! The apostle Paul even said that there will be different glories of brightness in the resurrection as there are different glories of the stars (1 Corinthians 15:35-44). Which star will you shine like?

Isaiah 61:4
"And they shall build the old wastes, they shall raise up the former desolations, and they shall repair the waste cities, the desolations of many generations."

We know much of this is taking place in Israel right now from the desolation of many generations, but many of those cities in Israel are going to be destroyed again. Matter of fact, one of the vials poured out in the book of Revelation will cause a great earthquake. It will level every city in the world (Revelation 16:17-20). Now that's an earthquake! No one will escape this judgment on the Earth that are still here. Isaiah 13:13 says, "Therefore I will shake the heavens, and the Earth shall be removed out of her place, in the wrath of the LORD of hosts, and in the day of his fierce anger." There will not be a city left standing. But in this future promise of Isaiah, the returning remnant will begin to rebuild the cities.

Isaiah 61:5

"And strangers shall stand and feed your flocks, and the sons of the alien shall be your plowmen and your vinedressers."

Some of this promise is going on in Israel right now, but there's going to come a time when foreigners will come in the land freely and do the agricultural work. You don't see that today, but they're going to be glad to be able to do it because they want to be part of it when God begins to bless the land even greater than now. Who wouldn't want to be in Israel in those days seeing the great light rising out of the heavenly Zion and the glory of God? "I want to do something here! I want to plow the fields! I want to collect the fruit! I want to prepare the wheat and the barley and the oats! I want to do all these things!" That's what it says; strangers shall come and do these things.

Isaiah 61:6

"But ye shall be named the Priests of the LORD: men shall call you the Ministers of our God: ye shall eat the riches of the Gentiles, and in their glory shall ye boast yourselves."

The gentiles are those who are still alive on the Earth who didn't call upon the name of the LORD earlier. They're going to begin to bring their wealth into the land of Israel unto the redeemed Israel. The Israel that was led off into captivity and brought back is the redeemed Israel, along with the woman of Revelation 12. This is the woman who has been taken care of and protected by God and trained for three and a half years in the wilderness. They will be the leaders of physical Israel. They may even be the 144,000 of Revelation 7. However, the child of the woman is the remnant of the remnant of Israel that got raptured. As we read in Revelation 12, they will join with the saints who believe in that heavenly Zion. So the heavenly Zion will be comprised of Saints and a certain remnant of Israel. The physical Zion in Jerusalem will be comprised of another remnant of Israel.

In the book of Enoch 41:1, when speaking of the secrets of heavens, it says, "And there I saw the mansions of the elect and the mansions of the holy." The holy and the elect will dwell together. The elect is Israel, the holy are the saints, and they're going to dwell together in Zion. Enoch 50:1 tells us, "And in those days a change shall take place for the holy and elect." This is talking about the rapture. He also says that the whole world will see the rapture. Remember what Yeshua told his disciple Thomas, "Because you have seen me, you have believed, blessed are they that have not seen and yet have believed"

Enoch 50:2b-3 says, "And he will cause the others to witness this that they may repent and forgo the works of their hands. They shall have no honour through the name of the Lord of Spirits." There's no such thing as a secret rapture. The whole world will see the rapture take place. Enoch goes on to say that at that point, many will repent and turn to God when they see that, but they will have no honor. What does this mean? It means that you who believe by faith and not having seen some great miracle of God like the rapture will have great honor. The rewards of those that have not seen will have great honor. The rewards of those who believe because they saw is different from the rewards of those who believed by faith. That's what Enoch is talking about.

The tabernacle of Moses is an example of a believer's walk. One should look at the placement of all the tabernacle vessels and curtains to understand it is the gospel message. After coming through the door of the courtyard (Yeshua is the door), you come to the brazen altar which is the place of blood atonement. Appropriating this blood washes one's sins away. This represents Yeshua's sacrifice and atonement, the cross of Yeshua. Having passed this altar, one is now in the outer court. However, it takes washing at the brazen laver to get into the inner court which represents Zion where God dwells. We should desire to be in this inner court. That's where the presence of God is. That's where the Ark is. That's where the Menorah is, the table of showbread, the altar incense of gold. That's all in the inner court.

One cannot enter the inner court without washing at the brazen laver. If he failed to wash, and tries to enter the inner court, he would be struck dead as it was stated to the priests of Aaron in Exodus 30:20. The brazen laver was made of the polished brass mirrors of the Hebrew women. It represents humility, repentance, washing of the word, and filling of the Holy Spirit. Look at yourselves, see who you really are, and cleanse yourself. By that repentance, you now have a right to enter in the inner court. Anybody who appropriates just the brazen altar, the blood of the lamb of God, the Messiah, become outer court believers and will have salvation and eternal life. However, they cannot become inner court dwellers if they don't wash at the brazen laver.

Those who pass through the brazen altar symbolically, appropriates the blood of the lamb for the forgiveness of sin and they will be welcomed into the outer court for salvation and eternal life. However, they cannot pass on to the kingdom, which is the inner court, if they don't symbolically wash at the brazen laver. As stated in the Revelation letters to the seven churches, it is about overcoming that gets you in the inner court to rule with the Messiah. Keep in mind that your candlestick can be removed from the house of the LORD and your garments can be removed or stained and your crown can be given to another. Walk in the righteousness of the Messiah.

We should desire everything that God has for us. He says we need to wash, repent, and be filled with the Holy Spirit. That's what we have to do. That's why all your salvation scriptures never talk about anything like that. The salvation scriptures say to trust in the LORD, appropriate His blood, and call upon His name. But to be kingdom-minded, you must be born again. That's part of the repentance and filling of the Holy Spirit. That's why the brazen laver comes into play hugely in our day. Now, some people go from the brazen altar, the brazen laver, right into the inner court in a full sweep. Not only believed in the LORD, but repented and were filled with the Holy Spirit all in one sweep. Others spend their entire life in the outer court. They need to repent and stop doing the things they shouldn't be doing; putting God's name to shame in many ways with the things they do. Some find it later on; some find it many years after they received salvation. But that brazen laver is a huge, huge concept that we must understand.

Isaiah 61:7-8

"For your shame ye shall have double; and for confusion they shall rejoice in their portion: therefore in their land they shall possess the double: everlasting joy shall be unto them. For I the LORD love judgment, I hate robbery for burnt offering; and I will direct their work in truth, and I will make an everlasting covenant with them."

The word *confusion* actually means "for their shame, dishonor, insult." So for their shame, their dishonor, they will possess second rank (double) behind the inhabitants of the heavenly Zion but they still will rejoice in their portion. They will still be glad just to be part of God even if not the heavenly Zion. They will still be glad that they received salvation. However, they must still face the Great White Throne Judgment after the millennium. They will rejoice in their portion, God's promise for them. Because of their forefathers, God will allow them to have the land and Jerusalem. More than likely, their shame is their rejection of Yeshua and His followers. But for the saints of Zion and the raptured remnant of

253

Israel, they shall receive everlasting joy.

The LORD will lift up Israel. When the word "double" is used, it must be kept in mind the word can also mean second rank or second place. In comparison to Zion, Jerusalem will definitely be ranked second. That word *shame* in verse 7 could also mean the persecutions that Israel or any believer goes through. The people who reject you, people who make fun of you, family members who shun you. All of us have probably put up with some kind of shame in our lives for believing in the LORD.

That's why Yeshua said count persecution as all joy, for great is your reward. Every time you have a righteous persecution—now, why do I say righteous persecution? If you do bad and are persecuted, there's no reward. You start calling somebody bad names and he punches you in the face, there's no reward for that. Unfortunately, some people believe otherwise. They become really obnoxious and call people names, then they wonder why somebody just poked them in the nose. That's not works of righteousness, that's dead works. Being obedient to the things of God is righteous works. More than likely this isn't what God had in mind about shame. For true believers, receiving double doesn't even come close to what God has for you.

Isaiah 61:9
"And their seed shall be known among the Gentiles, and their offspring among the people: all that see them shall acknowledge them, that they are the seed which the LORD hath blessed."

Israel is coming back into the land from their captivity. So their children and their children and their children after that will be blessed, and the gentiles will acknowledge those children. God's promises are amazing! If you were a blessing to the LORD, He will shower blessings upon your seed. You should claim that. Do you have children who are struggling? Claim that blessing on them. Now, if you led lives that influenced your children negatively beforehand, then you have to clean up and pray. But you see the promise here that even the children of this redeemed group is going to be blessed and the gentiles recognize it as they come back into the land because of the promises God made to Israel at that time.

Isaiah 61:10

"I will greatly rejoice in the LORD, my soul shall be joyful in my God; for he hath clothed me with the garments of salvation, he hath covered me with the robe of righteousness, as a bridegroom decketh himself with ornaments, and as a bride adorneth herself with her jewels."

Again, we are talking about Zion here—both the physical and spiritual. When you are clothed with the garments of salvation, that is your new raiment that will shine. That's part of the reward system. It is the garment of salvation; those with these garments do not die. It's not talking about the physical remnant that's just came out of captivity. They will not have garments of salvation. It's for those who are part of both Zions who will have garments of salvation. Death still is in play here. During the millennial reign, the people who live on the Earth in the flesh will still die. The inhabitants of Zion, the saints in Zion, have passed from death to life eternal. Not even the lake of fire will harm them.

Those who live in Jerusalem also have a promise. They will live longer, but they will eventually die. Death is the last enemy to be destroyed and it is destroyed at the Great White Throne Judgment after the thousand-year millennial reign (Revelation 20:14). Prior to that, death will still continue. Even during the millennial reign people will die. So putting on the glorious garments of salvation pertain to the children of the heavenly Zion as a bridegroom that decks himself with ornaments and a bride that adorns herself with jewels. The heavenly Zion is the bride—the bride of Messiah, the bride of Christ, which is Zion, the New Jerusalem.

Isaiah 61:11

"For as the earth bringeth forth her bud, and as the garden causeth the things that are sown in it to spring forth; so the Lord God will cause righteousness and praise to spring forth before all the nations."

Isaiah 62:1

"For Zion's sake will I not hold my peace, and for Jerusalem's sake I will not rest, until the righteousness thereof go forth as brightness, and the salvation thereof as a lamp that burneth."

Righteousness will rule the day on the Earth. The presence of God and the heavenly city will cause all to believe and work as they should.

Isaiah 62:1 is talking about the heavenly Zion and Jerusalem. For Zion's sake, He will not rest until that city is in its fullness of glory and shining like a giant beam, to be seen beaming from the Earth. The glory of God and the saints and the elect that are in it, shining in that city. All of our glory is given to us by God. We can't shine ourselves, but He puts His light on us and we begin to shine with His glory. Here we have a commandment to give God no rest until Zion and Jerusalem are shining like a torch in all the Earth. Are we praying for that?

Isaiah 62:2

"And the Gentiles shall see thy righteousness, and all kings thy glory: and thou shalt be called by a new name, which the mouth of the LORD shall name."

This is about the heavenly Zion. How do the gentiles see your righteousness? They will see your light, your glorious garment of light that's going to shine, that brilliant light, and you shall be called by a new name. Do you know that two churches in Revelation 2:17 and Revelation 3:12 will be called by a new name that no man knows? These are those who overcome. They will be part of Zion and they will have a new name.

As I mentioned before, the intensity of your garment light depends on being an overcomer, being obedient to God, and being a worker of righteous works. Your salvation depends on faith and the grace of God but your position and rewards depend on your righteous works.

Isaiah 62:3
"Thou shalt also be a crown of glory in the hand of the LORD, and a royal diadem in the hand of thy God."

We learn in 2 Timothy 4:8 that those who overcome are given a righteous crown. We also learn in James 1:12 that those who overcome are given a crown of life; this is also mentioned in Revelation 2:10. First Peter 5:4 says you'll receive a crown of glory. Some believers will not get a crown at all for their poor walk with the Lord. If you do get a crown, what is it going to look like? What are you going to have on it? Will there be jewels on it? Will it be made out of gold? It all depends on your walk with God, but not everybody receives a crown. In the book of Revelation, the 24 elders are the only ones mentioned having crowns and they have thrones, too. Those who overcome shall sit on thrones with the Messiah and rule the nations with a rod of iron (Revelation 2:26-27). This is a great honor that God has for all believers who strive and work with Him and are obedient to Him. Yeshua says, "If you love me, keep my commandments" (John 14:15).

Those who say the law is gone are making a huge mistake. The law is not gone. In some aspects, there has been a manifestational change. For instance, sacrifices are on hold because there is no temple. Some laws apply only when you're in the land of Israel. But one thing's for certain, the moral and ethical laws have not changed. Even if you just say Yeshua fulfilled the ceremonial and sacrificial laws, that's a manifested change of those laws since they were shadow laws speaking of Him (Colossians 2:16-17). He would have fulfilled those particular laws. But saying He did away with the law is silliness, especially when you make certain deductions like, "Are we required to repent?" Yes, of course we are.

Repent of what? Sin. What's sin? Violation of law. Law is in effect. Yet the naysayers will agree that we must repent but they don't consider the law is valid. They don't know sometimes what they say.

Even Yeshua said in **Matthew 5:17-19**

"Think not that I am come to destroy the law (Torah), or the prophets: I am not come to destroy, but to fulfil. For verily I say unto you, till heaven and Earth pass, one jot or one tittle shall in no wise pass from the law, till all be fulfilled. Whosoever therefore shall break one of these least commandments, and teach men so, he shall be called the least in the kingdom of heaven: but whosoever shall do and teach them, the same shall be called great in the kingdom of heaven."

There you have it. Are you ready to be great or be the least in the kingdom of heaven?

Isaiah 62:4
"Thou shalt no more be termed Forsaken; neither shall thy land any more be termed Desolate: but thou shalt be called Hephzibah, and thy land Beulah: for the LORD delighteth in thee, and thy land shall be married."

Again, we're talking about the land here. So the captives of Israel that are coming back in the land, God will consider that He's married to them again and no longer will the land be desolate. It'll be called Beulah and means "Delight in the LORD."

Isaiah 62:5-6
"For as a young man marrieth a virgin, so shall thy sons marry thee: and as the bridegroom rejoiceth over the bride, so shall thy God rejoice over thee. I have set watchmen

upon thy walls, O Jerusalem, which shall never hold their peace day nor night: ye that make mention of the LORD, keep not silence."

The LORD will betroth Israel and Jerusalem again. In Hosea 2:19-20, the LORD says He will betroth His people again whom He apparently divorced due to idolatry like He did to Israel in Jeremiah 3:8. And now the LORD will cling to them as a bridegroom and rejoice over them.

Who are these watchmen? They are those who make mention of the LORD. Do you make mention of the LORD? It's talking about believers in Yeshua. It's talking about before the actual redemption of Israel takes place, before the heavenly Zion comes down from heaven and before Jerusalem becomes a holy city. If you are one of those who call upon the name of the LORD, you are actually commanded by God to not be silent until Jerusalem is holy again. You are told to give Him no rest until Jerusalem is a praise in all the Earth.

Isaiah 62:7

"And give him no rest, till he establish, and till he make Jerusalem a praise in the earth."

That's a commandment! You are to constantly say, "LORD, make Jerusalem a praise in the Earth!" Why are we so linked to this? Every believer in Messiah should feel a strong link to Israel. That's what draws us to pray for Israel. What is it that draws us to understand and support Israel? It's because we're part of the bigger picture of Zion—both the physical and heavenly! We're part of that city. Israel right now is unredeemed but a day is coming in which they will become redeemed. They're an unredeemed brother right now, but they will become a redeemed brother. So we have this tie to them, this love for them. That's why we say yes, we'll pray for the peace of Jerusalem. Yes, we'll pray for God to make Jerusalem a praise in the Earth. Not only because He told us to, because we're driven to. We have our heart in this that we must do these things because it's the spirit of God that pulls us toward these things.

Isaiah 62:8-9
"The LORD hath sworn by his right hand, and by the arm of his strength, Surely I will no more give thy corn to be meat for thine enemies; and the sons of the stranger shall not drink thy wine, for the which thou hast laboured: But they that have gathered it shall eat it, and praise the LORD; and they that have brought it together shall drink it in the courts of my holiness."

This is a big theme throughout the Bible where God tells Israel that because of their wickedness, "You plant and somebody else eats. You make wine, somebody else drinks. You make bread, somebody else eats it." This is part of that blessing and curse thing that we read in God's Word in Deuteronomy. If Israel doesn't walk in the holiness and righteousness of God, then somebody else is going to eat their fruit. This applies to everyone today, too. If we don't walk in the things of God and walk in the holiness of God, somebody else is going to eat our fruit. You wondering why you're always struggling financially, why your car breaks down, or why the washing machine quits working? Why these things happen to you all the time? You're probably not walking in the precepts of the LORD and somebody else is eating your fruit.

The same rule that applies to Israel applies to everyone today and those that call upon the name of the LORD. Those blessings and curses that Deuteronomy talks about—the law is not cursed, it's disobedience to the law that is cursed. Yeshua took that for us. He took the curse of the law so we won't be punished for violating the law in the life to come. But as long as you're alive, the blessings and curses apply in your life. So, when you don't walk according to the obedience of God, things happen to you. Someone else will eat your fruit. When man walks in obedience to God, then he sits under his own fig tree and vine as mentioned before.

Isaiah 62:10-12

"Go through, go through the gates; prepare ye the way of the people; cast up, cast up the highway; gather out the stones; lift up a standard for the people. Behold, the LORD hath proclaimed unto the end of the world, Say ye to the daughter of Zion, Behold, thy salvation cometh; behold, his reward is with him, and his work before him. And they shall call them, The holy people, The redeemed of the LORD: and thou shalt be called, Sought out, A city not forsaken."

I don't know about you, but I want to be part of this; I want to be part of Zion. I want to be called the "redeemed of the LORD." Who wouldn't? But how do you get redeemed? You call upon Him, but you also repent and be obedient. When I say "repent," that means to turn from your wicked ways and walk in holiness, according to God's holiness and not our own. It doesn't mean just saying "I'm sorry" and never changing. That's called worldly repentance. Godly repentance is necessary to help you change your life. Godly repentance will work a work in you. Godly repentance requires understanding you have sinned against God and man. It requires a change in your life and a renewed mind, and it requires God to help make that change. We have to seek God daily. If you think you're going to repent once a year, that's not good enough; it has to be daily. Have the LORD on your mind always.

We make mistakes, we know we make mistakes, but we should be a work in progress striving for Zion at all times—working out our salvation as Paul said. He didn't say work *for* salvation, but work *out* our salvation (Philippians 2:12). The only way to get salvation is by the grace and mercy of God. That's the blood atonement at the brazen altar. Once we are saved, we have to work out our salvation step by step, precept upon precept, and we keep moving forward until we shine like God wants us to shine. Even a righteous man falls seven times but he gets back up, dusts

261

himself off, and calls on the LORD until he doesn't fall anymore. The danger is when you don't get back up. Back to Isaiah 62:10, notice that the LORD will create a highway and gather out the stones for a safe easy journey for the captivity to come back to Israel. This will occur after the sign (standard) of the Son of Man appears and the Lord will lead them.

Isaiah 59:20
"And the Redeemer shall come to Zion, and unto them that turn from transgression in Jacob, saith the LORD."

So here you have a definition of two different groups. The Redeemer shall come to Zion, the place of the saints. But He'll also come unto those that turn from transgressions in Jacob. The Redeemer will also appear to the rest of Israel that isn't part of the heavenly Zion and cause them to turn from their sins in repentance.

Isaiah 59:21
"As for me, this is my covenant with them, saith the LORD; My spirit that is upon thee, and my words which I have put in thy mouth, shall not depart out of thy mouth, nor out of the mouth of thy seed, nor out of the mouth of thy seed's seed, saith the LORD, from henceforth and for ever."

Of course, this is again speaking of the children of Jacob. They're the ones who will be having children in the millennial reign, and the rest of the world, too, but, Jacob in particular. The world has to be repopulated. There are many thoughts of how many people will still be alive on Earth after the tribulation. Some people suggest that as much as three-quarters of the world's population will die. So if there are seven billion people in the world now, can you imagine how many billions of people are going to die in the Tribulation? But then they which are alive when Yeshua comes back shall all know the LORD, and their seed after them and their seed after them for a thousand years that repopulate the world. There will be no more sickness and no more death in the land of Israel and Jerusalem until one is very old. That promise is not mentioned for the world. It may occur but it is a promise for Israel. Albeit, the world is going to repopulate at a fast rate as there will be no wars. The world's population is growing fast even today but it is constantly slowed down by plagues, diseases, and wars. Just think when millions of people were killed in just one war! Over 30 million died in World War II alone. That won't be taking place in the millennial reign, so the world will be repopulated rather fast during that time.

The Spirit of God will be given to Israel as seen in Joel 2. They will dream dreams and have visions. The Spirit of God will direct them and lead them. This is what Jeremiah 31:31 is talking about: "Behold the days come, saith the LORD, that I will make a new covenant with the house of Israel, and with the house of Judah." And in verse 33 Jeremiah says, "I will put my law in their inward parts and write it in their hearts, and will be their God, and they shall be my people."

Isaiah 60:1
"Arise, shine; for thy light is come, and the glory of the LORD is risen upon thee."

Risen upon who? The heavenly Zion! The New Jerusalem! This is a rapture scripture and is to be taken literally. He will place His light on the saints and elect. They will shine and the glory of the LORD will beam out of them. So when Yeshua said, "You are the light of the world," He meant it literally. How many times do we just take those kind of scriptures and say, "Okay, I'm a light. That's nice. Light on; light off. I think today I'll let my light shine. Today, I think I'll turn it off." No! When you are given the glory of the LORD, arise and shine! The rapture has just occurred. You're taking on your new body, you're going to be bright and magnificent! This light of God will shine continuously while we are in the heavenly Zion, we may have the ability to tone it down or shut off our light when we leave Zion to minister. Even Yeshua showed his light and turned it off again on the mount of transfiguration before Peter, James and John. Because you're going to be in resurrected bodies, you don't need to sleep. Your light will shine all the time in Zion!

This is why it's important to understand the difference between the heavenly Zion and the physical Zion at Jerusalem. In Jerusalem, people will still live in their normal bodies. They have honor and God's with them; He's taking care of them, but it's not the heavenly Zion. This brilliant light of God on the saints is so brilliant that anybody in the flesh would probably perish just standing in front of that brilliance. The light of the heavenly Zion will put the sun to shame, as scripture says in Isaiah 24:23. Yet Isaiah 30:26 says the sun in the Zion at Jerusalem will be seven times brighter. So it appears that the light from the heavenly Zion will also light the physical Zion at Jerusalem. God will protect those in Zion at Jerusalem from the brilliant light.

There are probably other ways to look at this but it is not easy to understand the two Zions and how the inhabitants in the physical Zion at Jerusalem will handle the light from the heavenly Zion. Remember, however, that the two are connected somehow. The rest of the world couldn't handle the brilliance of the light. As far as the sun being seven times brighter, I think it just means that the light over that area is seven times brighter than the sun. I don't believe it means the sun is actually seven times brighter. A normal flesh could not survive that, only those in their resurrected bodies. The heavenly Zion is the home of the raptured saints consisting of Jews and gentiles and the light from this Zion will cast its light upon the Zion at Jerusalem.

This is a glorious time! That's why eyes have not seen nor ears heard the things God has for those who love Him. Can you imagine that? When you're raptured and God says here's your new garment, whoa, man! Where are the sunglasses?! He's going to give you a garment of light.

A side note to consider here. During the millennium in Ezekiel 44:15-19, the prophet speaks of the priests ministering before the Lord God in their holy garments in the inner court. Yet when these same priests go to the outer court to minister to the people, they must remove their holy garments and put them on again when they return to the inner court. Is it possible that this is talking about the saints? While they are ministering to the Lord God, they have on their glorious garments and then they remove their light before ministering in the outer court before the people.

If this is true, then we will have the ability to turn our glory on and off. A precedent was set by Yeshua when He went with Peter, James, and John to the Mount of Transfiguration. On the mountain Yeshua showed His glory and the Father spoke. Afterwards Yeshua transfigured back into His earthly body. By the way, it appears that the inner court of heaven will be the heavenly Zion while the outer court could be the physical Jerusalem.

Isaiah 60:2
"For, behold, the darkness shall cover the earth, and gross darkness the people: but the LORD shall arise upon thee, and his glory shall be seen upon thee."

For the rest of the world outside of Jerusalem, it says darkness shall cover the Earth and gross darkness the people, but the LORD shall rise upon you and His glory shall be seen upon you. What does that mean? We talked about a believer getting their garments of praise and God's light will be placed on them. When one shines like the luminaries as Daniel 12:3 talks about, the rest of the world in comparison shall be like a gross darkness? It's not talking about sin—which would be the typical definition of something like that. He's talking about the millennial reign here, the period where the light is coming out of Zion with a great brightness. In comparison to Zion; the rest of the world is in darkness. The sun will still be shining. The rest of the world still has to plant their crops, the rest of the world still has to survive and eat. You can't do that without the sun. But in comparison, the brightness that is out of the heavenly Zion compared to those outside the walls of Jerusalem will be considered gross darkness. When the LORD appeared at Mount Sinai, a thick darkness surrounded the mountain. Moses entered the darkness while the people backed away. Could it be that the gloriousness of our God can be viewed only by those whom God chooses and this darkness is there to protect everyone else from the brilliance of Zion's light.

I would say that this is probably in reference to what other scriptures say when outer darkness is mentioned. Outer darkness is not hell, but it is further away from the light of the glory of God in Zion and is a protective barrier to those in the flesh. Look at the examples in the scriptures of those cast into outer darkness; the man who didn't have on a wedding garment and tried to come to the wedding feast. When the King asked him, "Where is your wedding garment?", all he could do was stand there and stutter. The King said, "Bind him and cast him into outer darkness" (Matthew 22:13). This man wasn't thrown into hell. If he was going to hell, he'd have already been there, and he's surely not coming out of hell to attend a wedding feast of the LORD. He probably got in somehow from outside of the walls of Zion or Jerusalem; he got in, and he was cast back out. That's outer darkness, being away from the light of the LORD. The outer darkness is really back into the world. And yes, there will be weeping and gnashing of teeth there. Only in Zion are there no tears. It is not a promise for the world during the millennium.

The servant with the one talent is another example. He believed, he was a servant, but he was fearful of the Lord so he buried his talent instead of using it like he was supposed to (Matthew 25:14-30). So when the Lord came back to collect his due, the unprofitable servant said, "Here, Lord, I knew you were a hard man so here's your one talent back." What did the Lord do? He said, "You wicked servant! Take the one talent from him and give it to the one who has ten who invested properly and cast this one into outer darkness where there is weeping and gnashing of teeth." The wicked servant wasn't thrown into hell; he was removed from Zion and perhaps even Jerusalem. He was cast outside the light of Zion where he would not enjoy the light of the LORD and have his own glory, but would be shameful to the rest of the world. He did not lose his salvation but he lost honor.

In comparison to the light of Zion, the rest of the world is outer darkness. Nine out of ten commentaries will tell you that outer darkness is hell because they don't know what to do with it, they don't understand, they have no concept. So they just say it's hell. The problem with saying it's hell is then—well, gee, if that one guy ended up in hell for burying his talent, that flies in the place of the promises of God for salvation. Trusting in the LORD, calling on the name of the LORD, trusting in His blood, by no works, by the grace and mercy of God, and you're saying, "I need to use this talent to keep out of Hell"?, that defies what the Word of God tells us, but it doesn't defy the concept of where your dwelling place may be—Zion, Jerusalem, or outside the walls. That's probably what outer darkness is referring to.

This should be a sobering thought for everybody. Again, God is not mocked. We are saved by the grace of God, but where we shall dwell and what we should look like and our rewards have everything to do with our righteous works and obedience to God. This is something that most of the Bible teachers today don't teach. They're going to be ashamed. You have to be an overcomer. You have to overcome the world. You have to be an overcomer to be part of the kingdom of God. Overcomers will dwell with God at His throne and have His name marked on them, along with the name of the city, and the name of the Messiah. All those promises require every believer to be an overcomer. As I would say, they're the ultimate tattoos. Maybe these marks are your ticket to get into the holy city.

Isaiah 60:4-5
"Lift up thine eyes round about, and see: all they gather themselves together, they come to thee: thy sons shall come from far, and thy daughters shall be nursed at thy side. Then thou shalt see, and flow together, and thine heart shall fear, and be enlarged; because the abundance of the sea shall be converted unto thee, the forces of the Gentiles shall come unto thee."

Once the Messiah comes and begins to reign out of Zion and His saints are there with Him, the whole world will begin to migrate toward Israel and Jerusalem. They will become believers, they'll begin to understand, their eyes will be opened. Multitudes and multitudes will all come to know the LORD. Talk about revival! A huge revival! They will all come to the light that is beaming out of Zion. It can probably be seen anywhere around the world. They all just came through a horrible tribulation and they hear that the King of kings and the Lord of lords is dwelling out of Zion and Jerusalem, so they are going to want to come and check it out. It says everyone's heart will be enlarged and be believers. Keep in mind, sin is not yet gone. Remember at the end of the millennium, Satan gathers the nations again to make war on Jerusalem.

The scripture also says during that time, all shall know the LORD, and His spirit will be poured out upon all flesh (Jeremiah 31:34; Joel 2). So it isn't going to be an instantaneous thing. It may take awhile, but as the nations come up toward Jerusalem to see this thing that's happening, many begin to believe on the LORD and be converted. Eventually, the whole world will know the LORD. What a great revival that will be! The forces of the gentiles is speaking of the gentiles' wealth. They will bring their wealth to Jerusalem to honor God and His Messiah.

Isaiah 60:6-7
"The multitude of camels shall cover thee, the dromedaries of Midian and Ephah; all they from Sheba shall come: they shall bring gold and incense; and they shall shew forth the praises of the LORD. All the flocks of Kedar shall be gathered together unto thee, the rams of Nebaioth shall minister unto thee: they shall come up with acceptance on mine altar, and I will glorify the house of my glory."

These names just mentioned are all the Arabian countries from Edom all the way down. They will bring their camels with riches. That's why the scripture says Israel and Jerusalem shall receive the forces or riches of the gentiles. Jerusalem shall receive the riches of the wicked, and the righteous will inherit the wealth of the wicked. When Zion is in her glory and the LORD is ruling out of Jerusalem, all the nations will begin to bring their wealth and their glory into Jerusalem! The gentiles will bring everything they have to honor God and will be coming into Jerusalem at that time.

Isaiah 60:8
"Who are these that fly as a cloud, and as the doves to their windows?"

When Isaiah saw this vision, he asks, "Who are these that fly in and out of these windows?" Who or what do you think he's talking about? It's the saints who dwell in the heavenly Zion. They have a mansion in the heavenly Zion as promised by Yeshua! They are traveling in and out of the windows! Isaiah doesn't understand how the whole saint/Zion thing is working, but he sees people flying in and out of the windows like doves. So right out of nowhere, he asks, "Who are these people who fly out of their windows?" That is not anybody in the flesh and blood, that is not those who come back into the land out of captivity who are farming the land. These are the redeemed of God, Zion!

Those in the heavenly Zion or New Jerusalem have the ability to fly. Did you not know that? You can fly! It said we don't know yet how we shall appear, but we know we shall be like the Lord (1 John 3:2). What did the Lord do after He was resurrected? He just kind of came and went and appeared as He wanted to, didn't He? He could walk through walls if He wanted to and He could eat if He wanted to. The saints are going to be able to do those things also. God will give them that kind of ability with their resurrected bodies. How wonderful and magnificent it's going to be! The saints will still have some physical attributes, yet they're going to have many spiritual attributes. The angels always wanted to be like men and men always wanted to be like angels, but the saints will have the best of both worlds. Isn't that awesome? Saints are going to fly out of their windows! No need to push a button on the elevator. They will fly! So when we sing that song, "I'll Fly Away," it's probably talking more about the rapture, but it can apply to this also. The saints will fly like doves out of the window!

Isaiah 60:10

"And the sons of strangers shall build up thy walls, and their kings shall minister unto thee: for in my wrath I smote thee, but in my favour have I had mercy on thee."

It says God punished Israel and He's going to do it again. Whatever happens to Israel, He does to the nations, too. Don't ever be high-minded and think, "Well, Israel deserved it!" Where Israel goes, so goes the rest of the nations. If God is going to punish Israel, He will punish the nations, too. Every nation that God rose up against Israel in the past were also punished and some completely destroyed. What happened to those nations? They're gone. What happened to Israel? They're still around. So don't ever forget that. Even a greater judgment comes upon those nations. In this scripture, the nations and kings will provide Israel help in every area. These sons of strangers will provide help in building walls and will minister to them. It will be their honor to do so.

Isaiah 60:11-12

"Therefore thy gates shall be open continually; they shall not be shut day nor night; that men may bring unto thee the forces of the Gentiles, and that their kings may be brought. For the nation and kingdom that will not serve thee shall perish; yea, those nations shall be utterly wasted."

During the millennial reign, anybody that does not serve Israel will perish. They will be utterly wasted. The wealth of the Gentiles will be brought unto Israel and Jerusalem. Even in the heavenly Zion where the holy ones and the elect dwell together, the world will pay homage.

Although the world may enter the gates of the physical Jerusalem, they may not be allowed in the New Jerusalem or heavenly Zion. In God's eyes, the saints are also part of Israel, whether Jew or Gentile. The saints are part of the olive tree whether natural or grafted in as stated in Romans 11:14-21.

Whatever promises are given to Israel also apply to those who believe in Yeshua. If God punished Israel for their disobedience, He will also punish the saints for their disobedience. One cannot say, like many used to say years ago, "All the churches have the blessings today and not the curses." Well, it's true that Yeshua took our curse. When we go into the next life, He took that curse, but while we're alive on this Earth at that time, those curses can fall on us also. Never forget that.

Isaiah 60:13-14
"The glory of Lebanon shall come unto thee, the fir tree, the pine tree, and the box together, to beautify the place of my sanctuary; and I will make the place of my feet glorious. The sons also of them that afflicted thee shall come bending unto thee; and all they that despised thee shall bow themselves down at the soles of thy feet; and they shall call thee; The city of the LORD, The Zion of the Holy One of Israel."

Not only will those who afflicted Israel come bowing at their feet, but those who afflict the saints shall also come bowing to them. That's why the LORD says if you are persecuted, count it all as joy and pray for those who persecute you. What did He tell the disciples when they said, "Lord, call fire down from the sky and burn him up!" (Luke 9:54)? He said, "No, that's not what I came for." He came to redeem, not to destroy. So when you're being persecuted, pray, because there's going to come a time when those persecutors will bow down before you as a saint or dweller of Israel. Those that afflicted believers or Israel will bow before them. The world will bow—not in worship but out of honor and perhaps fear.

Several times in the Bible when an angel appeared before somebody, that person fell on their face. What did the angel always say? "Get up! Don't bow before me!" Perhaps the saints and redeemed Israel may be saying things like that. But for the saints, when the world sees them in their glory, they're going to probably fall on their face immediately. They may be terrified of the saints! Can you imagine that? But the grace of God will come out of you. The saints will probably tell them the same thing: "Get up, don't bow before me." This, of course, is assuming that the world can see the glory of the saints face-to-face. It may also be that the gentiles that come, bow down to the holy city of Zion which is the habitation of the saints.

Isaiah 60:15-17

"Whereas thou has been forsaken and hated, so that no man went through thee, I will make thee an eternal excellency, a joy of many generations. Thou shalt also suck the milk of the Gentiles, and shalt suck the breast of kings: and thou shalt know that I the LORD am thy Saviour and thy Redeemer, the mighty One of Jacob. For brass I will bring gold, and for iron I will bring silver, and for wood brass, and for stones iron: I will also make thy officers peace, and thine exactors righteousness."

All things before that caused rejection will now reverse. The earthly Zion, Jerusalem, and land of Israel will now partake of the gentiles when Messiah rules. The redeemed will now prosper. Even the officers and exactors (taskmasters) will rule, and judge with wisdom and righteousness. One of the primary duties of the saints is to judge the nations, including Israel. Saints will also start off with judging the bad angels (1 Corinthians 6:3), and judging the enemies of Israel. Afterwards, the saints will be there as a judge for all the people of the world and Israel that will come looking for a judgment. The LORD will make it possible for His redeemed and the saints to judge properly. His spirit will be so strong in them that they will be able to do it.

Isaiah 60:18-22

"Violence shall no more be heard in thy land, wasting nor destruction within thy borders; but thou shalt call thy walls Salvation, and thy gates Praise. The sun shall be no more thy light by day; neither for brightness shall the moon give light unto thee: but the LORD shall be unto thee an everlasting light, and thy God thy glory. Thy sun shall no more go down; neither shall thy moon withdraw itself: for the LORD shall be thine everlasting light, and the days of thy mourning shall be ended. Thy people also shall be all righteous: they shall inherit the land for ever, the branch of my planting, the work of my hands, that I may be glorified. A little one shall become a thousand, and a small one a strong nation: I the LORD will hasten it in his time."

There will be no more wars in the land or borders of Israel and physical Zion. Swords will be beaten into plowshares. The walls of salvation and gates of praise seem more about the heavenly Zion but could apply to both Zions since they will be linked. It is the light of the heavenly Zion that shames the sun. The saints there will shine in glorious garments of light given to them by God from His everlasting light. Yeshua said He is the light of the world and also said that those who follow Him are also the light of the world. So if the saints are the light of the world, then those who believe in Him should shine for all to see. We need to allow Him to work in our lives so we shine with the glory of God even now.

He's going to make the saints judges and rulers as well as kings and priests. This glory that God has for those who believe is just one example of what Paul was talking about when he said eyes have not seen nor ears heard of the things God has for those that love him (1 Corinthians 2:9). Every believer should walk in God's glory even today—not with a prideful heart, not with a prideful mind, but with humble hearts, knowing that you didn't accomplish this. The LORD did. You cannot lift yourself up, but let the Lord lift you up. Great rewards will come upon those who trust in Him.

Do we strive for those rewards? Yes, because Yeshua said so! Don't create a false humility. *Oh, I don't want any rewards, I'm just happy the way I am. Whatever the Lord wants to give me, I'm just happy with that!* No, it pleases the Lord that you are striving and running and being obedient to Him and desiring His promises! Strive for the things God wants to give you. It's in His heart to give it to you; He wants to give it to you. Would you tell the Lord, *No, Lord, don't give me that! Oh Lord I'm a humble servant. Don't give me those things! Oh Lord, just let me have salvation, that's all I want, Lord.* The Lord's going to look at you like, "What?!" Not by our works, not by our pride, but by the things that he has promised us that we hold onto those things. When you look into that brazen laver, you do it with all humility, with the washing of the word, with the washing of the spirit, and repentance—all those things that are required to get into the inner court are important. Anything with pride will not be allowed into the inner court. You cannot allow your pride to be lifted up.

Revelation 20:4
"And I saw thrones, and they sat upon them, and judgment was given unto them: and I saw the souls of them that were beheaded for the witness of Jesus, and for the word of God, and which had not worshipped the beast, neither his image, neither had received his mark upon their foreheads, or in their hands; and they lived and reigned with Christ a thousand years. But the rest of the dead lived not again until the thousand years were finished. This is the first resurrection."

This is where they get the concept of the millennial reign, which means a thousand. Once Yeshua sets up His kingdom in both Zions and Jerusalem and on the whole world, He's going to rule for a thousand years with people living and dying and being born on the Earth, except for those in the first resurrection. The first resurrection is a series of raptures of the 24 elders (Revelation 5:9-10), martyrs (Revelation 6:9-11), and the multitudes (Revelation 7:13-15). These raptured saints will actually rule and reign with the Messiah out of Zion and out of Jerusalem. The 144,000 of Revelation 7 is a different group of the 12 tribes of Israel who are in the flesh and they will rule out of the physical Zion. They may also be the "woman" of Revelation 12. Both groups will have the Father's name written on their foreheads. 144,000 is only a symbolic number indicating the government of God. First Corinthians 15:23 speaks of every man in his own order when talking about the rapture. There will be more than one.

Many times believers talk about the scriptures pertaining to Israel and how we love Israel, but sometimes as a believer, you may look and say, *Well, where are we as believers in all of this?* You are Zion the New Jerusalem! Out of Zion and in Jerusalem, the LORD will reign. His throne will be in the physical Zion temple. However, He and the lamb are the temple thereof in the heavenly Zion, and we will rule with him as scriptures say.

Quite often in the Bible, you'll read the term "Zion." The LORD's talking about Zion *and* Jerusalem; they're two separate things. He may mix "Zion" in with the term "Jerusalem" so you have to look at the context of His words to understand what He is talking about at that time. Is it the New Jerusalem which is the heavenly Zion or the Temple Mount in Jerusalem which is the physical Zion? In Jerusalem, people will be born, live, and die, but with great promises that will take place during the thousand-year reign. But not in the heavenly holy city of Zion! That Zion is eternal. It's the city made by the hands of God and not made by the hands of man that Abraham was looking for. That's why when you believe in Yeshua and are born again for the kingdom of God, once you pass from this body, you will not just have eternal life, you will dwell in the holy city of Zion on the tops of the mountains above the physical city of Jerusalem. This New Jerusalem is the kingdom of God that is full of saints which are kings and priests.

Earlier scriptures of Zion mention several aspects of the city. Some say it's the city of David; it's the place where the temple is; it's where God dwells, but when the prophetic scriptures speak about Zion, it is where the temple of God is! That's where the light will shine, and the people who dwell there will have no need of the sun. It can be difficult to differentiate the holy city of Zion from the physical city of Zion, and Jerusalem. Sometimes the concepts are intermixed. When you say "Jerusalem," it could mean Zion or the city of Jerusalem or both, but the holy city of Zion in particular can be the New Jerusalem, or the heavenly Zion, or in particular the inhabitants of this holy city.

That's why Isaiah 52:1 says, "Awake, awake; put on thy strength, O Zion; put on your beautiful garments." That's a rapture scripture. What garments? The garments that God has promised to those who are His, who are walking in righteousness, who have overcome. He will give you dazzling white garments, beautiful garments that you will put on, and you will be glorious! How glorious depends on how you served in the kingdom of God and obeyed Him. Just like Daniel 12 says, some will shine like the luminaries, like the sun, and others will be more shameful to look at. In other words, for example one could compared a million-watt lightbulb to a ten-watt lightbulb. The ten-watt bulb is shameful when compared to the million-watt bulb but everyone will be happy and will rejoice together because God is the true judge. The believers together are going to join with the glory of God in Zion and the whole place is going to be lit up. All those millennial promises that have to do with Zion and Jerusalem will be fulfilled.

A lot of people (Bible scholars, Bible teachers, pastors, and teachers) think all these things they have read about in Isaiah of the millennial promises pertain to the whole world. No, they pertain to Israel,

Jerusalem, and Zion. The nations of the world will flood into the land, the earthly Zion, and Jerusalem to see these things taking place. The world will not be allowed in the heavenly Zion or New Jerusalem.

In case you missed something, I am saying that the New Jerusalem (heavenly Zion) will be here during the millennial reign of the Messiah and beyond. The last two chapters of Revelation are about the millennial period and not afterwards. The promises mentioned in those chapters can be found in Isaiah's words about the millennium.

Revelation 21:1
"And I saw a new heaven and a new earth: for the first heaven and the first earth were passed away; and there was no more sea."

The following scripture talks about the heaven and Earth passing away and it comes from Isaiah 65:17.

Isaiah 65:17
"For, behold, I create new heavens and a new earth: and the former shall not be remembered, nor come into mind."

We just read that in Revelation 21:1 God's going to create a new heaven and a new Earth, and here in Isaiah 65:17 and Isaiah 66:22 we see it again. After Isaiah speaks of the new heaven and earth, he goes on to say that men will come before the LORD to worship on the new moon and the Sabbath and will pass by the judgment place of the wicked when they come to worship. Are they referring to the same event, or are there two different events? Now, most scholars will tell you they're two different events, and that's the way I've always felt in the past. But, the more I study of the promises of the millennial, particularly the things that Isaiah has to say, almost all those scriptures in Revelation 21 are mentioned in Isaiah. So I began to think, *Maybe we're not seeing the whole picture here.*

I discovered the concept about the last two chapters of Revelation being part of the millennium when I was teaching on the book of Isaiah followed by the book of Revelation. I want you to see Revelation and Isaiah in a deeper way and understand that the holy city of Zion will be here during the Messiah's reign. It may be something different than you learned in the past and you may not agree with it. Well, praise God that's okay. This has nothing to do with your salvation or position in the kingdom to be able to understand these things. Remember the puzzle concept: make sure the piece fits.

People always assumed that Revelation 21 and 22 must flow in chronologically after Revelation 20 which has the Great White Throne Judgment. Revelation does not work that way in all places. For instance, in Revelation 9 the beast is mentioned, but he's not even described until Revelation 13. So it does eventually move in a forward position, but you have to understand Revelation does this kind of back-and-forth stuff. It's like the stock market—up and down, up and down—but overall hopefully it's moving forward. What I'm suggesting to you in your studies is to take a close look here. It's very possible that chapter 21 is still talking about the millennial reign. That being the case, the new heaven and Earth will begin at the beginning of the thousand-year rule of the Messiah and not after the Great White Throne Judgment.

What does it mean by New Heaven and New Earth and no more sea in Revelation 21:1? More than likely the New Heaven is talking about the heavenly Zion hovering just above the mountains. The New Earth is most likely talking about the land of Israel. The physical millennium temple that Ezekiel describes is bigger than Herod's temple and will require some land changes. Perhaps the "New Earth" concept has to do with the scriptures about mountains being made low and valleys being raised (Isaiah 40:4) as well as other scriptures. Remember that the word for earth is eretz which can also mean the land of Israel. Both Isaiah 65:17 and 66:22 talk about new heaven and earth and yet speak of people coming to worship the LORD at Jerusalem on the new moon and Sabbath days. This doesn't seem to indicate a complete new world and heaven. It is most likely pertaining to the land of Israel. What does it mean in Revelation 21:1 about there will be no more sea? More than likely this is about the Dead Sea. There is a good chance that when water flows from the throne of God in Jerusalem to the Dead Sea that it will be healed and have fish. Perhaps the Dead Sea will fill to the ocean and no longer be a separate sea but I doubt it. Basically, we really don't understand the term "no more sea."

Isaiah Chapter 65 and 66 have many descriptions of what the millennial period will be like. Isaiah 65:17 speaks of new heavens and earth. Yet afterwards in verse 20, it speaks of people being born and dying at an old age after the New Heaven and Earth. Yet, in Revelation 20:14, death is destroyed after the Great White Throne Judgment of Revelation 20:11-12. So it stands to reason that death can happen during the New Heaven and Earth, which means the New Heaven and Earth will occur in the millennium period. As mentioned, Isaiah tells us that there will be death during the New Heaven and Earth concept. So it can be concluded to understand that Revelation 21 and 22 are descriptions of the millennial reign and not afterwards. New Heaven and Earth in Isaiah and Revelation 21 are the same. Another thought is to consider Revelation 22:15. It says when speaking of the New Jerusalem, that "dogs, sorcerers, whoremongers, murderers, idolaters, and liars are without," that is outside of the heavenly Jerusalem and cannot enter the gates. If one considers that this all happens after the great white throne judgment, and all judgments are over and sin along with death and hell are destroyed at the Great White Throne Judgment of Revelation 20:11-15, why are there still wicked outside the city of the new Jerusalem? The New Heaven and Earth concept is all about the millennial period with the new Jerusalem and its beaming light and the land of Israel where the land becomes a plain and mountains are brought low. The wild beasts of the land become peaceful and the land produces abundant fruit for all. It is not about the whole earth. It is possible that there may be some cosmos changes after the tribulation and when the heavenly Zion comes down. We will have to wait and see. We also must remember that God said the earth will always remain.

Isaiah 65:18
"But be ye glad and rejoice for ever in that which I create: for, behold, I create Jerusalem a rejoicing, and her people a joy."

This is a reference to both Jerusalems, heavenly and physically.

Isaiah 65:19
"And I will rejoice in Jerusalem, and joy in my people: and the voice of weeping shall be no more heard in her, nor the voice of crying."

We see here in verses 18 and 19 that the LORD is going to create Jerusalem a rejoicing. The LORD appears to be speaking of both Jerusalems. One is about how he creates the heavenly Zion and the other is about how he rejoices over the physical Zion. Can this be a reference of the new heaven and new earth? Do you not know that He has great joy in you? So when you beat yourself up, He doesn't do that; you do that. He rejoices over you constantly. He desires to hold you! He desires to dance with you! He desires to run with you if you invite Him. He's going to rejoice in you because He died for you. He made you righteous, He made you clean by His blood. So this voice of weeping is not going to be heard in Jerusalem or Zion. There will be no weeping there.

The promise of no tears is very prevalent in the scriptures in this restoration.

"The redeemed of the LORD shall return, and come with singing unto Zion; and everlasting joy shall be upon their head: they shall obtain gladness and joy; and sorrow and mourning shall flee away."
        - Isaiah 51:11

"...and the Lord God will wipe away tears from off all faces."
   - Isaiah 25:8

"And the ransomed of the LORD shall return, and come to Zion with songs and everlasting joy upon their heads: they shall obtain joy and gladness, and sorrow and sighing shall flee away."
   - Isaiah 35:10

"They shall hunger no more, neither thirst any more; neither shall the sun light on them, nor any heat. For the Lamb which is in the midst of the throne shall feed them and shall lead them unto living fountains of waters: and God shall wipe away all tears from their eyes."
   - Revelation 7:16-17

"And God shall wipe away all tears from their eyes; and there shall be no more death, neither sorrow, nor crying, neither shall there be any more pain: for the former things are passed away."
   - Revelation 21:4

This is talking about the new Jerusalem which will be synonymous with the holy city of Zion. In Zion, there will be no death and there will be no tears. When you read scriptures about gnashing and wailing and all kinds of stuff because people didn't do what they were supposed to do, they're not going to be in Zion. It does not mean they will lose their salvation, but they may find themselves outside the city walls and there may well be, in fact, wailing and gnashing of teeth. Like the parable of the ten virgins: the five foolish women finally got their oil—or maybe they didn't— but they came back and found the doors that led to Zion shut. They can't get in. Now there's going to be weeping and gnashing of teeth because they're going to miss out on dwelling in the glory of the LORD and all those promises that are inside that city. This is why Abraham said he sought a city built by the hands of God and not a city built by the hands of man. That's what we're striving for also, to look for that city.

Isaiah 65:20

"There shall be no more thence an infant of days, nor an old man that hath not filled his days: for the child shall die an hundred years old; but the sinner being an hundred years old shall be accursed."

This scripture is saying that in Jerusalem, people will not die early. Jerusalem will be blessed during this period of time,, but death has not been conquered yet. That's why Paul says death is the last enemy to be destroyed. We know that after the Great White Throne Judgment, death and hell are cast into the lake of fire. Death is destroyed, hell is destroyed after the last final judgment after a thousand years.

During the thousand years in the city of Jerusalem people will live a very long time. However, the promise is not for the rest of the world, just in Jerusalem. No infant shall die in Jerusalem. Of course you've already defeated death if you're in the holy city of Zion. Only those in resurrected bodies have defeated death and will live in the heavenly Zion. But in Jerusalem on Earth, no infant shall die, nor an old man that has not filled his days. If a child was going to die, he's going to be at least 100 years old.

I assume by reading this that someone who's not a child is going to live a lot longer than that. Or a sinner, being 100 years old shall be a curse. In other words, if there's a sinner at that time and he dies at 100 years old it's because judgment came on him. Well, wait a minute. So a sinner himself can live to be 100 years old? If he dies at 100, it's because he's cursed. But if he's not cursed, he could live 200 to 400 years or more. How long did people live before Noah's flood? Hundreds of years! None of them was quite over a thousand, but many of them came close.

Psalm 90:10 actually tells you how long God appointed man to live on the Earth today. It says you're going to live seventy years, and if you're strong, eighty years. I found that really interesting because those are the days that have been appointed to us now on this Earth. So when people die before 70, then they died before their time. And if you died earlier because of plagues, accidents, war, diseases, or whatever, you died before your time. The time appointed to you, minimum, was 70 years.

One of the worst things you can ever tell a family when they lose a child is, "Well, it was their time." It was not their time! They died through some other means, but it was not their time. So don't ever tell that to somebody who loses a child. Or, don't ever tell them, "God needed another angel in heaven." What if the parents say, "Well, *I* needed that child! What do you mean, God needed that child?" They're well-meaning phrases people use to try to comfort somebody, but they're very, very wrong. So don't counsel somebody like that or talk to somebody and say, *Well, God needed another angel in heaven; it was their time.* It was not their time and God did not need another angel in heaven. He has millions and millions of angels in heaven. He did not need another angel in heaven. But unfortunately, we live in a fallen world. People die, things happen, accidents happen, so sometimes people die before their time.

Revelation 21:4 tells us there is no death in the New Jerusalem. So Isaiah 65:20 is only talking about in Jerusalem, perhaps even in the land of Israel.

Isaiah 65:21
"And they shall build houses, and inhabit them; and they shall plant vineyards, and eat the fruit of them. They shall not build, and another inhabit; they shall not plant, and another eat: for as the days of a tree are the days of my people, and mine elect shall long enjoy the work of their hands."

This is talking about Jerusalem again, but it's also talking about the land of Israel. They will plant and eat their own fruit. Somebody else isn't going to come along and take it from them. They're going to build houses, and they're going to live in their own houses. Somebody else isn't going to come along and take their houses from them either. It happens a lot in this world. Somebody plants and builds, and another comes and takes it away. But that will not happen during this period of time. Their lives will be like the days of a tree. Some trees live longer than other trees, but many trees have lived over a hundred years; some trees hundreds of years.

Isaiah 65:23

"They shall not labour in vain, nor bring forth for trouble; for they are the seed of the blessed of the LORD, and their offspring with them. And it shall come to pass, that before they call, I will answer; and while they are yet speaking, I will hear."

What a wonderful promise that is! While the people in Jerusalem and Israel are trying to form the words in their mouth, God is hearing already. When they begin with all their heart to call out to God, He's already hearing them before they finish the words. Your words don't have to travel millions of light-years to get to him; He's as close as right next to you. You just can't cross that dimension, but He's right there. So as you're speaking, He hears you. That's how powerful God's Word is. This is a promise for all believers now and in the future. However, it will be a promise for those in Israel and Jerusalem during the millennium.

Isaiah 65:25

"The wolf and the lamb shall feed together, and the lion shall eat straw like the bullock: and dust shall be the serpent's meat. They shall not hurt nor destroy in all my holy mountain, saith the LORD."

The wild beasts will not destroy in the physical holy mountain of Zion, and perhaps even Jerusalem and perhaps the land. Other scriptures indicate it could be all three—the land, Jerusalem, and Zion. Most likely, people will not be eating meat or very little of it in Israel during this time. So those of you who really haven't thought about being vegetarians might want to get used to it now. If a saint visits the physical holy city of Zion, they can eat or not eat. You don't have to worry about it. But in Jerusalem and in the land, they will eat very little meat if any. Isaiah 11:6 also says the wolf, the lamb, the leopard, the kid goat, the calf, and the lion will be lying together and a little child shall lead them. Yes, a little child in God's holy mountain will be leading these carnivorous animals around like pets! "I want you to meet Leo, my lion, my buddy!" That's the way it's going to be. I am not sure if there will be animals in the heavenly city of Zion. Scripture is not clear on that except for the "horses" that Messiah and the saints ride on to the Earth. But the saints can leave the heavenly city and travel in the land of Israel and Jerusalem. They can certainly see the animals there.

Hosea 2:18
"And in that day will I make a covenant for them with the beasts of the field and with the fowls of heaven, and with the creeping things of the ground: and I will break the bow and the sword and the battle out of the earth, and will make them to lie down safely."

Earth is *erets* in Hebrew and can mean earth or land. More than likely, this is talking about the land of Israel. God is going to make a covenant with the beasts of the earth and may say, "Lion, you will no longer eat any meat and you'll be nice to my people. Wolf, you're not going to eat that lamb and you're not going to bite anybody. Snake, you were cursed from the beginning and I'm going to remove that curse; now you're going to play with the children." This is the covenant of the beasts that God will make during the millennial reign. The people of the land of Israel will lie down safely from war, violence, or wild beasts. Ezekiel 34:25 says, "I will cause the evil beast to cease out of the land." There we see that even the beasts will be nice in the land of Israel. The inhabitants of Jerusalem and Israel will have all kinds of wonderful pets and will not worry about anything sneaking up on them in the night to eat them. Remember, these people are still in the flesh.

Hosea 2:19-20

"And I will betroth thee unto me for ever; yea, I will betroth thee unto me in righteousness, and in judgment, and in lovingkindness, and in mercies. I will even betroth thee unto me in faithfulness: and thou shalt know the LORD."

Even in the land of Israel, God says he's going to betroth Israel and Judah together. Now wait a minute. I thought they were already married at Mount Sinai! Yes, they were married at Sinai but it appears they got divorced. In Jeremiah 3:8 God put Israel away for her adulteries and idolatry. And it says Judah also played the harlot with her adulteries and idolatries. So it appears that God put away both Israel and Judah. The LORD will call Israel His people once again. Keep in mind, you can't betroth somebody you're already married to. God put Israel away because of its wickedness, but He promises that He's going to bring them back and re-betroth himself to them, and forever to be with the LORD at that time. The LORD will not have two brides or, as I have heard, Israel is the wife and the saints are the bride. No. There is one bride and wife. To be married to the LORD requires redemption by the Messiah Yeshua. Both Israel and the inhabitants of the holy city of Zion will be married to the LORD.

Isaiah 66:18

"For I know their works and their thoughts: it shall come, that I will gather all nations and tongues; and they shall come, and see my glory."

When Zion is established and the glory of God is beaming out of Zion, the nations of the world will come to Zion—not to see God, but to see His glory. They will not actually be able to see God, but they'll see His glory. If they could actually see Him, they'd probably be destroyed because they are still in flesh and blood and couldn't handle the fire of His glory.

Isaiah 66:19

"And I will set a sign among them, and I will send those that escape of them unto the nations, to Tarshish, Pul, and Lud, that draw the bow, to Tubal, and Javan, to the isles afar off, that have not heard my fame, neither have seen my glory; and they shall declare my glory among the Gentiles."

What is Isaiah talking about here? "Escape." This means refugees or fugitives or those that escape from slaughter. This is the captivity. The LORD will bring the captivity back into the land, and then He's going to turn around and send many of them back into the nations to teach the nations the things of God. Who's doing this? Those who were in captivity. God has a particular group He's going to send out to do this. Some portion of the captivity will be evangelists and will go into the world to proclaim God's glory.

This could also mean the saints. This sign is different from the sign of the Son of Man that caused the captives to return. This sign is placed on these individuals. It could be a mark of God or to sanctify them to evangelize the world which could work for Israel or the saints. The word "escape" here can mean to escape by flight or to deliver or to slip away, or it could be a rapture concept. The captives really don't escape, the LORD leads them away.

Isaiah 66:20-24

"And they shall bring all your brethren for an offering unto the LORD out of all nations upon horses, and in chariots, and in litters, and upon mules, and upon swift beasts, to my holy mountain Jerusalem, saith the LORD, as the children of Israel bring an offering in a clean vessel into the house of the LORD. And I will also take of them for priests and for Levites, saith the LORD. For as the new heavens and the new earth, which I will make, shall remain before me,

287

saith the LORD, so shall your seed and your name remain. And it shall come to pass, that from one new moon to another, and from one sabbath to another, shall all flesh come to worship before me, saith the LORD. And they shall go forth, and look upon the carcasses of the men that have transgressed against me: for their worm shall not die, neither shall their fire be quenched; and they shall be an abhorring unto all flesh."

What does that all mean? These Jewish evangelists will bring their brothers from around the world to Jerusalem. They will bring offerings and come to worship the LORD on the new moon and the Sabbath. Remember that the law (Torah) is not gone. As a matter of fact, in Isaiah 2:3 the prophet says, "for out of Zion shall go forth the law [Torah], and the word of the LORD from Jerusalem." Torah will be in full effect during this time. Sacrifices will come back and the feasts of the LORD will be honored. Chapter 2 of Isaiah is talking about the millennium reign of Messiah Yeshua, and all flesh will come to worship before the LORD at Jerusalem.

When the people come to Jerusalem to worship before the LORD, they're going to see the carcasses of people in judgment. In Revelation 14:10, we learn that those who follow the beast of Revelation and receive his mark will be tormented with fire and brimstone in the presence of the holy angels, and in the presence of the lamb. Isaiah 66:24 says when people come to worship the LORD, they will see the bodies of the transgressors being burned. This will be in a valley west of the Jerusalem walls, called the Gehenna (Gehinnom) Valley, also known as Hinnom Valley. All those who receive the mark of the beast will be thrown into a furnace of fire in this valley.

Today, Gehenna is a park with a stadium right outside the west wall of Jerusalem. It's a valley where Israel used to sacrifice children to the false god Molech. During Yeshua's time on Earth, it was used as a garbage dump. It could be the same place referenced by Him when He said, "where their worm dies not, and the fire is not quenched." So as people are coming to worship the LORD, they're going to see this valley and they're going to see the destruction of the flesh of those who receive the mark of the beast burning in that valley. Probably the fire will come out of that valley for the whole thousand years of the millennial reign. The people won't be alive in it, but you're going to see the evidence of their burning for a thousand years. Now that's kind of a dichotomy if you think about it. People will come to worship the LORD and as they pass by this valley, they will see the judgment of God. It will constantly remind one of the consequences of turning against God.

Let's look at a couple of scriptures from Enoch that backs up what Isaiah is saying.

Enoch 48:9
"And I will give them over into the hands of mine elect; and as strong a fire, so shall they burn before the face of the holy; as lead in the water they will sink before the face of the righteous and no trace of them shall be found anymore."

What is "the holy"? It is Zion. So before everyone in Zion, they are going to see the wicked bones burning in this valley. They will be handed over to the elect in Israel and Jerusalem who will put them in the valley.

Enoch 90:26
"And I saw at that time how a like abyss was opened in the midst of the earth full of fire and it brought those blinded sheep, and they were all judged and found guilty and cast into this fiery abyss and they burned. Now this abyss was to the right of that house and I saw those sheep burning and their bones burning."

289

The house is the physical temple of God, and the abyss is this Valley of Gehenna. So even during the millennial reign, you're going to see the remains of judgment still taking place in this valley. That's why Yeshua talked about this valley when He said, "Their worm dies not, and the fire is not quenched" (Mark 9:44). That's an alliteration phrase indicating that the judgment will continue. They're not being tormented all that time. They'll probably die pretty fast when they're thrown in that pit, but the evidence of that judgment will continue even on your way to worship the LORD in Jerusalem. These individuals under judgment here are those also spoken of in Revelation 14:10-11 that receive the mark of the beast. They will perish quickly in the fire and their spirits will go to hell. The smoke of their torment will rise for at least the millennium.

The saints will worship the LORD in the heavenly Zion, but they can see this judgment also. The nations of the world that are coming to Jerusalem to worship the LORD will definitely see that judgment. What a spectacle that will be! They will see the glory of Zion and the light that puts the sun to shame, and as they are walking toward the physical Zion in Jerusalem, they will see this valley with smoke rising out of it and be reminded of God's judgment. They may say *"Wow, LORD! You made all these animals nice and friendly, and we're not going to die until we're really, really old. Do You have to show us all this stuff, too?"* Yep, as a reminder. Why? Because men can still sin. The scriptures says everybody will know the LORD, but it does not mean that they are righteous. They will all know the LORD "For the earth shall be full of the knowledge of the LORD, as the waters cover the sea" (Isaiah 11:9) but it does not mean they will not sin. That only applies to the inhabitants of the heavenly Zion. Sin is only eliminated in the heavenly Zion.

This is one of the other concepts that perhaps Revelation 21 and 22 are talking about during the millennial reign. Revelation 21:27 says, "And there shall in no wise enter into it [New Jerusalem] any thing that defiles, neither whatsoever works abomination or makes a lie: but they which are written in the Lamb's book of life." Further on, in Revelation 22:15, it says, "For without are dogs, and sorcerers, and whoremongers, and murderers, and idolaters, and whosoever loves and makes a lie." People who do such things will not enter that holy city of Zion, also called the New Jerusalem for they are without (outward, away, out of, out of the doors, outside) the city. Those who do such things will remain outside the walls of Zion. So sin can still be present. I'm sure this concept will apply also to the physical Zion.

It always creates a problem with people studying Revelation because they're saying, "Why are there even those kind of people around if the Great White Throne Judgment is over and all wickedness is destroyed?" That's a good question. But if Revelation 21 and 22 belong in the millennial period, now you know why it can apply. There will be sinners on the Earth during this whole time. *Gee, I thought all sin would be done away with!* No, not yet, because Satan still will have influence again eventually. He will be locked up for a thousand years. At the end of the thousand years, he is let out. What does he do? He convinces the nations to attack Jerusalem again! Another Gog-Magog war. Satan will cause the world to sin greatly again.

During the millennium people will sin and will not be allowed in any holy city. Anyone who has sin in their life will not be able to enter the city. So the rest of the world may not receive these same promises as Zion and Jerusalem, and perhaps even in the land of Israel. I don't know what the promises will be like in the other lands. It doesn't talk about that in the Bible, but one thing I do understand is that there will be sinners, even during the thousand-year millennial reign.

Psalm 102:16
"When the LORD shall build up Zion, he shall appear in his glory."

In other words, when the LORD has built up the heavenly Zion and all the children who are to be in Zion are complete, He will appear in

His glory. As people believe and become born again and become part of Zion, there will be a final number where the LORD will say, "the last one." When He has built up Zion—that is, the last one that's going to be counted as Zion—you may say, *Why is there a number?* He's building houses for everybody who believes! I don't think He built spare houses. He knows who's going to be there. It'll be in the millions and there's a good chance that when Revelation 21:2 says, "I John saw the holy city, new Jerusalem coming down from God out of heaven, prepared as a bride adorned for her husband," it's not after the Great White Throne Judgment. It's during this millennial reign that the new Jerusalem comes down (which is Zion) and hovers over Jerusalem.

This is why Isaiah 60:8 asked, "Who are these who fly in and out of these window?" He's looking at the believers in Zion, and the new Jerusalem that the LORD had prepared a house for has come down and is probably hovering right above Jerusalem. That's why it's called a high mountain. It may be fifteen hundred miles high! The physical Jerusalem's elevation is not very high at all, but the LORD is always talking about Zion being a high mountain.

Also consider this: If the New Jerusalem is to come after the Great White Throne Judgment of Revelation 20, does the bride have to wait a thousand years to get her city and mansions? No! This holy city will come just after Yeshua finishes His judgments on the Earth. This city will probably continue into eternity but it will be here for all the world to see up to and beyond the Great White Throne Judgment. God desires for the world to see the city from afar off to honor the saints who were obedient unto God. When this city is complete, the Messiah will come.

Psalm 102:21-22

"To declare the name of the LORD in Zion, and his praise in Jerusalem; When the people are gathered together, and the kingdoms, to serve the LORD."

After the LORD has built up Zion, He will declare the name of the

LORD in Zion which will be Yeshua. And His praise will be declared in Jerusalem by the nations of the world.

Isaiah 4:1
"And in that day seven women shall take hold of one man, saying, We will eat our own bread, and wear our own apparel: only let us be called by thy name, to take away our reproach."

Seven women taking a hold of one man. Poor guy! This will happen especially at the beginning of the millennial reign. Why? All the armies of the nations of the world will gather against Jerusalem and it would probably be safe to say that most will be men. God will destroy those armies. So if all the armies of all the nations of the world come against Jerusalem and God wipes them out, there is going to be a shortage of men on the Earth. It'll be so bad that seven women are going to take hold of one guy and say, "Can I be your wife? Give me your name; I'll do anything! You don't have to feed me; I'll bring my own food. You don't have to give me clothes, I'll bring my own clothes. Just take away my reproach!" Another scripture that says men will be as rare as the gold of Ophir during that time (Isaiah 13:12). Many men will be slaughtered.

Remember that during the Tribulation period, comets, asteroids, or angels will fall out of the sky and destroy one-third of all ships in the ocean. What's in those ships? Mostly men, especially in military ships. There will be a real shortage of men when it all starts coming down. Here we see the evidence that mostly men are going to be destroyed in warfare as God fights them. (Just a side note: Did you know that in Islam they say that Allah hates women, that hell will be mostly full of women? Isn't it interesting that there will be more women on Earth after the Tribulation than men.

Isaiah 4:2
"In that day shall the branch of the LORD be beautiful and

glorious, and the fruit of the earth shall be excellent and comely for them that are escaped of Israel."

There are two concepts here. One is the branch and one is about the fruit of the Earth being excellent for those escaped of Israel. What is the branch? It's Yeshua, but it also goes along with John 15:15 that says, "I am the vine and you are the branches. He who abides in me and I in him the same brings forth much fruit. For without me you can do nothing." He is the branch, but He's also the vine. So when we believe, we become a branch to Messiah. It's talking about Zion. The escaped of Israel here is talking about deliverance and can be Israel or saints. The fruit of the earth can mean that the returned captives will produce great fruit and the land will respond to them. Israel produces wonderful fruit today, but it will be nothing compared to what will happen during the millennial. Amos 9:13 says during this time, "The plowman shall overcome the reaper." The harvest will be so plentiful that it becomes planting time again before the initial harvest is complete.

Isaiah 4:3
"*And it shall come to pass, that he that is left in Zion, and he that remaineth in Jerusalem, shall be called holy, even every one that is written among the living in Jerusalem:*"

That word "left" could mean *remain, rest, survive, retain, left behind*—all those concepts. Again, two concepts: those who are left in Zion and those who remain in Jerusalem. Zion and Jerusalem are two separate thoughts taking place. Not only is Zion called holy, but Jerusalem is called holy also.

Isaiah 4:4-5
"*When the LORD shall have washed away the filth of the daughters of Zion, and shall have purged the blood of Jerusalem from the midst thereof by the spirit of judgment,*"

and by the spirit of burning. And the LORD will create upon every dwelling place of mount Zion, and upon her assemblies, a cloud and smoke by day, and the shining of a flaming fire by night: for upon all the glory shall be a defence."

Zion and Jerusalem will have their abominations cleansed. Zion will have their sins washed away by the blood of Yeshua and Jerusalem by the spirit of judgment with Yeshua's return to judge the world. The LORD will create a cloud, smoke, and the shining of fire upon every dwelling place of Zion. This is speaking of the New Jerusalem, the heavenly Zion where Yeshua said He would prepare a place for the saints. The glory will be a defense. It is interesting to note that the word "defence" in Hebrew is *chuppah*." It is a canopy, especially a wedding canopy. It gives a different meaning to it when you see that. The glory of God shall be a *chuppah* to Zion.

The cloud over Mount Sinai when the LORD appeared to the Hebrews has also been referred to as a *chuppah*. It was then that the LORD took the nation of the Hebrews for a wife. This cloud of glory over Zion also will show that the inhabitants of Zion are married to the LORD. *Chuppah* can also mean "chamber, closet and nuptial bed." In other words, the wedding bed, for the bride of the Messiah. This is why in Revelation 21:2 the New Jerusalem is referred to as a bride adorned for her husband.

Isaiah 4:6
"And there shall be a tabernacle for a shadow in the day time from the heat, and for a place of refuge, and for a covert from storm and from rain."

It appears that this heavenly Zion will be a cover for Israel and Jerusalem. This huge city will hover above the physical land and Jerusalem. Those who live in the heavenly Zion will have no need of protection from the elements with their power and resurrected bodies. The heavenly city is supposed to be 1500 miles long, wide, and high. However, there is something else to consider. Revelation 21:16 says the city will be 12,000 furlongs in height, width, and length. The word in Greek for furlong is *stadion*, from which we get the word stadium. It also means race or race course and the root means "to stand." "abide." "covenant." "appoint." and "continue." This seems to be very much in line with what the apostle Paul says in running the race, finishing the race, and seeking for that "incorruptible crown" and the "mark of the high calling." It also goes with the idea of being an overcomer as was spoken to the seven churches of Revelation. Those who dwell in this heavenly city will be all that and more.

Isaiah 30:26

"Moreover the light of the moon shall be as the light of the sun, and the light of the sun shall be sevenfold, as the light of seven days, in the day that the LORD bindeth up the breach of his people, and healeth the stroke of their wound."

This is certainly an interesting scripture. Is it metaphoric or will it be real? Obviously if our luminaries really do shine that brightly, those on the earth will perish. Perhaps it is just in reference to how bright the heavenly Zion will be. It certainly is possible that this light will shine not only in the heavenly Zion but also in Jerusalem and the Temple Mount, or physical Zion. This will occur when God has restored Jerusalem and has completed His work on the heavenly Zion and those inside—the inner court if you will. The light of the moon shall be the light of the sun.

How is He going to do that? How is He going to make the moon as bright as the sun and the sun be seven times its brightness? It's because of the glory shining out of the heavenly Zion, the glory of the LORD and the millions of saints who will be there and the glorious garments that God has given them that will shine like the luminaries. That's why they say they will have no need of the sun, for the glory of the LORD will be the sun unto them during this time.

This is another clue that the New Jerusalem will be here during the millennium. Revelation 21:23 and Revelation 22:5 both say that the city will have no need of the sun because the glory of God and the Lamb will be the light in it which will be given unto the saints to shine.

Isaiah 19:19

"In that day shall there be an altar to the LORD in the midst of the land of Egypt, and a pillar at the border thereof to the LORD."

So the LORD is going to have an altar in the land of Egypt near the Israeli border for the Egyptians to offer sacrifice unto the LORD. Egypt will come to know the LORD, especially after a horrible judgment comes against them during the Tribulation.

Isaiah 19:20-23

"And it shall be for a sign and for a witness unto the Lord of hosts in the land of Egypt: for they shall cry unto the LORD because of the oppressors, and he shall send them a saviour, and a great one, and he shall deliver them. And the LORD shall be known to Egypt, and the Egyptians shall know the LORD in that day, and shall do sacrifice and oblation; yea, they shall vow a vow unto the LORD, and perform it. And the LORD shall smite Egypt: he shall smite and heal it: and they shall return even to the LORD, and he shall be intreated of them, and shall heal them. In that day shall there be a highway out of Egypt to Assyria, and the Assyrian shall come into Egypt, and the Egyptian into Assyria, and the Egyptians shall serve with the Assyrians."

There's going to be a great highway moving from Egypt through Israel into Assyria and the people will be coming to the house of the LORD. Now we read in other scriptures that God will actually destroy Egypt and it will be wasted for 40 years (Ezekiel 29:10-16). So obviously this promise comes after that, after God has destroyed Egypt. That's why He says, "I will heal Egypt." All of a sudden His promises will come upon Egypt and Egypt will be healed and will serve the LORD, just as Assyria will at that time.

Why is He specifically talking about Egypt and Assyria? Those are the two main places where the captives will be sent. It shows a great mercy of God. Here, they're the ones who helped destroy Israel and led the captive off into Egypt and Assyria, yet the mercy of God—after the Messiah comes back—will restore them. What a great promise. If the Messiah can go that far to restore Egypt and Assyria, He can surely restore anyone who needs to be restored, God will have mercy on these two nations that will do tremendous harm to Israel. This shows the absolutely amazing grace and mercy and the love of God taking place.

Joel 2:23-27
"Be glad then, ye children of Zion, and rejoice in the LORD your God: for he hath given you the former rain moderately, and he will cause to come down for you the rain, the former rain, and the latter rain in the first month. And the floors shall be full of wheat, and the vats shall overflow with wine and oil. And I will restore to you the years that the locust hath eaten, the cankerworm, and the caterpiller, and the palmerworm, my great army which I sent among you. And ye shall eat in plenty, and be satisfied, and praise the name of the LORD your God, that hath dealt wondrously with you: and my people shall never be ashamed."

The restoration of Israel is a promise and it will happen. After all the destruction of the Tribulation, God will restore everything in that land. The prophet is using the analogy of locusts and how they destroy everything in their path, which will be the damage the nations did, as well as the damage the army of Joel does (Joel 2:2-11) and other judgments of

God.

Joel 2:32

"And it shall come to pass, that whosoever shall call on the name of the LORD shall be delivered: for in mount Zion and in Jerusalem shall be deliverance, as the LORD hath said, and in the remnant whom the LORD shall call."

Those who call upon the LORD today will be delivered. As Zechariah 12:10 says, when Israel looks upon Him whom they have pierced and recognize it is Yeshua, then they will call upon him by saying "Blessed is he who comes in the name of the LORD" and will be delivered. As mentioned before, this will begin the release of the captives. Another group of Israelis will flee into the wilderness (Revelation 12 concerning the woman). Yet there will be a remnant in Jerusalem who will be called up to the heavenly Zion with the multitudes of gentiles who already call upon the name of the LORD (Revelation 12 concerning the male child).

Joel 3:16-18

"The LORD also shall roar out of Zion, and utter his voice from Jerusalem; and the heavens and the earth shall shake: but the LORD will be the hope of his people, and the strength of the children of Israel. So shall ye know that I am the LORD your God dwelling in Zion, my holy mountain: then shall Jerusalem be holy, and there shall no strangers pass through her any more. And it shall come to pass in that day, that the mountains shall drop down new wine, and the hills shall flow with milk, and all the rivers of Judah shall flow with waters, and a fountain shall come forth out of the house of the LORD, and shall water the valley of Shittim."

Where is Shittim? It is the place where the Hebrews crossed at the

Jordan river near the northern end of the Dead Sea. The Dead Sea is pretty desolate; nothing lives in it. When it says "dead," it's dead. Now, scientists recently said they actually found bacteria in it that manages to survive, but other than that, everything is dead in that sea. It says in this verse that water is going to come forth from the house of the LORD and water the valley of Shittim that shall flow into the Dead Sea.

Zechariah 14:6-8

"And it shall come to pass in that day, that the light shall not be clear, nor dark: But it shall be one day which shall be known to the LORD, not day, nor night: but it shall come to pass, that at evening time it shall be light. And it shall be in that day, that living waters shall go out from Jerusalem; half of them toward the former sea, and half of them toward the hinder sea: in summer and in winter shall it be."

Zechariah 14 says there will be living waters going out from Jerusalem. Half of the water will go to the former or eastern sea (the Dead Sea) and half will go to the hinder or western sea (the Mediterranean Sea). So water's going to come out in both directions from the throne of God. The Dead Sea will become alive and the fishermen will catch fish. Where there was no life will now teem with life. This will happen during the millennial reign. No more will it be termed the Dead Sea at all. There'll probably be water skiing on it and boating. I don't know if that will happen or not, but there will be fish in it. Wonderful, wonderful things are going to happen.

So out of the very throne room of God, water is coming out and it shall flow—part to the Mediterranean Sea and part to the Dead Sea.

Ezekiel 47:8

"Then said he unto me, These waters issue out toward the east country, and go down into the desert, and go into the sea: which being brought forth into the sea, the waters

shall be healed."

We're talking about the water flowing out of the throne of God and going east toward the Dead Sea and it will be healed.

Ezekiel 47:9-10
"And it shall come to pass, that every thing that liveth, which moveth, whithersoever the rivers shall come, shall live: and there shall be a very great multitude of fish, because these waters shall come thither: for they shall be healed; and every thing shall live whither the river cometh. And it shall come to pass, that the fishers shall stand upon it from Engedi even unto Eneglaim; they shall be a place to spread forth nets; their fish shall be according to their kinds, as the fish of the great sea, exceeding many."

The water coming out of the throne of God shall flow towards the Dead Sea and the waters shall be healed. In other words, it will become fresh water and fish will start to live in it. The fishermen at Engedi— which is a small town halfway down the Dead Sea west coast near a little freshwater creek that runs out of the hills—will cast forth their nets and catch fish. The hills of Engedi is where David hid from King Saul. There are no fish there today but there will be in the millennium.

In Ezekiel 47:12, we see that there are trees along this river bank that will provide fruit for food every month and the leaves are for healing for those in the land.

In Revelation 22:1-2, we learn about another river in the New Jerusalem. It is possible that it is tied to the Ezekiel's river coming from the throne of God in Jerusalem. However, there is a difference in its description from the Ezekiel 47 explanation. This river is called the River of Life and it is pure and clear as crystal. It comes from the throne of God in the heavenly Zion. Unlike the Ezekiel's river, this river has the Tree of Life which bears 12 types of fruit and like Ezekiel's river, its leaves are also for healing. Revelation 2:7 promises the church of Ephesus that if they overcome, they will eat from the Tree of Life which is in the midst of the paradise of God. This tree is for the saints who overcome and it will be in the New Jerusalem.

In Zephaniah 2:3-13, the prophet basically tells us that Gaza and Escalon, the western coast which is the land of the Philistines, will now be Israel's. All the coastline will belong to the remnant of the house of Judah. The Cherethites will belong to Israel. That word "cherethites" actually means *executioners*. It's saying the enemies of Israel will belong to Israel. Moab will be as Sodom, Ammon will be as Gomorra. Egypt will be destroyed, but we also see that God will heal Egypt. Ethiopia will be slain, Assyria will be slain, but God will also restore Assyria. As God begins the millennial reign, He will destroy all these nations that come against Israel. But then He will restore them in His mercy. Praise God for that because if He can do that for them, He can do it for anyone.

Isaiah 40:9
"O Zion, that bringest good tidings, get thee up into the high mountain; O Jerusalem, that bringest good tidings, lift up thy voice with strength; lift it up, be not afraid; say unto the cities of Judah, Behold your God!"

The prophet is saying, "Zion! Say to the cities of Judah 'Behold your God!'" We have a commandment as believers to try to reach Judah, the Jewish people, and the cities of Judah, and say, "Behold your God!" That's what should be in our hearts at all times, telling the Jewish people, "Behold your God!" If you are part of Zion, you have a commandment right here that says, "say to the cities of Judah 'behold your God!'" This is why believers who are filled with the Holy Spirit and knowledgeable in the Word of God are strong supporters of Israel. They may not really know why, but the Spirit of God is bearing witness with their spirit to support Israel.

Believers should say, "Behold, Judah, your God! Do you not

understand? Grab hold of your God! Do you not understand what's coming? Do you not know that you need to have your sins washed away and your blood purged of its iniquity? Behold your God! Embrace Him! Call upon Him! For in deliverance shall be in Zion and deliverance shall be in Jerusalem!" We have great responsibilities for those of us who say we are Zion.

This deliverance will also be in Jerusalem shortly after the armies of the nations surround the city. A remnant of Judah will be delivered up to God at that time from Jerusalem. Another remnant will flee into the wilderness and God protects them for three and a half years. They appear to be the ones who will rule out of Jerusalem in the flesh and conduct service for the people. Perhaps it's the 144,000 of Revelation 7.

Isaiah 2:2

"And it shall come to pass in the last days, that the mountain of the LORD's house shall be established in the top of the mountains, and shall be exalted above the hills; and all nations shall flow unto it. And many people shall go and say, Come ye, and let us go up to the mountain of the LORD, to the house of the God of Jacob; and he will teach us of his ways, and we will walk in his paths: for out of Zion shall go forth the law, and the word of the LORD from Jerusalem."

The LORD's house will be on the top of the mountains. This heavenly city will hover above the mountains over Jerusalem. All nations shall flow unto it. It is interesting that the word "nations" can mean gentiles or people, and "flow" can mean to stream like a river, but it also means to shine, beam, light, or burn. I believe it is talking about the inhabitants of the New Jerusalem. They will shine so brightly, there is no need for the sun. The saints will flow in and out of the heavenly Zion, yet others will flow into the physical city of Jerusalem and Zion. Those not of the first resurrection (Revelation 20:5-6) cannot enter the heavenly city.

From Jerusalem goes the word, but out of Zion goes forth the law which appears to be talking about the heavenly Zion. Why is the law coming forth out of this Zion? Because the saints of gentiles and certain elect of Israel are going to be sitting on thrones with the Messiah as kings and priests. They will judge the nations. They will judge angels. The saints will have thrones next to the Messiah and what they say will be law. They will be incredible judges. Even today, a saint may be thinking, *I can't do that!* But God will empower you to do those things. You may even say, *I don't want to do those things!* Well, you should. He will empower you to do those things, but the law will go forth from Zion and the word of the LORD from Jerusalem. It's an important concept.

Isaiah 2:4

"And he shall judge among the nations, and shall rebuke many people: and they shall beat their swords into plowshares, and their spears into pruninghooks: nation shall not lift up sword against nation, neither shall they learn war any more."

There shall be no war during this period of time until the end of the millennial period when Satan goes out and deceives the nations again (Revelation 20:7-10). After he is let out of his prison, he comes to attack the holy city. God destroys the nations at that time that come against the holy city. Satan will be thrown into the lake of fire and will deceive the nations no more.

At the end of the millennium reign of the Messiah, the Great White Throne Judgment of Revelation 20 will occur. Everyone who has ever lived will be resurrected to be judged by their works. Those not found in the Book of Life will be thrown into the lake of fire to be destroyed—both body and spirit.

Those who are in the first resurrection will not be judged but will dwell forever with God and the Lamb. There is still time to be part of the first resurrection. Call upon God's Messiah now and you shall be delivered.